RATIONING IN THE SECOND WORLD WAR

SPUDS, SPAM AND EATING FOR VICTORY

RATIONING
IN THE SECOND WORLD WAR

SPUDS, SPAM AND EATING FOR VICTORY

KATHERINE KNIGHT

The History Press

In memory of my parents, Walter Fritz Alfred and Ruby Bell, and of my sister Jane

First published in 2007
This edition first published in 2011

The History Press
97 St George's Place,
Cheltenham, Gloucestershire, GL50 3QB
www.thehistorypress.co.uk

Reprinted 2014, 2021

British Library Cataloguing in Publication Data.
A catalogue record for this book is available from the British Library.

ISBN 978 0 7524 5946 2

Typesetting and origination by The History Press
Printed in Great Britain by TJ Books, Padstow, Cornwall

Contents

	Acknowledgements	6
	A Note about Weights and Money	8
	Introduction	10
1	Fairer Shares	13
2	Food Values and Valuable Foods	36
3	The Housewife, Her Kitchen and What She was Told	57
4	Dig for Victory and Vegetables	85
5	Country Life	104
6	The Wild Harvest and Preserving	125
7	Towns	138
8	The Black Market and Grey Areas	160
9	Let's Have a Party	175
10	Austerity and Recovery	189
11	Representative Recipes	203
	Appendix: Friends and Memories	221
	Notes	224
	Bibliography and Further Reading	232
	Index	236

Acknowledgements

For permission to reproduce copyright material the author and publishers gratefully acknowledge the following:

The account of his father's bakery business in Awsworth, Notts. David Bexon.

The poem by Tom Earley, 'For what we have received' from *All These Trees*, Gwasg Gomer (Gomer Press, 1992).

Extract from the Foreword to *They Can't Ration These*, by the Vicomte de Mauduit, reprinted 2004 by Persephone Books (www.persephonebooks.co.uk).

Extracts from *When the Lights Go On Again*, ed. by Pam Schweitzer, an Age Exchange Publication, 2000. Pam Schweitzer and The Age Exchange Theatre Trust.

Extracts from John Barnett's *Plenty and Want* (Penguin, 1968) and *Liquid Pleasures* (Routledge, 1999). Taylor and Francis Group.

Text extract from *Warne's Everyday Cookery* © Frederick Warne & Co. Ltd., 1926. Reproduced by permission of Frederick Warne & Co. Ltd.

An account of wartime substitutions in Jersey by Mrs Cecile Mallet. Nancy Yates.

Extracts from articles from *The Times* newspaper:

'Aluminium for aircraft – an appeal to women.' © *The Times*, London, 10/7/1940.

'Underground food train – snacks for shelterers in the tubes.' © *The Times*, London, 15/11/1940.

'Helpers for the harvest – 500,000 volunteers wanted', from the labour correspondent. © *The Times*, London, 18/2/1943.

'Infection of milk – doctors appeal for pasteurization.' © *The Times*, London, 19/2/43.

'Labour for the harvest – minister's call for 500,000 helpers.' © *The Times*, London, 22/4/1943.

'No increase in rations – more fish and eggs', by the food correspondent. © *The Times*, London, 15/8/1945.

Quotations from papers and ephemera held by The National Archives and the Department of Printed Books, The Imperial War Museum, are Crown Copyright.

Excerpts from wartime broadcasts by Dr Charles Hill and Lord Woolton, from the BBC Written Archives, are published under PSI Licence.

Every effort has been made to trace all copyright holders, but this has not always been possible. The publishers would be glad to put right any errors or omissions in future editions.

Acknowledgement and thanks to the Age Exchange Reminiscence Centre, Blackheath Village, for permission to photograph some of the articles in their display.

Many thanks for his help to my son, Robert Knight, who holds a BA (Hons) degree in History. He gave me valuable introductions and advice on resource materials.

A Note about Weights and Money

During the Second World War, Britain was still using Imperial weights and measures and a system of pounds, shillings and pence, both of which made children dread arithmetic lessons.

However, they were a part of everyone's lives at that time, so I have only converted weights and measures in my text to modern equivalents when describing food values and recipes which you may like to try out in the twenty-first-century kitchen.

The conversion of weights and measures is straightforward.

The ounce (oz) is about 28g; 30 or 25g are usually used to approximate quantities in metric recipes. 16oz = 1 pound (lb), about 450g, or rather less than half a kilogram.

The pint is still familiar (beer and bottled milk still sold thus). It contains 20 liquid ounces. Its metric equivalent is 550ml, rather more than half a litre. There are 2 pints to a quart, 4 quarts or 8 pints to the gallon.

Household measures are described on page 63.

The main monetary unit was a pound, as it still is. It was divided into 20 shillings, and each shilling was made up of 12 pence. At the start of the war at least the penny could be further divided into 2 halfpence or ha'pennies, or 4 farthings. Farthings faded out with inflation.

£ s d were the written abbreviations. For example, four pounds, eight shillings and ninepence ha'penny became £4 8*s* 9½*d*. If no pounds were involved, a forward slash divided shillings from pence: six and eightpence was written 6/8*d*. Two shillings would be 2/- and a penny three farthings 1¾*d*.

Inflation has made conversion of money almost meaningless. To say that we had 5p worth of meat per week would imply starvation, which was not the case. It may be more helpful to compare prices with wages. Even so, wages increased in the course of the war by about 45 per cent for men, more for women who were catching up a little.

The weekly average figures in January 1944 were:

Adult men	£6 4*s* 2*d*
Women of 18+	£3 4*s* 6*d*
Male youths under 21	£2 6*s* 11*d*
Girls under 18	£1 14*s* 3*d*

The calculations were based on 6 million workers, including those in agriculture, where wages were notoriously low.[1] Professional people would earn considerably more than the average, and a salary of £1,000 per year made you well off.

Introduction

The trouble with history is that we know what happened. It is like reading the last page of a detective story before the beginning. But for people living through and creating events in the Second World War there was no guarantee of a happy ending, with the villain arrested and the victim someone else. For children particularly, caught in conflict beyond comprehension, there was uncertainty and fear. There was also courage, humour, common sense, selfishness, bureaucracy – and Spam. We did not know how things would turn out but could only hope for the best.

Thus this book is written from two points of view. I researched the period as I would any other, but then applied a personal reality check of what I could remember from my own young experience. Of course this was limited, so I asked others for their recollections as well.

I was only six years old in 1939. I grew up in Cornwall, at Porthcurno, just round the corner from Land's End. My father worked for Cable & Wireless Ltd, a company which owned the undersea telegraph cables forming a vital link with America and the rest of the world. He became the manager of the cable station there. The staff and their families made up a more or less self-contained community.

It was thought likely that the cable station would be a target, either of a commando raid or more likely bombing, and so a large artificial cavern was blasted into the steep side of the valley. As much essential equipment as possible was transferred there. Soldiers were also stationed to protect the area. I can remember that my father was issued with a wood-chopping axe with which to wreck the delicate machinery in case of imminent invasion.

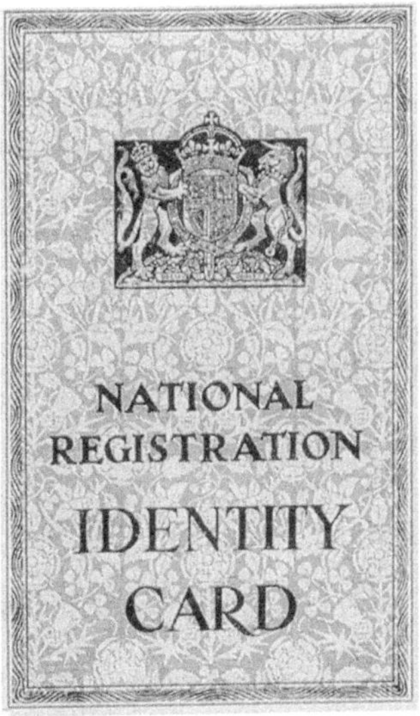

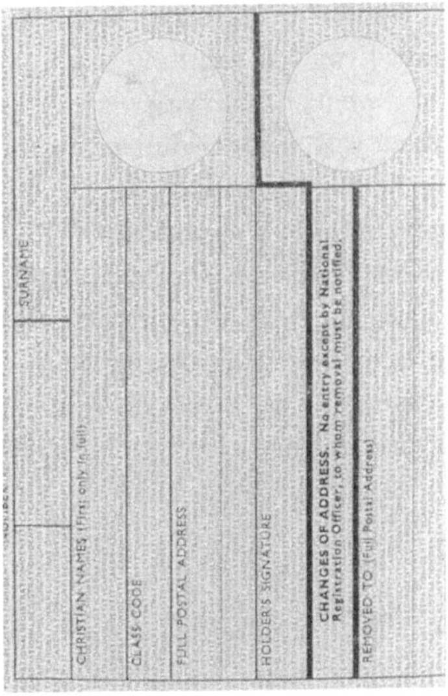

Everyone was registered with an individual number. The identity card was meant to be carried all the time, and produced on demand. It was linked to the issue of the ration book.

The axe remained unused, gradually turning rusty in the damp of winter. The anticipated attack did not happen, and in the later years of the war the area was thought sufficiently safe to receive evacuees from London. I was lucky compared with many others, but of course shortages and rationing affected my family like everyone else's. (The site is now a successful museum, the Cable & Wireless Porthcurno and Collections Trust, telling the story of its technology, the place and its people.)

So although this book, finished in 2007, must give an account of the past, I hope there is enough in my own and other people's memories to bring to life a picture of the home front with particular emphasis on food. It describes the rations that were available, other things that could be grown and gathered for the kitchen, and how the housewife managed (for most of the time) to put reasonably palatable meals on the table. There are accounts of radio broadcasts and advertisements which helped to teach the art of making do and good nutrition.

But the most elusive thing to capture is the emotional truth of the past. I can tell you how many ounces of cheese we had per week, how we managed with few eggs and many potatoes, but how we felt about it all is more difficult to convey. I can only ask you, if you are under the age of sixty-five, to try to imagine how you would have responded to our challenges.

There are perhaps other questions too: suppose such shortages arose again, maybe as a result of climate change, would the experience of the past help ordinary people to survive? Better still, could we adapt some war-time methods of saving and sharing food and fuel with a generous spirit of neighbourliness?

1

Fairer Shares

One of the most fundamental human terrors is that of famine. Not enough to give your children. Not enough to eat yourself. Outright starvation is the worst. People with big heads and limbs like sticks, children too feeble to cry. The images are still shockingly familiar in the twenty-first century. The skeleton shook its angry bones in the cupboards of Whitehall in the 1930s when war seemed likely. It was clear that another conflict would be partly one of attrition, with vital supplies reduced as they had been in the Great War. Britain began re-arming, repairing its military machine, but it was also realised that 'Food is a Munition of War.' Britain was importing most of its food. If supplies were completely cut off the population would starve. How should the government react? What could be done to increase home-production, safeguard essential imports and make sure that everyone had a reasonable share? It was time to blow the dust off files which referred to similar problems in the previous struggle with Germany.

RATIONING: THE PRECEDENT OF THE FIRST WORLD WAR[1]

Submarine attacks had led to food shortages by December 1916. The consequent rise in food prices, and long queues, had led to industrial unrest in 1917 and 1918. Fats, sugar, meat and bacon were rationed in 1918, at the flat rate per person per week of 4oz fats, 8oz sugar, 15oz beef, mutton or lamb and 5oz bacon.[2] Rationing continued until 1920. To make it work, there had to be government control of both imports and home-grown produce, and a Ministry of Food was set up. (It was abandoned after restrictions were lifted in 1921.) It was decided to

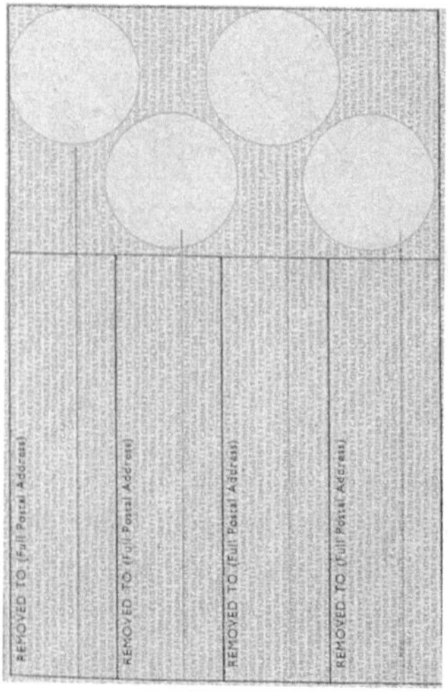

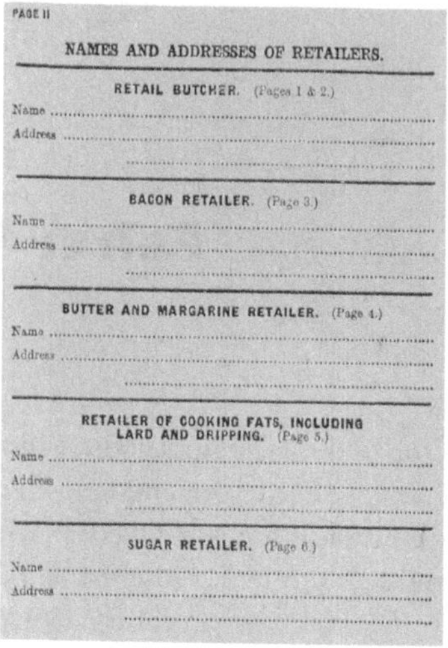
PAGE II

NAMES AND ADDRESSES OF RETAILERS.

RETAIL BUTCHER. (Pages 1 & 2.)
Name ....
Address ....
....

BACON RETAILER. (Page 3.)
Name ....
Address ....
....

BUTTER AND MARGARINE RETAILER. (Page 4.)
Name ....
Address ....
....

RETAILER OF COOKING FATS, INCLUDING LARD AND DRIPPING. (Page 5.)
Name ....
Address ....
....

SUGAR RETAILER. (Page 6.)
Name ....
Address ....
....

Above, left and right: This was the first ration book to be issued, in 1939, ready for rationing in 1940. The pages of instructions show what was planned, but not all of this happened. For instance coupons were not surrendered for restaurant meals.

allow the same quantities to everybody in order to be fair. Bread was subsidised, and though there was a campaign in 1917 which urged people to eat 25 per cent less, it remained available. Of course different people needed different amounts of food – your bedridden granny was never going to eat as much as your brother the blacksmith.

Retailers and consumers had to be closely associated, as the shops got their supplies in proportion to the number of customers registered.

The system was accepted by the public as a success, generally speaking, though May Byron, a cookery writer of the time, had serious reservations:

> Of course, the fundamental idea of rationing was standardisation, equalisation: i.e., that nobody shall have more than anybody else. Equally of course, like all theories of standardising and equalising, it won't work out in practice … the households numbering from one to three person have a desperate struggle to make ends meet on meat-ends

> and scraps. Their perplexities are multiplied in inverse ratio to their tickets [coupons] ... This is a question only to be solved by good management.[3]

However, good might come from facing the difficulties. She foreshadowed the propaganda of the Second World War when she said:

> I conjecture that, sooner or later, we shall emerge from this dire emergency a great deal cleverer than we were before; having acquired all sorts of knowledge, and exploited all manner of possibilities, which we should have regarded with a stare of blank bewilderment in 1913.[4]

This hope came to not much. Nutritional standards generally remained at half-mast for the next eighteen years.

FOOD BETWEEN THE WARS FOR RICH AND POOR

Before 1939 social inequalities were far more obvious than they are today. Many people were ill as a result of poverty or ignorance or both. We should not be complacent, with obesity becoming literally a widespread problem, and poverty contributing to faulty choices. But many on low wages in the years of the Depression suffered from outright deficiencies. Commenting on the findings of John Boyd Orr in 1936, John Burnett wrote:

> But there was abundant evidence that it was particularly in the lower [income] groups that physical under-development, predisposition to rickets, dental caries, anaemia and infective diseases such as tuberculosis were most marked, and that their incidence was due – at least in part – to the inadequacy of protein and vitamin intake.[5]

It might have been expected that country people were better fed than those in towns, but Burnett dispels this idea:

> It was tempting to think in the 1930s that poor diet and malnutrition were essentially urban problems associated with unemployment, overcrowding, lack of fresh air and other difficulties of life in towns. A survey of nutrition in Cuckfield Rural District Council, a rural area

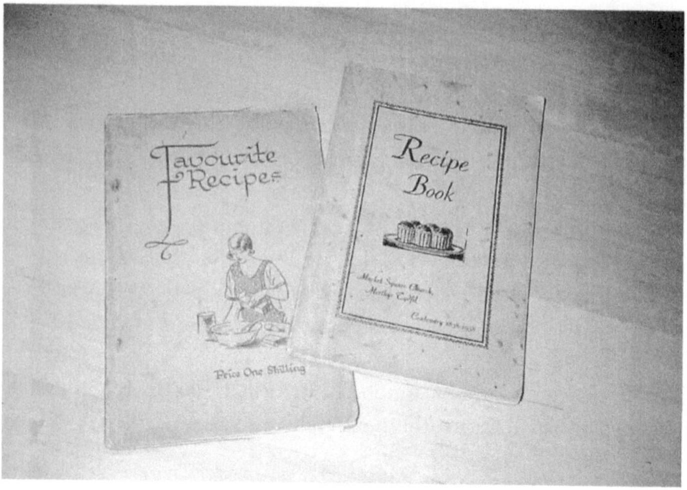

Many pre-war housewives owned modest cookery booklets.

> with no unemployment problems, completely disproved this belief and showed that in 1936, as a century earlier, the agricultural labourer was the worst-fed of English workers. Ninety-nine children out of 304 examined were of sub-normal nutrition – a proportion of 33 per cent.[6]

V.H. Mottram, a professor of physiology at King's College, London University, and his wife gave good advice in a book published in 1932, *Sound Catering for Hard Times*. It was based on necessary quantities of total calories, first-class protein (that is, protein of animal origin, such as meat or cheese), vitamins and minerals. It was intended, not for the very poor, but for the down-at-heel middle class. Several economies could be made by a man facing a reduced income or a tax rise: 'He cuts down his wife's dress allowance, he sends the boys to the local grammar school [instead of to a public school, though nothing is said about the daughters' education], he says he will mow the lawn himself and he waters the cat's milk …'[7]

But above all, savings could be made by switching from expensive foods to cheaper ones, without sacrificing food values. The Mottrams gave a collection of these economy recipes, with costs that show

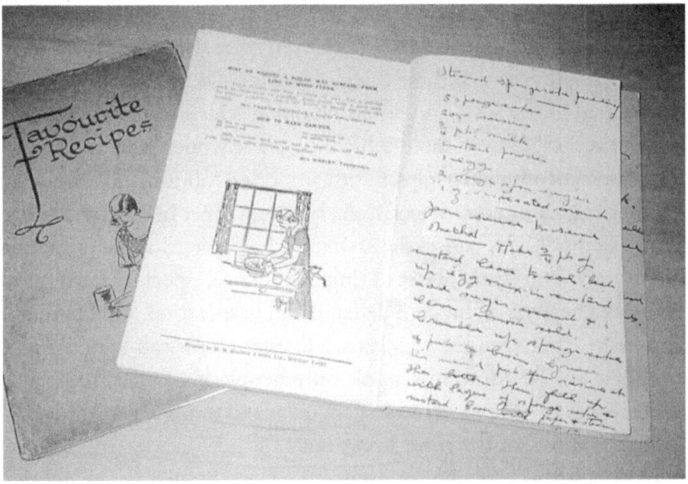

It was common to add recipes to booklets. Some even had blank pages for this purpose.

startling evidence of inflation over the last seventy years. Soups cost from 5½*d* per 1,000 calories or four portions (vegetable soup), to an extravagant 3*s* 1¼*d* for a tapioca cream soup attributed to Mrs Beeton. The meat stock in this cost 11*d*, and added very little to its food value. Two pounds of cod cost 2/-, whereas salmon was 5/- for 1¼lbs. A duck for roasting cost 4/6*d*, while the same weight of boiling fowl, that is 3lb, would set you back only 3/-. Boarding-school-type puddings, high in carbohydrates, were cheap anyway. For instance 1,000 calories of plain suet and treacle pudding (also from Mrs Beeton) cost 2½*d*. Leave out the treacle, and the cost could go down to 2¼*d*. It is noticeable that the food is priced down to the last farthing! A baked custard for one person was nourishing, but with a quarter of a pint of milk and one egg, it was probably too expensive at 3*d*.

The authors list the foods which provide the cheapest calories, for the 'really poor'. These include haricot beans and other pulses, white flour, white and brown bread, margarine and suet, pasta, rice, sago, tapioca, potatoes, dates, currants and figs, sugar and treacle, the cheapest cuts of mutton, cheese imported from New Zealand and bacon. They point out that this catalogue does not cover essential vitamins and minerals, and the book shows how these may be included, but the list is depressing to read, and the food would have been even more depressing to eat. But a lot of people regarded these things as staples, and they were certainly represented in the basic and points rationing which were to come.

Next is the group of foods which the 'merely poor' may add to the list, butter, cornflour, parsnips, raisins, imported mutton and lamb, and cheaper cuts of imported beef, milk, herrings, sweet biscuits and some pork. The book emphasises the savings to be made by switching from home-grown meat and butter to Empire produce, especially from New Zealand. There was naturally a demand for cheaper food, and this made imports rise between the two wars, a disaster for British agriculture.

Finally in the Mottrams' book only people beginning to escape poverty will be able to afford British meat and more vegetables, with fruit, fish and eggs the most luxurious of foods.[8]

How was this actually experienced? Maybe academic generalities need to be related to real people. For instance, the poet Tom Earley described his childhood meals as part of a large family belonging to the mining community in Mountain Ash, South Wales.

For what we have received[9]

We were not vegetarian from choice
but from necessity; meat cost too much
and allotment salad seemed free.
So there were fragile young
lettuces in season and small
shining globes of radishes,
spring onions which chilled
the throat (jibbons we called them)
and deep purple flesh of beetroot
fleetingly reminding us of meat.

In autumn we finished our meal
with blackberry pudding or wimberry pie,
whichever fruit our eager indigo fingers
had picked that golden day.
My mother had a hand for pastry,
especially for apple tart

made on a large flat dish
and served geometrically neat
with exactly equal slices
making fair shares for all.

In winter we had a thinner time
sometimes dinner was half a banana
with bread and margarine, though
there was always tea, hot, strong and sweet.
All week we waited for the Sunday joint.
The smell of mint or parsley
can still arouse in me
the excitement we felt
for the small sweet mountain mutton
when it arrived on our table.

Shoulder of lamb with its crisp
brown crust of fat across the top
or breast of lamb, fragrant
with green parsley stuffing
speckled with herbs and chopped
onion, was served with spring greens
and yellow waxy new potatoes
tiny from our own garden.
But the meat was the thing:
we were not vegetarian from choice.

Tom Earley

A middle-class diet was 'based upon bread, butter, milk, fish, meat, eggs, vegetables, fruit, game and poultry.'[10] This was high in protein and fats, adequate in vitamins and minerals and certainly sufficiently calorific.

Typical cookery books of the time confirm the impression of good living for the lucky and prosperous, though recipes had become somewhat simpler than Victorian ones. For instance an *Everyday Cookery* published in a revised edition in 1937, was written '... chiefly for people of moderate income, although a few of a more elaborate and expensive character have been included.'[11] Indeed they were. Twelve specimen menus covered breakfasts, luncheons and dinners for each of the four seasons. A spring breakfast consisted of baked eggs, tomato sauce, potted meat and banana salad. A summer luncheon might be salmon mayonnaise, roast fowl, bread sauce, potato chips, asparagus with cream sauce, and cherry flan and cream for dessert. Dinner was a more elaborate meal than luncheon anyway, and in winter particularly one needed to be well fed, so one might have oysters *au naturel*, tomato soup, fried whiting, fillets of beef à la St Aubyn, roast partridge, salad, potato straws, bramble cream, with cheese and biscuits to fill any spare capacity.[12]

The book as a whole is comprehensive and, perhaps, nostalgic for Edwardian days. Stocks and soups, sauces, gravies and batters are the preliminaries, and then the chapters follow the usual order of courses at dinner. *Hors-d'oeuvres* were needed to stimulate appetite, and then came two-dozen pages on fish, both freshwater and saltwater, and shellfish. Entrées and Made Dishes were important, but 'one entrée is usually considered sufficient nowadays, as dinners are much simpler than formerly. Sometimes the remove is dispensed with ...'[13] If not dispensed with, the remove was a solid meat course, often a whole joint of beef, mutton, or pork, roast, braised or boiled, served with potatoes and other vegetables – the fundamental scheme of the 'meat-and-two-veg' meal which still persists. The remove might also be omitted if a Roast course was included, poultry or game with accompaniments of salad, gravy and such. There is a large section on vegetable dishes, including the timeless baked or jacket potatoes and peeled potatoes roasted with the meat. Cold service dishes such as mayonnaise of whole salmon often appeared on party occasions, in what we would call a buffet meal. Plainer cold entrées such as chicken cream could be served up for luncheon.

Meatless dishes overlap the food of the poor, described by the Mottrams above. The book continues with pies, puddings, savouries, breakfast and supper dishes, cakes and beverages. And all this in the revised edition of a mainstream publisher just two years before the outbreak of war.

This poverty and plenty together made up the background against which government planners had to impose their scheme of food distribution and control when war came. Clearly the affluent classes felt the greatest culture shock, as meals were simplified, portions reduced, variety severely limited. But for those who had previously known real hunger, there was to be a guarantee of a minimum quantity of essential foods at reasonable prices.

RATIONING: PRELIMINARY PLANNING BY THE GOVERNMENT IN THE 1930S[14]

With the experience of rationing in 1918 almost fresh in their minds, the planners set to work when war looked probable. Sir William Beveridge had been a permanent secretary at the first Ministry of Food, and in 1936 he became Chairman of the subcommittee on rationing.

Control schemes for cereals, meat, fats, tea and sugar were worked out. It was essential that everybody should be guaranteed a proper share, so it followed there had to be strict organisation of supply and distribution. A Ministry of Food would spring into being immediately on the outbreak of war. It would own bulk stocks of foods and imported food, and also whatever was produced on British farms. It would also be responsible for contracts with overseas suppliers. At the outbreak of war therefore the plans were already in place. Stocks had been built up to some extent, arrangements for transport and storage made, and – important in a democracy – legislation for government control of food was drafted. Fifty million ration books had been printed in readiness (for a total population of 48 million) by the summer of 1939.

Other ministries were also involved. The Ministry of Agriculture and Fisheries extended its scope. The Board of Trade had responsibility for consumer goods apart from food, and the Ministry of Supply was in charge of salvage efforts, a campaign not unlike the recycling schemes in operation today. They were helped by the Women's Voluntary Service, which had been set up in 1938. Fuel rationing came under the direction of the Ministry of Fuel and Power.[15]

IMPORTS AND LOSSES

Before the Second World War Britain was nowhere near being self-sufficient in food production:

> Britain was dependent on imports for 92 per cent of her requirements of fat, for 51 per cent of her meat and bacon, 73 per cent of her sugar and 87 per cent of flour cereals, as well as for a large proportion of the cheese, eggs, vegetables and other everyday foods consumed at home.[16]

Part of the reason for the high level of imports was the encouragement of Empire trade, and as already mentioned there was a demand for cheap food. The country was vulnerable to a naval blockade, and when war came the U-boats, as the submarines were called, were especially deadly.

They hunted like wolves in packs, fanning out to intercept merchant shipping. They were fast on the surface, low in the water and easily overlooked. They shadowed the convoys and attacked at night. There were not enough escort vessels, and the ships were most vulnerable in mid-Atlantic. After the fall of France more bases were available for the U-boats, with the worst losses for allied shipping happening in early 1941, when in February to April 1,600,000 tons went down,[17] with a corresponding toll on seamen's lives.

Available British shipping was needed to carry troops too. It was obvious that imports would have to be cut back severely, which meant an enormous switch into production at home. Imported food was reduced by almost half from 22,026,000 tons to 11,032,000 tons by 1944.[18] Bulky cargoes were eliminated or compressed, as with boneless meat. Shipping space was not the only consideration either – food from abroad had to be paid for, until Lend Lease agreements eased the country's considerable cash-flow problems in mid-1941.

ORGANISATION OF RATIONING[19]

The challenge at the start of the war was to make sure that the whole population was kept in good health and, as in 1918, to distribute available goods fairly through the rationing and control systems. A fractious public was the last thing the government wanted, when the goodwill of the workers was essential to the coming war effort. (In fact, fair shares remained a part of Labour's social policy after the war.) It was thought that rationing would check inflation on food prices, enable the creation of reserves, and prevent queues. It was only partly successful in the last aim.

There was Cabinet debate about the best way to distribute supplies. Should there be extra meat, for instance, for workers doing heavy physical work? And what about the needs of growing boys? Oh, yes, and growing girls too. It was decided that it would be too complicated to differentiate between many kinds of groups,[20] so it became the stated aim of the Ministry of Food 'to provide the maximum possible, ration for all consumers rather than to give more to some at the expense of the remainder',[21] but in fact there were many common-sense adjustments. For example, extra milk and vitamin foods were allowed to children and pregnant women, and there was a larger ration of cheese for agricultural and other workers who couldn't take advantage of canteens. The armed services were fed under separate rules. Service people on leave were issued with temporary ration documents. In any case, bread and potatoes were unrationed during the war, and communal feeding arrangements, such as British Restaurants, were expected to supplement the rations.

The controls applying to institutions will be described in later chapters, but for the moment there is enough to say about the ordinary household rations.

In the autumn of 1939 the so-called 'phoney war' delayed the start of the scheme, as nothing very much seemed to be happening to Britain. But in January 1940 rationing kicked off with bacon and ham, butter and sugar (preserves came later, and included jam, marmalade, mincemeat, honey etc.). Meat, tea and cheese followed. Margarine and cooking fat were added to the butter to make a 'fats' ration. Fresh meat went on the ration in March 1940. Unlike the other basics sold by weight, it was restricted by price. At first you could buy 1/10*d* worth, but there was a low point of 1/- in March 1941, and again in 1948. The system itself was a good one, allowing people to choose between small amounts of prime cuts such as steak, or larger quantities of cheaper parts, mince for instance. It meant that none of the carcase was wasted because demand was spread. Meat at this time cost very roughly 1/- a pound on average. Cheese was rationed in the spring of 1941.

At the beginning these were the ordinary rations for an adult per week, with some later variations during the war years in brackets:

Bacon and ham	4oz	(max. 8oz)
Sugar	12oz	(varied between 8oz and 1lb)
Tea	2oz	(max. 4oz)
Meat worth	1/10*d*	(max. 2/2*d*, min. 1/-) Children had only half.

Cheese	1oz	(max. 8oz usually 2 or 3oz.)
Preserves (per four weeks)	8oz	(max. 2lb usually 1lb. Sometimes sugar could be taken instead.)
Butter	4oz	(min. 2oz)
Butter plus marg.	6oz	(mostly static, though proportions varied)
Cooking fat	2oz	(max. 3oz, min. 1oz)[22]

The 'points' system was different. It was introduced in December 1941, covering canned fish, meat and beans, but later a whole range of foods such as dried pulses and dried fruit, biscuits and cereals were included. Each of these were given points values, and you could buy what you liked within the limit of your allocation of points coupons. 'Personal points' were for chocolate and sweets. There is more about this below.

Another method of sharing food in short supply was through distribution schemes. You had to register for some things, such as milk, others were supplied as available, with the purchase registered on the ration book. Foods so controlled included oranges, fresh and dried eggs as well as liquid, dried and condensed milk. (Condensed milk was later switched to the points system.) Unlike the basic rations, these foods were not guaranteed. You could not feel let down if there were no oranges, for instance, but were grateful when some did appear (briefly) at the greengrocer's. There was a system of priorities applying to some groups of people, especially expectant mothers and children, for milk and eggs in particular, and they had to be supplied before the ordinary ration-book holder.

Rationing went on far past the end of the war, and some foods became even scarcer in the first years of peace than they had been at the height of the conflict. Bread, for instance was first rationed in July 1946, and stayed so for two years afterwards. Meat was the last food to be freed, in June 1954. Rationing of many foods was phased out over several years, with a marked decrease in 1950 when the points rationing scheme ended in May.

Organisation of the system was detailed and formidable. At the top of a bureaucratic mountain sat the Minister of Food, with his civil servants around him. Then came nineteen Divisional Food

Basic weekly rations for an adult in the summer of 1941: 2oz butter, 2oz cooking fat, 4oz margarine, 2oz cheese, 4oz bacon, 8oz sugar, 2oz tea and approximately 1lb of meat – worth 1/2*d*.

Offices – eleven in England, five in Scotland, two in Wales and one in Northern Ireland. (The number was later reduced.) They linked with, and supervised, the work of the Food Control Committees at the next level down. There was plenty to do, as there were 1,520 of these Food Control Committees at the beginning of the war.

The Committees typically had ten to a dozen consumer members, five more representing local retailers and one to give the shop workers a voice. They covered the same area as a Local Authority, and brought some democracy into the system, though nominees had to be approved by the Minister before being appointed for a year at a time. They were responsible for enforcing the Government's Rationing Orders, and dealt with the authorisations for retailers and various catering businesses, canteens, hospitals etc. so that they could obtain supplies.

Lower down again came the 1,220 Food Offices or Joint Food Offices, which became important to everyone because they administered local rationing arrangements under the direction of the Food Control Committee above them. For example, this was where you had to go to justify the issue of a new ration book if you had lost your first one, or to produce a Certificate of Pregnancy to get the documents for extra meat, priority milk and vitamins.

In 1943 the local Food Offices were combined with the parallel National Registration Offices, which issued identity cards, so that you could do business with both under one roof, cutting out a bit of bureaucracy, and proving 'of great convenience to the public as well as administrative saving.'[23] As there were 50,000 civil servants employed by the Ministry of Food by 1943,[24] there must have been scope for considerable saving.

RATION BOOKS

The ration book was the passport to getting enough to eat. A National Registration Schedule had been compiled in October 1939, and everyone had been assigned a National Registration number, which actually contained both letters and numbers, such as WBTC 95:1. Your first ration book, complete with a serial number, was sent through the post. It had to show your name, address and National Registration number, and was valid for a year. You got the next year's book by detaching and sending off a postcard, until year five. After that you had to collect a new one from the Food Office, showing your identity card and the relevant page of the old book. You were wise to grab your ration book (and of course your identity card and gas mask) to take with you when sheltering from an air raid.

The scheme was designed to share out food as fairly as possible, so everybody was entitled to the rations. Even royalty were issued with the document, with the implication that the privileged would get exactly the same treatment as everyone else. The Imperial War Museum has Queen Mary's ration book on display for example. (Queen Mary was the grandmother of Queen Elizabeth II, who was a teenager during the war.)

There were several different types of book. The most common, for adult civilians, was the buff-coloured R.B.1 (Ration Book 1). R.B.2 was for babies and infants up to five years old. The holders of these green books had half an adult ration of meat, and no tea after mid-1942, but priority for milk, eggs, and some vitamin foods. R.B.2 was issued to expectant mothers too, for extra meat and priority for milk etc. but the number was later changed to R.B.7, a grey one. R.B.3 seems never to have been issued. R.B.4 (blue) was for children from five to eighteen, allowing the same quantities as adults but with priority for milk and for bananas when they started to be imported again after 1946. R.B.5, like 3, is not mentioned, but R.B.6 was a weekly seaman's ration book, 'for the special needs of merchant seamen in the home and coastwise trade and of certain classes of fishermen, when at sea.'[25] They were entitled to a higher scale of rations. It was modified for other marine workers too.

There were further ration documents from time to time, including temporary ones for those who were without proper books for any reason, or who were away from home for short stays, or for Service personnel on leave. Special coupons were issued for extra soap for babies for instance. Extra rations and priorities were documented for vegetarians (extra cheese, no meat), for some invalids and for the dietary needs of some religious groups.

Once your ration book had arrived by January 1940, you had to go along to a shop – you could choose which one – to register for the various groups of foods. The retailer's name and address had to be entered on each page of coupons. To save trouble you could deposit a whole page of coupons with the shopkeeper – with your name and address filled in, naturally ... You were not obliged to register with the same shop for all the rations. If you wanted to, you could buy your bacon at one shop for instance, your sugar at another. In practice however most people stayed with one grocer, though getting their meat at a separate butcher.

The ration book contained coupons which could be 'spent' on the various foods. At first they were valid for only a week at a time, but this was impractical, and soon you could exchange most of them at any time during each four-week period, but not before or after. Bacon could be bought in the designated week or the week after, but the meat ration had to be bought in the current week only, or you missed your chance. Tea coupons were exchanged for a whole month's ration at a time. As the ration started off at 2oz per adult per week it saved having to weigh out very small quantities.

At first the shopkeeper had to cut out the coupons from your book. I remember seeing them collected in a series of old tobacco tins ranged on the counter of the village shop. Then he had to count them and send them off to the Food Office to renew his entitlement to supplies. This was tedious and inefficient, so the system was changed to allow cancellation of coupons, left in the book, with a cross made in ink or indelible pencil. Tea coupons continued to be cut out in the shop, as you could buy tea anywhere you saw it and did not need to register. However, you were never allowed to cut out coupons yourself. To do so invalidated them.

Having counted his coupons and sent in the details of his registered customers to the Food Office, which kept registers of retailers and rationed goods, the shopkeeper received buying permits so that, in his turn, he could replenish the rations from his wholesalers. Later the coupons were disregarded for wholesale allocations, and the system worked on the number of registered customers kept on record.

There were some drawbacks to absolute precision. Because there were always some people with temporary ration documents that could not be registered, the shop had to have a slightly larger allocation than was justified by their regulars. Customers moved about a lot too, because they were evacuated, went into the Services, or were bombed out. (The shop might be bombed too.) Records therefore became inaccurate. Some retailers were said to be quick to register new customers, slow to record that some had left.[26]

It seems amazing now that all this worked as well as it did. It had to be administered by a proliferation of office workers, all in the absence of computers of course. As it was an offence either to buy or to sell more than the authorised amount of rations, the retailer had to be both efficient and honest.

WINNING ON POINTS

With the arrival of Lend Lease foods in 1941, the supply of scarce canned foods eased a little. But there were nowhere near enough to ration them in the same way as sugar or meat. It would have been difficult to allow a ration of one quarter of a pilchard per head every two months for instance. The points system was a brilliant idea, both because it spread and regulated the demand for sparse foods, and because it allowed the public some choice of what to eat.

Lord Woolton, the Minister of Food at the time, gave a special broadcast to explain what was going on. Just after lunch on Sunday,

2 November 1941 he spoke on the Home Service of the BBC.[27] He started by acknowledging that both he and his listeners had been worried about unrationed foods.

> Canned foods have been difficult to obtain. We hadn't got them. Well, now we have some of them; canned meat, canned fish, canned beans, and we hope to bring in more. Our friends in the United States have been helping us very generously … Now we have to distribute that food fairly. And that's what this Point Scheme is all about.
>
> But there's something new about this plan. It's a rationing scheme. But up to now we've been accustomed to think of rationing as restricting consumption, so that people should have less than they've been used to. But this Scheme is just the opposite; because of the help our American friends have given us, we're going to have more of these things than we've had for a long time, and they'll be new things …
>
> The Points Plan gives you freedom. You can buy these new goods where you please and when you please in the four-week period. You're free to spend your Points on any foods that you choose on the list, and you can go to any shop you like to make your choice. Everyone doesn't want the same thing every week. We want variety …

Lord Woolton made it sound as if these foods were going to be plentiful, but as it turned out you could only buy a very limited amount. If you splurged out on a can of the new Spam, for instance, that would take up your whole monthly allowance, which meant you had to forego many other foods. The scheme, which started at the end of 1941, applied at first, as Lord Woolton said, to canned meat, fish and beans. More and more foods were added: rice, sago and tapioca, dried pulses, dried fruit including prunes, figs, dates and apple slices, more canned vegetables, canned fruit, condensed milk, breakfast cereals, and cereal products like oatcakes, exotic cheeses (after the war), biscuits of all kinds and syrup and treacle. These last were valuable if you had a sweet tooth and could not manage on the ordinary sugar ration.

At the beginning, each person had sixteen points a month, but the number went up to twenty-four, then varied with food stocks. There were highs of twenty-four points per month in the spring of 1942 and again in 1944 for instance. The points values of the different goods also changed according to availability and demand:

'if the public rushed for one particular variety or size of container, its points value was raised; if it sold slowly, the value was lowered.'[28] It created a flexible way for the Ministry of Food to control supplies.

It might be difficult to keep up with the changes, what was in and what was not, and to judge your best buy. The Ministry did its best to keep people informed by publishing *Food Facts* advertisements at the beginning of each four-week rationing slot.

Larger families were able to manage their points allocation better than smaller households. If you had a lot of ration books, you could buy a variety of canned goods, biscuits, dried fruit and breakfast cereals for instance, but a smaller total of points had to be concentrated on fewer things. This month a meat loaf, next month cornflakes.

In theory you could go to any shop, though the retailer was allowed to keep back points goods for their registered basic rations customers. This of course led to preferential treatment when things were short, and allegations of 'under the counter' trading. If as a stranger you were told there were no chocolate biscuits available, for example, but saw the next customer walk outside with a packet tucked into her basket, it naturally led to resentment.

The points coupons were cut out and counted, and the shop could then get hold of goods to the same points value. Later there was a Points Banking System, which operated like a bank account. On paying in the points he had cut out of customers' books the shopkeeper was credited. When he ordered goods from his wholesaler his points account was debited accordingly. Although there was the hassle of cutting out and counting coupons, it meant that the foods followed demand pretty closely.

'Personal points' were another name for coupons for sweets and chocolate, which were first rationed in the summer of 1942. The coupons varied from time to time in the quantities they would entitle you to buy, but you could spend them as you liked during the month in which they were valid. For example, you could buy a whole block of chocolate, 8oz size, which would take the whole of your sweet ration for a month at the outset. Or you could spread it out to buy 2oz of toffees or peppermints or anything else available, every week. The total quantity soon went up to 1lb a month, and varied throughout the rationing period mainly between 12oz and 1lb a month. There was a touch of humanity on the part of the authorities, as they generally allowed a few extra ounces at Christmas, and children were allocated an extra 8oz in December 1944 and 1947.[29]

You were allowed to detach these pages of coupons from the full ration book, and spend them where you liked, as you did not have to register with a retailer. Children often wanted to choose their own sweets, and could do so in this way – their mothers would probably not have let them go off to the shops with the whole of the precious ration book in case it got lost. It was useful, as well, to people living in residential accommodation where they had to hand over the main book to the management.

SOAP

It may strike the modern reader as strange that soap rationing was organised by the Ministry of Food. However, the raw materials, fats and oils, 'are in some cases the same as those used in margarine, compound fats, etc.'[30] The Minister of Food had a hard choice, in other words. He had to decide on behalf of the people if it would be better for them to be clean or well fed. (I can remember the taste of wartime margarine, and on second thoughts, wonder if there *was* all that much difference between margarine and soap.)

The soap ration was not particularly generous. There were four ration units of soap per person per month, sometimes only three after the war. For each ration unit you could buy *either* 4oz hard soap, for scrubbing floors, *or* 3oz toilet soap, *or* 6oz soft soap, *or* 6 to 12oz of soap powder, depending on its strength, for washing fabrics in general, *or* 3oz soap flakes, often preferred for washing woollens, *or* ½ to 1 pint of liquid soap, again depending on its strength. Detergents as we know them were not developed until after the war, but when they became available they were unrationed. Scouring powder of the Vim type was also free of coupons.

However difficult it was to wash with a limited supply of toilet soap, personal hygiene was not abandoned. Women's magazines carried many advertisements to persuade women to prefer one brand over another, and the feminine need to be appealing was emphasised. Shampoo powders and toothpaste were unrationed, and men could still remove their whiskers, as shaving soap was coupon-free. (If you ran really short of toilet soap this was something worth knowing too.)

As there were no disposable nappies in wartime, babies needed additional soap. They had one coupon a week extra for their laundry. Chimney sweeps were also allowed an extra coupon a week after 1945. Coal was still used extensively for heating homes, and coal fires meant sooty chimneys. Coal workers, including miners, also had extra, with special arrangements for pithead baths where these existed. Employers of workers in other dirty jobs could get a special ration if they provided washing facilities for their employees, and there were allowances for laundries and washerwomen if these still existed at such a time of social change. Washing machines were not yet part of the normal kitchen.

PRICE CONTROLS AND SUBSIDIES

Food had been 'rationed' by price for hundreds of years. Market forces drive up the price of food if there is a shortage, of course, unless the government intervenes. During the First World War food prices more than doubled between 1914 and November 1918, for example.

Inflation during the Second World War was feared – if food prices went up, so too would demands for wage increases. A threatened increase in the cost-of-living index of seven points in November 1939 was therefore countered by the government agreeing to temporary subsidies. The short-term expedient became a long-term policy, though at a ballooning cost to the Exchequer. Government subsidies were half the deal. The other half was control of prices, which meant that food did not go up and the cost of living was stable; though still about 25 per cent to 30 per cent above pre-war levels. This had the desirable effect of keeping industrial peace, with huge benefit to the war effort.[31]

It was not of benefit only to the war effort. Price controls and subsidies coupled with full employment meant that food became more affordable than probably ever before. John Burnett comments:

> To keep bread at 9d. the 4-lb. loaf, eggs at 2s. a dozen, meat at 1s. a pound and cheese at 1s. 1d. was in itself a remarkable contribution to social policy, and its cost, in the form of food subsidies which in 1944 totalled

> £152 million, was a relatively small price to pay. Coupled with almost full employment and steadily rising wages, food control produced a marked increase in the standard of living of that poorer third of the population who, in the thirties, had existed below nutritional adequacy; if the dietary standards of the upper third had to be temporarily lowered there were possibly gains to their health and digestion also.[32]

The prices he gives compare with the Mottrams' of 1931 to show that there had really been only moderate inflation. Bread in 1931 had cost 7*d* for 4lb, eggs at 2/- a dozen were the same, cheap meat in 1931 cost from 9*d* to 1/-, though British meat was more, and New Zealand cheese had been 9*d* per pound.[33]

UNRATIONED FOODS

It would have been impossible to ration or control all foodstuffs, especially the more perishable ones, which could not wait for bureaucratic machinery to distribute them.

Most importantly though, it was government policy to leave the two main carbohydrate foods, bread and potatoes, outside the rationing scheme, though bread was rationed for two years after the war, and there were a few months when potatoes were controlled by a distribution scheme due to a bad harvest in 1947. There had been a campaign during the First World War to reduce the amount of bread consumed, and there was a hint that people might be asked to eat less in total. *Woman* magazine of 21 September 1940 carried an advertisement from the Ministry of Food:

> Get fit not fat on your war diet! Make full use of the fruit and vegetables in season. Cut out 'extras'; cut out waste; don't eat more than you need. You'll save yourself money, you'll save valuable cargo space which is needed for munitions; and you'll feel fitter than you ever felt before.[34]

Food values will be described in more detail below, but carbohydrates are used by the body to generate energy. The more active your life, the more you need. There was therefore a large variation between different groups. A miner at the coalface would have starved if he had

had only the same amount as a schoolgirl of seven, and it would have been very unwise to restrict total calories. Nevertheless there was a touch of control at times. In late 1942 grain was in short supply, so the government raised the price of bread and reduced the price of potatoes to compensate. A publicity initiative helped to make the change more palatable to the public, so to speak.[35] Flour was also unrationed until after the war.

Vegetables were another great standby against hunger, as well as contributing many valuable vitamins to the national wellbeing. They were the focus of the 'Dig for Victory' campaign which will be described in Chapter 4. There were propaganda drives: Doctor Carrot joined Potato Pete in poster campaigns, humorous anthropomorphic figures with a serious purpose.

Of unrationed protein foods, fish was in great demand. But demand exceeded supply and it could almost be said it was rationed by the amount of time a housewife could spend standing in the queue. Restaurants were restricted in the amount they were allowed to buy, to stop them getting more than their fair share, and to leave some for the patient woman with the string bag. People living on the coast or near a riverbank could get lucky.

Offal and sausages were in much the same position. They did not usually require coupons, but were scarce. (They did occasionally form part of the meat ration.) Your registered butcher's shop was the most likely place you might find the odd kidney, bit of liver, or a slab of tripe to cook with onions – if you had the onions, which disappeared at the start of the war. Later you could grow your own. Sausages were made from all the odd scraps of meat available, and bought with gratitude to stretch the ordinary ration, or for breakfast. There might be other titbits as well. A woman talking to me on a bus described how her mother had bought marrow-bones off-ration from the butcher. Her mother boiled them to extract the fat, which she used to fry chips, and then burnt them as extra fuel. 'They were lovely chips,' I was told.

Game of all kinds was also unrationed, but available mainly in the country, where you might be able to get a wild rabbit or hare for the pot, as described in Chapter 5. If you kept chickens for eggs, you were unlikely to waste a bird past its lay-by date.

In fact, the average housewife spent only a little more than half her food money on rationed goods.[36]

Foods usually free of coupons but often scarce. Sausages and offal such as kidney or liver were mostly unrationed, though they slipped occasionally into the meat allowance. Fish and vegetables, especially potatoes, were never rationed during the war.

★ ★ ★ ★ ★

The nation's food habits were shaken, stirred and rehashed through the long years of rationing and controls. Nutritional standards that had been so very uneven during the early part of the century became more nearly equal for all, with better health as a social aim and result.

The rationing system was successful, if tedious to administer. It was perceived to be fair to everyone, which was good for morale at all levels of society.

People are inclined to stay with the foods they know, and to be suspicious of changes. There was enough flexibility in the arrangements to allow for preferences, keeping people comparatively cheerful about the general restrictions.

Above all, nobody starved in this country, even towards the end of the war, as, tragically, so many did in the rest of Europe and Russia.

2

Food Values and Valuable Foods

GOOD FOR YOU

The challenge faced by the wartime Ministry of Food was immense. Although rationing policy was constrained by available supplies, for the sake of morale the Ministry had to ensure that enough familiar ingredients remained in the shops. It is notoriously difficult to change people's food habits. Yet they also had to supply all the proper nutrients to maintain public health. Admittedly, seventy years ago dietetic knowledge was not as detailed as today's, but the basics were in place.

J.C. Drummond was a Professor of Biochemistry at University College, London. With Anne Wilbraham, his second wife, he had written a classic history of English diet, *The Englishman's Food*, first published in 1939.[1] He was seconded to the Ministry of Food in October 1939, becoming its Scientific Adviser in 1940 just after the introduction of rationing. Though the initial plans were made without him, he held this influential position until the end of the war.[2] (He was knighted in 1944, but sadly he was killed in France with his wife and daughter in 1952.)

He could speak with authority because of his expert knowledge of nutrition and the history of British food. He was a reformer too, persuading Lord Woolton, the second Minister of Food, and then the Prime Minister, Winston Churchill, that the rationing scheme could only work with the goodwill of the food industry and retail trade, as well as public acceptance.[3] He was one of the forces behind the Food Advice Division of the Ministry of Food, which carried out a massive public relations exercise to persuade the housewife she could cook her way to victory. Above all he was determined to take the opportunity to improve the nutrition of pregnant women and children from the low level of the most vulnerable groups to an acceptable standard for everyone.

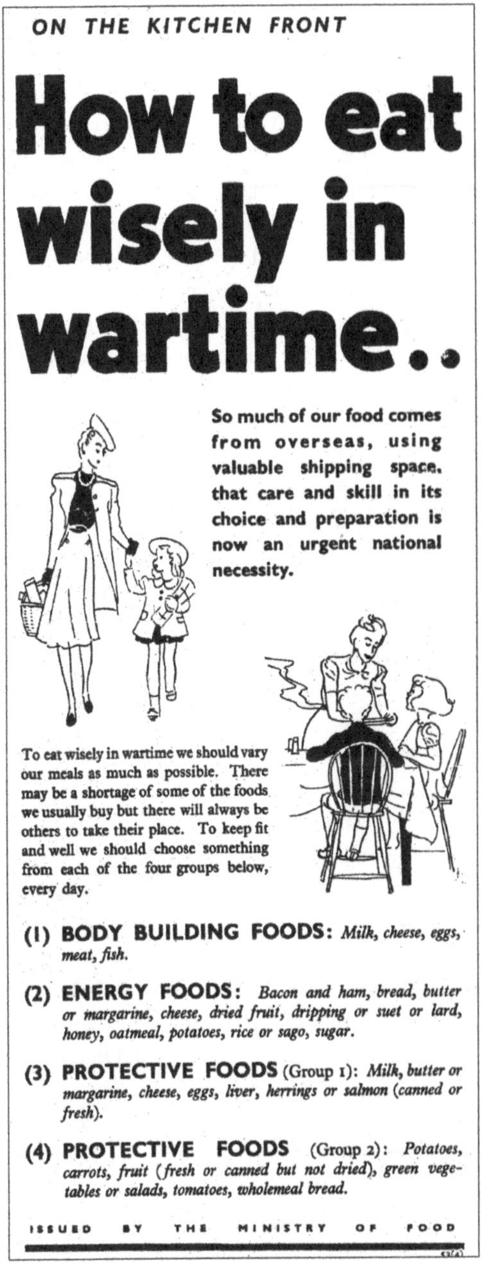
ON THE KITCHEN FRONT
How to eat wisely in wartime..
So much of our food comes from overseas, using valuable shipping space, that care and skill in its choice and preparation is now an urgent national necessity.
To eat wisely in wartime we should vary our meals as much as possible. There may be a shortage of some of the foods we usually buy but there will always be others to take their place. To keep fit and well we should choose something from each of the four groups below, every day.
(1) BODY BUILDING FOODS: Milk, cheese, eggs, meat, fish.
(2) ENERGY FOODS: Bacon and ham, bread, butter or margarine, cheese, dried fruit, dripping or suet or lard, honey, oatmeal, potatoes, rice or sago, sugar.
(3) PROTECTIVE FOODS (Group 1): Milk, butter or margarine, cheese, eggs, liver, herrings or salmon (canned or fresh).
(4) PROTECTIVE FOODS (Group 2): Potatoes, carrots, fruit (fresh or canned but not dried), green vegetables or salads, tomatoes, wholemeal bread.
ISSUED BY THE MINISTRY OF FOOD

How to eat wisely in wartime. The Ministry of Food turned out a huge amount of simple information on healthy eating. Notice how food was divided into four groups, without mentioning protein, fat, carbohydrate or vitamins.

In a key review in May 1940 he recommended making better use of grain by using 85 per cent of it in flour for bread, increasing the home production of milk and vegetables, including potatoes, and to use shipping space to the greatest nutritional advantage by importing cheese, powdered and condensed milk, canned fish and dried pulses, and obtaining concentrates of vitamins A and D to add to margarine during manufacture. This meant that other imports, such as bulky fresh fruit, meat and eggs had to be cut back. Between 1942–44 fruit imports were reduced by about 90 per cent.[4] He insisted that there should be no repetition of the 'Eat Less Bread' campaign of the First World War, which had led to weight loss and reduced efficiency of the workforce.

Lord Woolton (born Frederick James Marquis, 1883–1964), was also a reformer, with a background in both science and business. Even as an undergraduate he had been interested in social policies and the problems of poverty. He earned the nation's trust by his frequent broadcasts and common-sense approach, and, after Churchill, was one of the best known of wartime Ministers. (He moved on to become Minister of Reconstruction in 1943.)

What were the main facts then, about human nutrition which had to be taken into account?

HOW FOOD WORKS[5]

The human body, at any age, has to have a fairly steady supply of different components to keep it going. Put simply, protein is needed for growth and for repair. Fat and carbohydrate are necessary for energy. Vitamins and minerals in small quantities are also required for growth and repair, and for regulating biochemical processes. Some insoluble fibre, which remains unabsorbed, helps digestion by adding bulk to the mixture passing through the intestines. Water is essential too, even more vital than food itself. Dietetics would be easy if things were as straightforward as this, but as the body is highly complex and adapts well to different conditions, within limits, so too its proper nourishment is highly complex but adaptable.

Actually most foods contain a mixture of components, or nutrients, though in differing proportions. White sugar is the nearest you can get to a single nutrient, as it contains sucrose (a carbohydrate) and a mere trace of calcium. Meat is a mixture of protein, fat, water, minerals and vitamins. Fruit contains in general a lot of water and carbohydrate, with only traces of protein and fat but plenty of vitamins. Wheat has some protein and vitamins, but is mostly starch (also a carbohydrate). Butter is mainly fat, but also has a little water and fat-soluble vitamins. Milk is mostly water, but has very useful protein as well as fat, vitamins and minerals.

Cooked dishes are even more of a miscellany. For example, if you consider a Christmas cake you have to think about the individual ingredients and the nutrients they are made from – fat, sugar, eggs (protein, fat, minerals, vitamins), flour (starch, protein, minerals, vitamins), dried fruits and glacé cherries (mostly carbohydrate and fibre), maybe nuts (fat, protein, a little carbohydrate, minerals, vitamins), and then go on to spices and spirits, the marzipan containing almonds, sugar and eggs, plus the royal icing with sugar, egg white and lemon juice. Only the paper frill and plastic model of Santa Claus can be left out. But after you munch and swallow a slice of this cake, your patient digestive system churns it all up, separates and slowly breaks it down into simpler forms of carbohydrate, fat and protein, plus minerals and vitamins, that can be taken into the bloodstream, and in time used for energy or rebuilt into your very own substance. What you cannot digest you excrete. This is the process that all foods go through as they go through you.

Protein

Protein is made up of smaller 'building blocks' called amino acids. There are about twenty of these. Eight of them, plus another needed for infant growth, *must* be supplied in food.[6] Others can be made by the body itself from surplus amino acids.[7] The indispensable amino acids are most readily obtained from protein foods which are the nearest to human flesh – that is, from other animals (including fish). They used to be called 'first class proteins' but are now known simply as animal proteins. There are proteins in plants, too. They were called 'second-class proteins' in the past, but are now logically renamed vegetable proteins. Their amino acids do not occur in the same proportions as in animal proteins, so they are not as good a match for human beings. However, a small amount of something like milk or cheese can often make the balance right, and a properly worked-out vegetarian diet with a wide range of foods is perfectly healthy. In this context, soya beans are rich in protein, and the use of soya flour was encouraged during the war.

Unrationed fish was a valuable source of protein. The Ministry of Food urged people to make the most of it.

If you eat more protein than you need, it cannot be stored, but can be used for energy. However, this is a waste of resources, because protein costs more to buy than carbohydrate, and more land is used to produce food animals than to grow starchy crops.

Carbohydrates

Carbohydrates and fats are the main energy foods, oxidised or 'burnt' to give heat and motion. Carbohydrates break down in digestion ultimately to glucose. The starch in bread and potatoes, the sucrose of sugar, lactose of milk and fructose of a fine, juicy peach all give energy to the body. Some carbohydrate in the form of glycogen is stored in the liver and muscles as an instant reserve that can be used as needed, like cash in your purse ready for spending. But if you take in more carbohydrate than you need, as almost everybody knows, it is converted into fat, which can mean extra inches round the waist and internal padding bad for your life expectancy.

A modern concern is the speed at which carbohydrates are converted to glucose and released into the bloodstream. Rapid release causes a surge of blood sugar, which is controlled by the hormone insulin, made by the pancreas. Quick release carbohydrates tend to come from highly refined foods such as white bread, polished rice, sweets and glucose itself. Whole grains take longer to digest, and don't cause spikes in insulin production, which is better for us. This is the principle behind glycaemic index diets.

Alcohol is treated by the body as a source of energy too, though in our culture we enjoy it for other effects rather than thinking of it as a food. But beer for example may be a significant source of calories for those who drink it regularly.

Fats

Like carbohydrate, fat is used for living processes: to keep warm, breathing, and able to move about with your heart beating for example. There are some fat deposits in the normal body. It is useful to have a reserve of energy, like money in the bank that you haven't yet spent. (You can't draw on it quite as fast as you can the glycogen in liver and muscles.) But as with carbohydrates, excess means excessive where fat deposits bulge and arteries get clogged up. Modern medicine has implicated being obese with various kinds of disease, heart disease in particular. Some kinds of fat are better for you than others. In the 1940s, though, there wasn't much heard about cholesterol, or the differences between saturated and unsaturated fats. It is hardly fair to criticise the wartime diet for this however, not only because the science was not yet developed, but also because fat consumption was restricted anyway. If you look at any wartime photographs of civilians you may notice how few of them looked overweight.

Minerals[8]

Various minerals are essential too. The most important are iron, calcium and phosphorus, and sodium in balance with potassium. Others are chloride, magnesium and zinc. Traces of other minerals are also required, but it is unlikely that the diet will be deficient in these – fluoride, copper, selenium, iodine, manganese, chromium and cobalt, though table salt often has iodine added to it to make sure the thyroid gland functions properly. Fluoride nowadays is added to drinking water, but that is a post-war development, aimed at preventing dental decay in children.

Iron is required for the haemoglobin of blood, which gives it its red colour, and is used to carry oxygen round the body. If you don't get or absorb enough iron you become anaemic. Children need a good amount to build up their reserves. In wartime, pregnant women had an extra meat ration, to supplement their iron as well as protein. In fact even when not pregnant, women are still more at risk of anaemia than men, because they lose blood during menstruation, and therefore need to make up their losses with iron-rich foods. These include red meat and offal, particularly liver, eggs, and sardines, as well as green vegetables. Breakfast cereals nowadays have added iron, making them a better source than in the past. Curry powder contains a lot, but is not eaten in large enough quantities to be really significant. Cocoa powder and chocolate are enjoyable sources. It is noticeable that most of these foods were either rationed or in short supply in wartime. However, the good news is that the body recognises the value of iron, and recycles it when red blood cells die naturally.

Calcium intake was clearly an important preoccupation of the Ministry men during the war, especially as it concerned babies and children. Calcium phosphate is a major component of bones and teeth, and its main source for humans is milk and milk products such as cheese. If there is not enough Vitamin D in association with calcium, rickets can occur in children. In the rationing period, children and pregnant and nursing mothers were given first call on the fresh milk available. Dried household milk, made from skimmed milk, was also available, but was unsuitable for feeding babies, who needed the fat and vitamins of the liquid variety or proper babies' formula.

Sodium, present in salt, was likely to have been too plentiful in the diet rather than too scanty. Salt was used for preserving to some extent, and there was a lot in the popular Bovril and Marmite used as drinks or to flavour stews. It turned up too in canned meat such as corned beef and Spam. However in the 1940s there was less emphasis on the hazards of excessive salt, and it helped to give savour to meals that might otherwise have been too bland. It is noticeable that Ministry of Food recipes almost always included a pinch of salt, even in sweet dishes.

Vitamins

The vitamins have a long and interesting history. Their story became important when something about fresh fruit and vegetables, particularly citrus fruit, was found to prevent scurvy on long sea-voyages or castles under siege. This something is now known as Vitamin C or ascorbic acid, and does not, strictly speaking, 'prevent' scurvy – it is its *absence* that *causes* the sickness. The same is true of most of the vitamins, with deficiencies leading to many symptoms such as stunted growth, bad teeth, skin diseases, bad health in general and death in extreme cases.

It was established in 1906 that foods contained 'accessory factors' which were at first thought to be 'vital amines', shortened to 'vitamines', and later shortened again to 'vitamins' when it was found that not all of them were amines. They fall into two broad categories, water-soluble and fat-soluble. They were originally given letters to identify them. Vitamins A and D are soluble in fat for instance, and B and C are soluble in water. The letters used have now reached at least Vitamin P. However, they have proliferated, divided and subdivided, so that there is no longer a 'Vitamin B' but 'vitamins of the B complex', numbered from one to at least twelve. Then someone decided that it would be better to give the substances more scientific names, so that thiamin is the alternative name for B1, riboflavin for B2 for example.

Vitamins do not figure largely as such in the food propaganda of the war years. Instead, the foods that are good sources were referred to as 'protective foods'. But it is possible to see the scientific subtext.

Carrots (Vitamin A) were said to be a protection against night blindness. Cod liver oil, for children and expectant mothers, is particularly rich in Vitamins A and D.

Deficiency of the B group was less likely, as thiamin is contained in bread, potatoes, milk and meat, while riboflavin occurs in milk, meat and eggs. Children had priority for eggs.

Vitamin C is contained in many fresh foods, but is diminished or destroyed by heat. Even potatoes supply Vitamin C, though the quantity goes down the longer they are stored. The 'Dig for Victory' campaign was partly motivated by knowledge that fresh vegetables were essential for everyone's health, especially if fruit was scarce. To be on the safe side, children were supplied with concentrated orange juice, as fresh oranges were often unavailable.

Vitamin D is present in dairy foods, eggs and fatty fish such as herrings, and was added to margarine. It is also formed in the human skin in the presence of sunlight. Sunny summers are good, dark winters, with heavy clothes, are bad. As already mentioned, cod liver oil is a particularly potent source, and formed part of the Welfare Foods scheme which I shall describe later.

Calories

The level of food-fuel needed varies according to people's age, sex, size, and of course the amount of physical energy used in their lifestyle. It is convenient to measure the energy value of foods in kilocalories, abbreviated to kcal, or the colloquial term 'calories'. The food calorie is a unit of heat, equivalent to raising the temperature of a kilogram of water by 1°C. (This should not be confused with the 'small' calorie used in other scientific work, which is the amount of heat needed to raise the temperature of only 1g of water by 1°C.) Another unit is sometimes used nowadays, the kilojoule, or kj. But in this book I use 'calories' to mean food calories or kcal.

The calorie values of foods had already been worked out by the beginning of the war, together with estimations of the amounts required by different groups of people. You started with a measure called the 'basal metabolic rate' which is what a person at rest needs just to stay alive, heart beating, breathing, keeping warm and so on. Then you add the amount of heat energy used up by all the various things done during the day. For instance, just sitting takes up about 1 calorie per minute, walking 3.5 calories and jogging 6.5 calories. But these numbers vary between individuals. Extra energy is needed by pregnant and lactating women too.

If you look at the information on the back of food packaging, you will see that today the guideline daily amount for average women is 2,000 calories a day, with 2,500 for men. These recommendations are less than in the past, and compare with 2,200 for most adult women and 3,000 for moderately active men in 1969.[9] During the war, when people had to walk or cycle (very little petrol for cars) and rarely had central heating, they needed more still. For heavy work it would increase again. A person who is short of calories feels hungry, the body's signal that refuelling is required.

Fat has rather more than twice the energy value, weight for weight, as protein or carbohydrate. A gram of fat yields 9 calories compared with 4 calories for a gram of protein, or 3.75 calories per gram of carbohydrate. As an example applied to real food, this means that a slice of white bread, weighing 40g eaten alone will give you about 95 calories. If you spread it with 10g butter, you will get another 75 calories. If you decide to make it into a ham sandwich with 50g of canned ham, adding a further 60 calories or so, you end up with 230 calories.[10] (You don't need to worry about the mustard.) If you are a man this is a bit less than 10 per cent of what you need in a day, rather more than 10 per cent if you are an average woman. Calories don't tell you much about making healthy choices, but can be valuable statistically to estimate whether a diet is broadly adequate or not.

ESSENTIAL FOODSTUFFS

In 1940 an emergency study drew up an 'Iron Ration' plan based only on bread, fats, potatoes, oatmeal, vegetables and milk. It was never actually implemented, though it came close in the summer of 1940.[11] For the sake of morale at home it was thought that certain foods were non-negotiable. Bread and flour, potatoes and other vegetables, meat, milk, cheese, sugar and fats of various kinds were staples. Eggs and fish came close. Tea was valuable mostly because of its traditional psychological function – a nice cup of tea was always a comfort. These were the bread and butter, so to speak, of feeding the nation.

Additionally the needs of pregnant women, babies and children were given priority by the Welfare Foods Service, described below.

Bread and Flour: Brown v. White

Bread is the food that has, throughout history, aroused maximum emotion. Bread was a synonym for food itself ('our daily bread'), and a lack of it meant starvation. Bread and water were traditionally the basics still allowed to prisoners on punishment regimes.

It was also an indicator of social status. Even during the Middle Ages in Europe, the colour of the bread on your table said much about your position in society. Because it was more expensive and perhaps more digestible, white bread was regarded as superior to brown, and a wheaten loaf was of higher status than one made with a proportion of barley, rye or oats. Even so, early milling did not produce absolutely white flour, and the finest bread was cream-coloured (and more nourishing) than later white. Still, the palest available was usually preferred. Nineteenth-century food reformers suggested that brown bread was better for you, but it was a minority choice.

Flour is milled from wheat, of course. The cleaned wheat grains are torn apart, rubbed and sifted so that the inner starch grains are separated from the outer skins, which are not digestible. The inner covering of the wheat 'berry' is bran, and may or may not be removed. The actual embryo of the wheat is divided from the starch, or endosperm, which would give energy to the growing plant. This germ contains most of the protein, minerals and vitamins, but it may be separated from the starch in milling. (Hovis flour puts it back.) The proportion of the original grain left in the finished flour is known as the extraction rate, so that a fine white flour has a 70 per cent extraction rate, while wholemeal, as the name implies, keeps much more of the grain. Flour may be bleached to make it look more attractive.

At the start of the war, plain bread generally came as white, brown or Hovis, but there were also many regional kinds and shapes available. A browner bread began to be made, but was not compulsory until March 1942, when the changeover to an 85 per cent extraction rate became law. This was not entirely for nutritional reasons, but to make the most of the grain that was available, because shipping was a great problem at this time. There followed a short period when barley and a small proportion of oats were added to make the wheat go further.

Whether a flour is suitable for bread-making or not depends on how much gluten it contains. Gluten is a protein, and the amount varies in different kinds of wheat. When the flour is mixed with water, and kneaded either by hand or machine, the gluten 'develops' or forms a kind of elastic mesh, which gives bread its texture. Soft flours (less gluten) are more suitable for cake-making, where you want a tender effect. One wartime problem was that the wheat grown in Britain was generally soft, unlike the gluten-rich wheat from Canada, which could not be carried easily across the Atlantic.

Area Bread Officers were appointed by the Ministry. They were professionals who knew the capacities of the bakeries in their localities. Their job was to make sure that there was no interruption in supply so that the public should never feel threatened by shortage.

Even after heavy bombing raids, as on Coventry in 1940, the bread came through from nearby cities, when bakers worked twenty-four-hour shifts at times.[12]

On a local level, Peter Bumphrey, who was aged eight in 1939, demonstrates the importance of bread to the community. He lived in the village of Itteringham, North Norfolk, where his father was a farm foreman. In one particularly cold winter the three steep roads into the village were impassable because of snow and ice. There was no bread. Peter and his father got hold of a couple of carthorses and two huge sacks, and rode over the frozen fields to the nearest town of Aylsham, 5 miles away. They were able to fill their sacks at the baker's there, and rode back to rescue their village from the bread shortage.[13]

Nowadays, ordinary bread, though still important, is not as central to our diet as it once was. We eat more cakes and biscuits, as well as breakfast cereals, pasta and rice. Perhaps, too, bread is not as attractive as it once seemed. Factory-made loaves, sliced and pre-packed, contain various additives and enzymes, and rather less yeast, than in traditional doughs,[14] which, once upon a time, were produced just from flour, yeast, water and salt, with perhaps a little fat plus a dash of sugar to help the yeast ferment. Speciality breads, such as naan or focaccia are popular though, and probably more kinds of flour are available today than ever before.

Not all additives are bad. The fibre and phytic acid in wholemeal flour can hinder absorption of calcium and iron. Calcium carbonate was added in the war, to make up for this. Bread is now fortified with iron, thiamin and niacin, except for wholemeal, which contains enough naturally.

People ate the wholemeal bread when they had to in 1942, but they did not adapt to it willingly. Many switched back when white was freely available again in 1953. However, perhaps the British loaf should be compared to the 'bread' of parts of Europe, where in concentration camps, for instance, it was made from potato flour, peas and sawdust.[15]

National flour matched the National Loaf, and posed a few problems for the cook. It made cakes of closer texture than white flour, and pastry needed to be carefully prepared if it was not to be heavy and indigestible. Like bread, flour was available throughout the war. Cornflour, made from maize starch, was in shorter supply and was on points. A canny cook could add cornflour to lighten the texture of her cakes and pastry.

Potatoes and other Vegetables

Like bread, potatoes have traditionally been one of the most important energy foods, as, raw, they have a calorie value of 70 to 75 calories per 100g. They also have up to 2g per 100g of protein, and 14 to 16mg of Vitamin C, according to their freshness. The protein is not much compared with the 16 or 17g of carbohydrate per 100g, but as potatoes were eaten day in, day out, in fairly large helpings, their total contribution of protein and vitamins was significant. If they are made into chips the calorie value soars because of the added fat, rising to about 190kcal per 100g.[16]

Someone doing heavy manual work might welcome a filling meal such as fish and chips, and children with high energy needs have always liked them, but fat for domestic frying had to come out of the ration or some supplementary source such as marrow-bones.

Potatoes themselves were one of the crops most encouraged for home production, and many people grew their own on allotments or in a patch at the bottom of the garden in place of a pre-war lawn. Sir Jack Drummond of the Ministry of Food reassured housewives that potatoes were not in themselves fattening. 'Starch is not more fat making than butter: it is only over-eating which puts weight on the average person.'[17]

At any rate, potatoes were generally available (until a failed crop in 1947 led to a restriction to 3lb a week per 'normal consumer' until the following spring). Some of the most inventive thinking went into Ministry of Food recipes for potatoes and more potatoes. The housewife was encouraged to cook them unpeeled, because the protein and vitamins lie mainly just below the skin. Jacket potatoes are still recommended as a healthy choice. Actually they were cooked as a vegetable in all ways known to mankind, and also made into dumplings, pastry, scones, even cake. They had always been an ingredient in Cornish pasties, Lancashire hot-pot, shepherd's pie and similar country dishes.

Other vegetables were also very high in the Ministry approval ratings. For example, carrots were easy to grow, with a natural sweetness that appealed to children. They were promoted as preventing night blindness, a clever bit of propaganda, because everybody needed to be able to see as much as possible in the dark. This was a time when there were no streetlights because of the blackout. All lights showing at night, particularly from the windows of houses, were rigorously prevented by ARP Wardens. There was naturally an increase in road accidents too, when vehicle headlights were dimmed. RAF pilots were popularly supposed to feed on carrots for the same reason.

It is true that carrots are rich in Vitamin A, and true that a deficiency causes disturbance of vision, including impaired sight in dim light, as well as other undesirable symptoms in the skin, and stunted growth. But if one has enough there is no advantage in having extra. Carrots were taken for a spin!

All green vegetables were in favour as well, justified because of their vitamins and minerals. They are sources of Vitamin C of course, when eaten fresh or raw, and also of very useful amounts of potassium, calcium, iron and trace elements. Because Vitamin C is reduced or destroyed by heating, quick methods of cooking were recommended. The favourite was 'conservative' cooking, that is, the washed veggies were put into a saucepan with a scrape of margarine and a little water. They were cooked with the lid on for a short time, and then dished up complete with what was left of the cooking liquid. Or the vegetable water could be used for soups etc. In this way nothing was wasted down the sink, but conserved.

Cabbage was the prototype of greens. It was traditional and cheap, much used in schools and other institutions, but to be fair to the Ministry other vegetables were promoted too. A leaflet[18] dated January 1946 mentions savoy and red cabbage, spring greens, kale, spinach; the tops of broccoli, turnips, beetroot and broad beans 'which gardeners always pick off'; Brussels sprouts, cauliflower and broccoli, sea kale, peas, French and runner beans and broad beans. Interestingly it has a traditional country vegetable too, young nettles, which of course had to be picked using gloves. They were cooked as cabbage according to this leaflet.

Butter, Margarine and Cooking Fats

During the early twentieth century butter was the most acceptable accompaniment for bread. It is easily digested, and was traditionally used for making sauces, cakes and some pastries. Margarine was a cheaper substitute, generally perceived as inferior. It had been invented in France in about 1870, being made then from melted fats mixed with milk and salt, then chilled to make it solid.

The fats used varied considerably, but by the time of the Second World War vegetable oils and whale oil were used extensively. The oils had to be treated at high temperatures to make them solid. The process is called hydrogenation. These altered fats are now thought to be unhealthy.[19] Nowadays some people prefer a different kind of margarine on health grounds, as it can by made from polyunsaturated fats, which are better for the heart and arteries. However the different kinds of fat were not of great concern for the planners before the 1950s. Margarine as manufactured was thought to be as nutritious as butter, and had similar amounts of Vitamins A and D added to it. The Vitamin D was desirable to offset the shortage of eggs, which would otherwise be a good source.[20] You were allowed to take your butter ration as margarine, in whole or part, but not vice versa. Vegetarians and others who did not eat bacon on religious grounds gave up the bacon ration in exchange for vegetarian margarine plus an extra 2oz.

The wartime version of margarine was good for making shortcrust pastry, especially if used with cooking fat, and was satisfactory in cake. For many people, though, it was unpalatable on bread. Some people mixed their butter and margarine together, to improve the taste. At times when milk was comparatively plentiful you could siphon off the top creamy layer, and after a couple of days shake it up in a Kilner jar usually used for bottling fruit. The jar could be closely sealed. I remember it was one of my jobs to sit down and shake it solemnly for half-an-hour or so. A quarter of a pint of cream from the milk yielded a small knob of butter, but however little it was a welcome addition to the ration. In my family, and in others, everyone had an individual butter dish, so that nobody ate more than their share.

Cooking fat was a vague term, which described lard or a white fat, usually solid, made from oils. It was part of the fat ration and good for pastry and for frying. Housewives supplemented this by saving every scrap of dripping or fat from meat or bacon. It could be made fit for use, or 'clarified' by boiling in water, which was then allowed to get cold. The solid fat was then removed from the top. Marrow-bones were unrationed, if you could persuade your butcher to sell them to you. If they were broken and then boiled they yielded a satisfactory amount of fat, which could be used for frying. Shredded suet became part of the cooking fat ration in September 1945, but in March 1946 it was added to the points system.

Dripping toast, with marmite or the juices from the pan after a roast, was a delicacy.

Milk, Cheese and Eggs

These foods are important sources of protein, fat, the essential vitamins A and D, and the calcium needed for strong bones and teeth. Because milk production increases in spring, diminishes in winter, it was controlled by a distribution scheme, rather than being rationed – though it was sometimes difficult to tell the difference. Priority was given to the 'welfare' groups described below.

Cheese had been a traditional food of the country labourer, and a larger ration was granted especially to agricultural workers. Cheese is good in sandwiches, remaining fresh and appetising even after being in a lunch box for several hours.

Eggs were a problem, especially in towns. They are an excellent source of iron and Vitamin D, easily digestible, and an ingredient in many baked dishes such as cakes. They were one of the foods most missed when in short supply, and short the supply certainly was unless you kept your own hens. Many people did. Dried eggs, imported from America particularly under the Lend Lease Act of 1941, helped to restore the nutritional deficit, but weren't like the real thing. They had to be 'reconstituted' or mixed with water, or added to dry ingredients in baking with extra liquid to compensate. Some people made scrambled egg from the reconstituted mix, but it turned hard and watery and did not much resemble the genuine dish. Still, they were better than none.

Meat

Butcher's meat, along with bacon and poultry, was a significant source of protein, iron and various vitamins and minerals for many people. However, because it was expensive before the war it was eaten more often by the affluent than by the poor. During the war, as it was rationed by price not weight, consumption became much fairer, because money did not guarantee you a better deal. You could choose between a minuscule amount of fillet steak, for instance, or a larger quantity of stewing beef. Even so the ration covered only a few main meals. Canteen food or British Restaurants were meant to supplement the basic allowance. Offal did not require coupons, and helped to keep up protein intake if you could get it. Muriel Gibson remembers the butcher in the village of Corbridge, near Hexham. He would offer a little bit of liver from time to time to his registered customers, which was then enjoyed fried with bacon.[21]

Canned meat was also a valuable supplement. Most was on points, but corned beef formed part of the meat ration for much of the rationing period from the end of 1941 onwards.[22] I can remember that the butcher had a huge oblong block of it, from which he cut a few slices. These were separated from the raw meat with a piece of greaseproof paper, but I don't think he washed his hands between touching the raw meat and the canned stuff. None of us could afford to be fussy.

The famous Spam was one of the great successes of the war, having survived to this day as a tasty quick meal, especially with salad, although in wartime we had many recipes to vary it. Imported from America, it was made from chopped pork and ham, spiced to a special formula. It was nourishing, high in calories because it contained quite a lot of fat, and high on points value.

Fish

Cod, then plentiful in the sea, had been a very important protein resource for many poorer people and those living in institutions such as boarding schools. It was a cheap food before the war, and continued to be valued. As it was unrationed, it was necessary to queue for a share whenever the fishmonger had been supplied. Apart from protein, oily fish such as herrings supply significant amounts of Vitamin D. In white fish such as cod and halibut the vitamin is stored in the liver – hence cod liver oil. The crews of trawlers and inshore fishermen risked their lives not only from the natural hazards of the ocean but also from enemy action. The fishing fleet was much smaller than in peacetime, because so many boats and men were engaged in trawling for mines instead of fish.

Once fish had landed in cans, it was invariably on points, with salmon, sardines and tuna all carrying high values, pilchards more modest ones.

Sugar

One of the first foods to be rationed, sugar continued to be supplied throughout the war. From a purely nutritional point of view this is perhaps puzzling. Refined white sugar is sometimes referred to as 'empty calories'. It provides energy but unlike most other carbohydrates has almost no vitamin or mineral content. Unrefined cane sugar, such as black treacle, is different, containing useful amounts of iron. But the lowest income groups had, before the war, relied heavily on bread and jam to keep them going. Many people took sugar in their tea, too. I suspect that the sugar and jam ration was maintained so that these popular familiar foods would still be available, particularly for poorer people.

Then, too, sugar is a preservative, and so has a special relationship to fruit. Though there is not much Vitamin C left after boiling fruit for jam, sugar was often added to bottled fruit, valuable in winter. The Ministry was keen to make sure that fruit crops were not wasted if there was a glut, but it was difficult to predict if this would happen. There were extra issues during the jam-making season. But the extra sugar for jam did not gel, so to speak, in the summer of 1940, when the Ministry itself was in the throes of a house-move to Colwyn Bay. Manipulation of national stocks of sugar and jam became necessary, so there were times when you could exchange your sugar ration for jam, marmalade, fruit curd or honey – even for imitation honey, whatever that may have been. Sometimes you could make the swap the other way round, and get extra sugar instead of jam.[23] Mincemeat was included in the preserves ration too, but there was also extra sugar at Christmas later on in the war.

The psychological effect of sugar was important. Cakes, puddings and biscuits figured largely in wartime catering. They were and are comfort foods, the sweet things that people crave when they are under stress. Biscuits went with tea as emergency restoratives after air raids, for instance. The nutritionally valuable 85 per cent extraction flour had to be made palatable too. Sweet puddings and cakes were a way of doing this.

Tea

Tea continued to be imported. It is not a nourishing drink, as it has mere traces of minerals. Its food value depends on the amount of milk and sugar added. Its psychological value is immense, however. Tea had become our national drink from the nineteenth century, after its initial upper-class status during the seventeenth century. Indeed by the years of Depression, the late 1920s and early 1930s, it was being enjoyed all day long by all classes of society, with an annual average purchase of 10lb per person. A tea ration, generally of 2oz per week per adult, works out at about 6½lb a year, and the total rose to about 9lb taking into account supplies in canteens and so on.[24] Children lost their ration of tea in the summer of 1942 (perhaps it was thought that it was not good for them), but the over-seventies were granted an additional ounce a week from the end of 1944.

It owes its cheering effect to caffeine, like coffee. It is a stimulant, acting on the central nervous system to make a person feel more alert and less tired. Of course this was desirable when under stress, as for instance during an air raid or when on fire-watching duty after a hard day's work.

A tea break in itself was good for productivity, as a short rest refreshes both body and mind. As drunk with milk and sugar it gives a boost to energy levels. The founders of the Temperance Movement of the nineteenth century would have been proud of the sober civil servants as they poured supplies into the nation's cups.

Coffee did not become anything like as popular as tea until after the war, with the introduction of trendy coffee bars in the 1950s. It was not rationed, but was difficult to find.

Welfare Foods

Being poor before the war had meant bad health for children and high rates of infant mortality. Rationing was seen as a chance to improve things as a deliberate social policy, building on previous welfare schemes such as cheap or free milk for elementary school children. Hence there was tremendous emphasis on getting milk to those who needed it most during the war, especially pregnant women, nursing mothers, babies and young children. Expectant mothers also had extra meat. National Dried Milk was a baby food for infants to replace or supplement breast milk. (Not to be confused with Household Milk, which was dried skimmed milk, unsuitable for babies.).

Older children and adolescents had extra too, but not as much as the younger ones. (It was not all good news though. Milk was not universally pasteurised until the mid-1960s, so it carried some risk of bovine tuberculosis, as mentioned on page 169.)

National Dried Milk was supplied for babies. The message on the tin mentions cod liver oil and concentrated orange juice, which were also welfare foods.

Milk was subsidised, with a pint a day of cheap or free milk for expectant mothers and children under five, plus priority for more at full price. Schoolchildren had at least a third of a pint a day, free after the war when the scheme continued. (The squat bottles had cardboard lids with a hole for a straw, also thoughtfully supplied, as I remember.) In spite of its undoubted success, the scheme started to dry up in 1968. Secondary school children no longer received it, and in 1971, Margaret Thatcher, then Secretary of State for Education, stopped the free supply to primary schools except for children who had medical needs.[25] 'Thatcher, Thatcher, milk snatcher', was a slogan adopted by her opponents.

Another welfare food was concentrated orange juice, also supplied to expectant and nursing mothers and young children from April 1942. This was a rich source of Vitamin C, and was fairly well received. At the start, about a quarter of the entitled mothers bought it, rising to 45 per cent in 1945 but dropping back to 27 per cent by 1951.

A very well-meaning but less successful project was the supply of cod liver oil. This is an excellent source of Vitamins A and D needed to prevent rickets, and was given away free. But even at the height of its distribution, in 1947 and 1948, it did not reach 33 per cent of its potential uptake. Figures for Vitamin A and D tablets for pregnant women were slightly better, with a maximum of about 42 per cent in 1946.[26] Housewives were given a scolding in a *Kitchen Front* broadcast as early as 1942.[27] They were asked why they were failing to take up the vitamin foods – then blackcurrant juice and cod liver oil. They were told outright that a great many mothers were refusing to safeguard their babies' health.

There was much distress too among the Welfare Foods staff responsible for distributing it. A little newsletter for them, published by the Ministry of Food, *Keeping in Touch*, constantly exhorts them to try harder to persuade mothers to give it to the children. '500–800 international units are an anti-rachitic measure, and one teaspoonful of the National Cod Liver Oil Compound – 750 international units – ensures this.' Children in residential nurseries were given it 'in a matter of fact way' and took it in the same spirit, and if a baby was started on a drop or so at a month old there was less resistance later. You could always add a few drops on a portion of cabbage or potato (not a lot of help, I imagine). However, it was acknowledged that many children did not like it. 'If we could have found something that tasted nicer than cod liver oil we would have done so, but there was nothing to give anywhere near the same food value under present conditions.'[28]

My mother thought I ought to have it too, though I was too old for the free issue. I can remember it was poured into a teaspoon and offered with encouragement, but only an inflationary rise in pocket money would persuade me to try it – and after a while, no bribe was big enough.

But even if the vitamin supply was not as well received as it might have been, there was a marked improvement in children's health during the Welfare Foods period. Infant mortality in England and Wales fell from 59 per 1,000 live births in 1941 to 46 in 1944.[29] The birth rate itself increased too, and the numbers of women dying in childbirth declined. There was a baby boom, which reached its peak in the two years after the war.

3

The Housewife, Her Kitchen and What She was Told

The Second World War changed the position of women in society. There had obviously been some emancipation during the First World War, and in 1918 women won the vote at the age of thirty. This was subsequently reduced to twenty-one, like men, in 1928. They were very much under-represented in Parliament however.

For most of our history there had been plenty of jobs performed by women outside the home, particularly by the poor. Country women had always helped to bring in the harvest, for example. Many were servants before marriage and later continued to clean other people's homes as well as their own. Factory workers were certainly around between the wars, but largely doing such things as assembly work where their manual dexterity made them valuable. Better-educated women were entering the professions, and a large number were teachers and nurses.

But in the Second World War, for the first time in British history, women's paid employment was brought under Government control. In late 1941 women between the ages of nineteen and thirty, later extended to forty-five and even fifty, were expected to register for war work unless they had a child or children under fourteen years old. Some were considered 'immobile' if they had a home to run, and so were the wives of servicemen or sailors in the Merchant Navy, but those without family ties could be directed to work in essential industries in different parts of the land. They were sent to aircraft or munitions factories for instance. Alternatively they could join the Women's Auxiliary Services – the ATS, the WAAF, the WRNS and others – or could volunteer for the Women's Land Army.

The idea was that women who had up until then stayed at home would be more usefully employed on war work unless they had children to care for. The war expanded many skills and increased confidence. Although there was still a difference in wages, women were now earning more. Women's work was paid at about half the rate for men in industry. The unions were generally unhappy at the 'dilution' of the workforce by introducing women to do men's jobs, or what had formerly been thought of as men's jobs. However, the call-up or redirection of men left little choice but to accept them.

Women's Lib. was a long way off though. Education was patchy, and social attitudes ambivalent. Married women were still taxed as if their earnings belonged to their husbands, who were assessed on the joint income. (It was not until 1990 that they were taxed independently.) It was still the aim of many women just to get married, have children and make a home.

Even if they were working there does not seem to have been much sharing of housework if their husbands were still around. An advertisement for a Peek Freen pudding neatly summed up prevalent attitudes. 'Can a Warden Be a Good Wife?' it asks. A strip cartoon explains that the wife is working in the ARP, but her husband is unhappy because when he gets home his dinner is a cold one – yet again. But here is helpful Mrs Peek: her tinned pudding is ready to eat after being boiled in the can for (only!) an hour. The husband is no longer deprived or neglected, and the wife can continue to do her essential and dangerous job without feeling guilty …

In fact a lot of women remained housewives. In 1939, out of a total adult female population of 16.04 million, there had been 10.9 million women who were neither in work nor looking for it. By 1943 the figures had dropped to about to 8.75 million,[1] so that rather more than half were still doing what home-making women had always done, in theory. However, very many were also doing unpaid voluntary work or had part-time jobs or duties in civil defence organisations. In the country they might have the additional task of looking after evacuees.

Changing roles and harder work meant extra psychological stress. One can deduce this by reading women's magazines – especially between the lines. Advertisers would not have wasted money on items that would not bring a return, so one can assume there was a demand for the goods advertised. Just looking at *Woman's Own* magazine for June and July 1940 gives an interesting insight into the time.

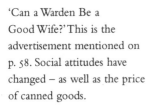

'Can a Warden Be a Good Wife?' This is the advertisement mentioned on p. 58. Social attitudes have changed – as well as the price of canned goods.

On the health front, there is an impression of an epidemic of headaches, mild constipation and a feeling of being 'run down'. Beecham's Pills ('Worth a Guinea a Box'), Aspro, Phensic, Eno's Fruit Salt, Fynnon Salts, Phosferine tonic [sic], Dr Cassell's Tablets to make you eat, sleep and feel better, are all represented. 'Ovaltine' takes up many column inches, promoting itself as an aid to sound sleep, largely because new-laid eggs were used in its manufacture (this in 1940, at least). Allenbury's Diet followed the same line – it was a 'predigested nightcap', and Horlicks took a scientific line, promising that at bedtime it would give you 1st Group Sleep – the most restful – compared with the 2nd and 3rd Groups.

Period pains were taken care of with pills, periods themselves made less of a nuisance with Tampax. At first there was a medical note: you could consult Nurse Jones, but a little later servicewomen were stepping out confidently on their own.

Anaemia was still in evidence: mothers were urged to watch their teenage daughters for the signs, which included pale cheeks and dull eyes, depression, backache and unhealthy food preferences.

Not much had changed, evidently – these symptoms had been described as 'green sickness' 300 years earlier. Now, however, you could give the girl Dr Williams Pink Pills, also good for menopausal symptoms. They cost 1/3*d* a box, or a triple-sized bargain at 3/-.

All these women, but especially those who were primarily housewives, were given unprecedented attention by the authorities. Their role as mothers and particularly home cooks was a large concern of the Ministry of Food. The BBC, film flashes, newspapers, magazines, leaflets and cookery demonstrations put them at the centre of a sustained campaign of propaganda and information that recognised how important they could be. They were essential troops on the Home Front.

KITCHENS AND KITCHEN EQUIPMENT

It is easy to overlook the difficulties of wartime home making, and of cooking in particular, because equipment was generally minimal. Today we have streamlined gas or electric cookers, or maybe ranges of the Aga type. Microwave cookers can heat through a ready meal in a few minutes. An electric kettle takes no time to boil for an instant hot drink. The refrigerator and deep freeze are indispensable. Stainless steel or non-stick pots and pans are easy to use and quick to clean. Our continuous work surfaces are covered with food processors, bread makers, ice-cream makers, coffee grinders and all the other electrical goods that have been invented to make life easier (though more sophisticated), available at the flick of a credit card.

In 1939, however, everything took longer and was more basic. There were no washing machines or dishwashers. The most up-to-date gas or electric oven stood on four legs, with a hygienic space underneath for sweeping or mopping the floor, which was often covered with linoleum, 'lino' for short. Lino had the questionable advantage of taking a good polish, applied by the housewife with a rag, and rubbed off perhaps with a duster over a mop. Too much polish and you were apt to skate dangerously across the shiny surface with a pan of hot boiled potatoes in your hand. The sink you were aiming for was most likely made of thick white glazed pottery, with a wooden or clip-on enamel draining board or perhaps just a table or shelf beside it. You could put a bit of cotton curtain on a spring-wire round the sink to conceal the bucket, scrubbing brush, and cardboard cylinder of Vim scouring powder, which belonged underneath it.

Not everyone had an up-to-date cooker, of course. Many rural houses were still not connected to an electricity supply, and gas was mostly confined to towns. In the country you might still be using a kitchen range left over from an earlier era, with its coal fire still exposed and arrangements for heating saucepans to the side or on top. Such ranges had an enclosed oven that needed skill and experience to manage if you were not to get an uncooked cake, or, on the contrary, a joint burnt to charcoal. Alternatively you might have a paraffin stove with burners rather like gas ones but smellier.

I remember the kitchen of most of my childhood. The house was a large one, belonging to Cable & Wireless, the company that employed my father at the cable station in Porthcurno. It was a hybrid, probably state-of-the-art in Edwardian times, with a coal-fired kitchen range that also heated hot water, and two sculleries which contained the deep butler's sinks. My parents put a new sink into the kitchen and an electric cooker to supplement the range. We had a refrigerator too, kept in a separate pantry, which sounds quite grand, though inconvenient because it was so far from the kitchen. It was certainly useful though. It kept food reasonably cold and made a limited quantity of ice (and ice-cream which in the war was remarkably similar to frozen custard). But it had one anti-social drawback. The motor, which ran intermittently, sounded like a modern jumbo-jet. Visitors would be cut off in mid-sentence and sleeping cats woke up howling.

In modest homes the galvanised iron or enamelled oval bath, used for laundry and probably a Friday night tub if there was no bathroom, was too big to go under the sink, so it might hang from a peg on the wall, or in an outhouse if there was one.

There was a lot of enamelled ware – breadbins, casseroles, jugs and kitchen waste bins were often made from it, either in white with a navy-blue trim, or cream with green. Saucepans might be of this kind too, or perhaps made from aluminium or old-fashioned cast iron.

A round wooden breadboard was essential for cutting slices off your loaf, because pre-sliced bread had not been thought of. It was probably round because many loaves in the past had been the round cottage loaf with its smaller bun shape stuck on top. Oblong tin-loaves were normal as well, but the traditional breadboard remained in use in many homes.

Rolling pins were usually made from wood, and so were the simple wooden spoons whose design remains more or less unchanged today.

Storage jars were made from glass or stoneware, mixing bowls of the still-popular thick white pottery with a cream exterior. Pudding basins were commonly simple white. Pyrex glass existed, and was useful for oven-to-table ware such as pie dishes. Cake tins were so called because originally they had had a thin layer of tin over steel, but tin was needed for the war, and was on its way out. Baking sheets had to be greased, as there was no non-stick finish yet. Food 'tins' were made of thin steel, lacquered on the inside, and were generally opened with a sharp bayonet-type of knife, requiring skill and strength if it were not to slip and give you a gashed thumb. It was still customary to refer to 'tinned food', not canned food as it is today.

As the war went on, a shortage of pots and pans developed. In July 1940 Lord Beaverbrook, the Minister for Aircraft Production, had appealed to patriotic housewives:

> Give us your aluminium. We want it, and we want it now. New and old, of every type and description, and all of it.
>
> We will turn your pots and pans into Spitfires and Hurricanes, Blenheims and Wellingtons. I ask, therefore, that every one who has pots and pans, kettles, vacuum cleaners, hat-pegs, coat-hangers, shoe-trees, bathroom fittings and household ornaments, cigarette boxes, or any other articles made wholly or in part of aluminium, should hand them over at once to the local headquarters of the Women's Voluntary Services.[2]

However, though thousands responded, the pans turned out to be unsuitable, a mountain of saucepans which never came to the boil. Meanwhile, back at the stove, the pots that remained started to wear out, and war production did not allow them to be replaced in quantity or quality. One of the Ministry of Food leaflets tells you how to cook several different items in one pan. Put the jam pudding and a meal roll in separate cocoa tins, lids on, and simmer in a large pan. Cook carrots and potatoes in the boiling water nearer dinner time.[3] Or you could steam vegetables over a boiling stew using a colander (if you hadn't sent it off to be turned into a Spitfire). If you had no lid you could put a plate on top instead. It was to be hoped that you had saved your frying pan, often made of iron, as this could be very useful not only for fry-ups of sausages and small portions of meat and fish, but for making such things as drop scones and oatcakes.

The meat ration was frequently made up of tougher cuts, so a mincing machine was invaluable. It had a screw clamp to fix it firmly to the table. You put the food into a small hopper on top, turned the handle, and a screw inside forced the food through the holes of round cutters. Cold cooked meat was made into shepherd's pie, rissoles and so on, and you could also mince suet and prepare baby food. The mincer could be taken apart to wash, but you had to be careful not to lose any of the smaller parts or it was useless.

To weigh ingredients you might have a spring-balance with a pan on top, a dial below to show the weight. Some people still had the old type of balance, with a pan on one side, a weight platform at the other. Sets of weights, which stacked together, usually came as 2lb, 1lb, 8oz, 4oz, 2oz, 1oz and ½oz, though as this was small and easily lost it was frequently missing. If you didn't have a set of scales – and they were comparatively expensive – informal measures were pretty well as good. A breakfast cup held 10 fluid ounces, or half a pint, and a full cup of flour held about 8oz. A teacup was ¼pint or 4oz. A tablespoon of a dry ingredient was an ounce, though you had to remember to 'round' it, having as much above as below the rim. A level tablespoon was therefore ½oz, and a rounded teaspoon ¼oz. Liquids could be measured in purpose-made jugs with quantities marked on the side, or measures improvised from cups. A milk bottle held a pint, as bottles still do.

SAVING FUEL (CARELESS COOKING COSTS LIVES!)

It was just as important to economise on fuel, as it was to use food to the best advantage. Ministry of Food advertisements and leaflets and wartime cookery books all had helpful tips.[4] First of all you should manage the top of your stove. One-pot cookery, described above, not only made full use of your one large saucepan but also saved fuel. Steamers were economical as well, as you could stack them one above the other to cook a full meal, especially if you put something such as potatoes in the base pan too. If you had one of the early models of pressure cookers, it was a splendid way of saving both time and fuel.

Pans for electric cookers ought to have had ground bottoms, so that they made good contact with the hot plate. If using gas, you should keep the flame underneath the base of the pan, not licking up round the sides where the heat would be wasted.

Soaking dried goods and porridge oats speeded up the cooking time. You could start cooking prunes for instance, or pulses, by covering them with boiling water and leaving them in a vacuum flask overnight.

Vegetables ought to be shredded or broken into small pieces, in order to cook them more quickly in the minimum amount of water. The pan was covered with a lid or plate. Two vegetables of the same type could be cooked together, like diced carrots, or carrots and parsnips. You could 'cook enough carrots and potatoes to last two or three days so that they are ready to use in vegetable pies, fish cakes, potato cakes, or potato and carrot pancakes,' though you should not cook greens in advance because they would lose 'so much health value when reheated.'[5]

Stewing and braising were good methods to use for meat, as only a 'glimmer of heat' was needed to cook it – though you needed the glimmer for quite a long time. If you were cooking a whole piece of meat it was better to bone it. A pot-roast was just as good as an oven baked roast (and possibly more tender). More dubiously you were advised not to overcook meat: 'Reheated meat is quite satisfactory if not overcooked the first time, and only heated through the second time.' Well, that would depend on the meat concerned. Beef would probably be all right, but pork should always be cooked through very thoroughly. In any case, reheated meat ought to be brought to the boil and kept there for several minutes, as it can be the home of some nasty food-poisoning bacteria.

It was better to cook food in several small dishes than one large one. Cakes and steamed puddings in individual basins cooked in far less time than in a conventional bowl.

You were meant to organise your baking so that the oven was always filled to capacity, not heated for just one or a few items. You could offer to cook a neighbour's dish if you had space. (This presupposed that you were on very good terms with your neighbours. They might not have wanted to hand over a precious joint to your possibly unskilled care, however well intentioned.) In any case you might plan a whole week's baking in one day. If you had the oven on in any case, you could wrap brown paper round the handles of your pans and put them into the oven as if they were casseroles.

In fact economical cooks had always tried to use the oven of the kitchen range in this way. First you heated it to the maximum required – to roast a joint, let us say. Underneath you would put the Yorkshire pudding, and underneath that the potatoes. On the floor of the oven you might have a rice pudding, which needs a long time but comparatively cool conditions. When the oven was turned off it would still go on cooking, so you could put in an egg custard, or your stale crusts to transform them into rusks for the baby. Oven management was even more of an art in the past, because thermostatic control is comparatively recent. Electric ovens had thermometers visible from the outside, so that you could turn the heat up or down to keep a constant temperature. Gas ovens were controlled by a 'regulo' number, which kept the oven at the correct heat. The temperature 400°F was the same as regulo 6, or 200°C.

It was a good idea not to use your cooker at all, or very little. You could have cold meals with hot drinks, or soup only, on some days. In an era when you frequently had a coal fire to heat your living room, you could do some of your cooking on that, using a trivet with a kettle on it, for instance. You could use the fire to make toast too, holding the bread on a toasting fork, saving grill power.

The hay box was an expedient much advertised. It was based on the principle of conserving heat by insulation. Hay was a convenient and cheap material in the country, but you could also use blankets, crumpled newspaper balls or pieces of old carpet (clean). First you needed to get hold of a wooden box or crate big enough to hold a couple or saucepans, or better, casseroles, with a bit of room to spare. You lined this with several newspapers, pinning them in with tintacks or drawing pins. Then you put a thick layer of hay etc. on the bottom.

After that you went back to the kitchen, prepared your stew or casserole, and brought it to the boil for a few minutes. With the lid firmly on, it was quickly transferred to the box, and about 4in thickness of hay packed tightly round and over the pans. A blanket, or hay-filled cover, went on top, and then the wooden lid of the box. After that you got on with something else of national importance and left the meal alone for several hours or even overnight for a porridge breakfast.

When you were ready to eat, you resurrected the casseroles/pans from their snug resting place, brought them to the boil again on the conventional cooker, and sat down to enjoy what ought to have been a perfectly cooked and thoroughly tender meal. You can see that not much fuel was used. The method was especially recommended for soups, stews, pulses, porridge and root vegetables.

This was fine for foods that were fresh and uncontaminated with bacteria. Even if they were, the preliminary and final boiling ought to have killed them off. But if the beginning or final stage was rushed, the long slow warmth could encourage their growth, so you might end up with food poisoning rather than satisfaction.

There were expedients for the time when you might be in a really desperate situation, borrowed from the Army or Boy Scouts' outdoor cooking methods. If you had no oven at all, but had access to a spade, fuel such as wood or coal, and a long piece of metal such as a bit of corrugated iron, you could make a kind of fire-pit.

First you dug a trench in the ground deep and wide enough to take metal pans. The bottom and sides you lined with bricks – possibly from a bombsite. You then lit a fire at the end of the hole nearest the way the wind was blowing. When you had a good hot pile of embers you scooped out the biggest ones onto the metal cover, leaving the smaller ones behind. Then you put in your pans of food to cook, covering them with the metal and embers. In this way the pans would have heat from both the bottom and top.

If the ground was very wet you could make an oven above ground, simply building the brick container at ground level and piling earth against the sides. The fire was lit, the pans covered as before.[6]

FOOD STORAGE

As food was precious, every housewife was exhorted to prevent spoilage, but it was easier to exhort than to execute. Some better-off households were lucky enough to own a refrigerator at the outbreak of war, and some of them ran an informal food-saving scheme by looking after a neighbour's meat ration, for example. The time-honoured cold slab of stone, slate or marble in the north-facing larder was the nearest most people got to cold storage however. This was one of the reasons why shopping took up so much time. You could not buy more than a few days' supplies in one go, or the stuff would go off, especially in hot weather. A summer *Food Facts* advertisement from 1943[7] has some helpful advice about keeping milk. First, tell the milkman where he can put your milk in the shade if you are out all day. When you come home, put it in a bowl of cold water on the larder floor, not on a higher shelf (heat rises). Put a piece of wet muslin over the bottle and dipping into the water. (Evaporation would cool the milk.)

You could sometimes buy butter coolers using the same principle. You put the butter on the dish, and covered it with a porous lid, which was kept wet. Another method was to scald the milk when you received it, and store it in a scalded jug covered as before. Bread was to be wrapped in a clean cloth and kept on a shelf or in a ventilated tin. New bread should not be put away warm, in case it went mouldy.

As there was such a shortage of aluminium there was of course no aluminium foil to wrap food, or clingfilm either. You could use the greaseproof paper that had wrapped your butter or margarine ration to stop cheese drying out, or cover food with plates, cups and bowls – whatever you had to hand. I remember that my grandmother used a little net cover, weighted with beads at the corners, to put over the milk in the jug. That would keep out flies at least. Very useful for storing packets of dry goods such as rice, pasta, sugar and so on were the large cubical biscuit tins which a grocer might let you have if you were lucky.

You would store most of your dry goods in free-standing cupboards, or you might have a dresser with shelves for china above and cupboards below. There was an item called an Easiwork cabinet, a forerunner of the kitchen unit, with cupboards above, a drop-down working surface at waist height, which you latched back when you had finished, and cupboards at floor level.

Packaging of dry goods was simple, often a cardboard box or drum for branded goods like Bird's custard. Dried egg came in waxed cardboard packages, sugar in blue paper bags. Tins were very much like our own, mostly round, but with some distinctive oblong shapes as for Spam. Biscuits were often sold loose, put into paper bags closed by twisting the top corners. As paper became scarce people would bring these back for reuse. It is difficult to imagine now, but this was a world without plastic bags. Vegetables were wrapped in newspaper or put straight into the shopping basket. Fish might get a piece of greaseproof paper

Some typical groceries. Essence of rennet was used to make junket. Jam-pot covers were essential for home-made jam.

before it too was wrapped in newspaper. A shopping bag itself might be homemade, of cloth or netted string, or you might have a proper basket with a sturdy handle across the top. This had the disadvantage that if it was heavy it banged against your legs as you walked home.

NUTRITION FOR THE PEOPLE

The majority of people had not been educated beyond elementary level, leaving school at fourteen. Recognising a gap in essential knowledge, the government initiated a sustained programme to make sure that all housewives should have the best advice available, a crash course in nutrition and cookery. What is now called the media was exploited fully. Firstly the national press carried many official advertisements. Leaflets were published and distributed by post or at Food Offices, and the radio (or wireless as it was then known) broadcast short and long talks on a variety of welfare subjects, including food. 'Food flashes' caught the housewife if she went to the cinema. Additionally there were of course ordinary cookery books, published to wartime economy standards.

The Ministry of Food was responsible for many helpful leaflets, giving recipes and advice on nutrition.

Official Advertisements

There were at least two series of advertisements, *LET'S TALK ABOUT FOOD* and *FOOD FACTS*. They appeared in national and local papers and magazines. Their content had the stamp of authority. They told you when the new ration books were due, and how to get them, for instance. Useful recipes and hints were included, together with pep talks about saving fuel, preventing waste and using Welfare Foods. A little book based on the recipes was published by Collins, price *6d*. It has a foreword by Lord Woolton himself, in which he acknowledges the recipes are simple, but hopes that posterity would learn from Britain's cooks.

Leaflets

Dedicated home economists at the Ministry of Food also produced a huge number of leaflets, giving recipes and advice along the same lines as the advertisements. They survive today in collections of ephemera as well as in reference libraries. The very first one extolled the virtues of oatmeal, 'the most valuable of all our cereals, more nourishing even than wholemeal flour. Oatmeal is one of the simple foods on which our forefathers lived and throve.'[8]

Subsequent leaflets included recipes for potatoes, carrots, planning meals, meals without meat, making the most of various rationed goods, suggestions for breakfasts, bottling, using semolina, using leftovers, making eggless cakes and puddings … There are at least a hundred of them, and probably many more if you count re-issues, because some of the recipes were recycled in slightly different combinations.

First of all the housewife was encouraged to look after family health, especially of children, by giving them carefully prepared meals of high nutritional value, using the rations and Welfare foods. By the end of the rationing period the housewife could not fail to know about 'protective foods', alias foods that contained essential minerals and vitamins, and 'body-building foods' containing protein. Nor could she possibly overlook the many virtues of the energy-packed potato.

For instance, there was a helpful leaflet with ideas for meatless meals, using fish, cheese, bacon and sausage meat, and haricot beans in various combinations. As a preliminary it states:

> Meat is a body-building food and can be replaced only by one of the other body-building foods.
>
> 1. The best are: Milk (fresh, household or canned), Cheese, Fish (fresh or canned) and Eggs (fresh or dried).
> 2. Second best are: Soya flour, Dried Peas, Beans and Lentils, Oatmeal and Semolina.
>
> Our bodies use a mixture of the two kinds very well.[9]

Another important example is a leaflet on green vegetables,[10] summing up earlier wartime advice. 'No country in the world grows vegetables better than we do, and possibly no country in the world cooks them worse.' This was due to excessive cooking and paring too much away. Probably the writer had potatoes in mind. Boiling vegetables and then pouring away the cooking water was a waste, as it contained valuable nutrients. You should use the vegetable water in soups, stews and so on.

A valid point was that 'When fresh fruit is short we need green vegetables more than ever because they all contain the important fresh fruit vitamin, Vitamin C.'

Some were more equal than others though: brussels sprouts, parsley and watercress were especially praised. (Parsley was a universal garnish, and you could grow your own on a windowsill.) You were advised to have a green leafy vegetable at least once a day.

Advice on using green vegetables is a world away from our own quick dash to the supermarket. You should (naturally!) grow your own if you could, and then pick them as you needed them. They had to be washed well but not soaked too long. Half an hour in cold salt water was enough 'for even the most tight-hearted cabbage.' (Insect life flourished on the allotment. Your family could be put off greens altogether by finding a cabbage-white caterpillar included.) You should boil the leaves in a covered pan in a little salted water, only just enough to keep the vegetables from burning. The vegetables should be 'steam boiled' for ten to fifteen minutes, which today we might think was more than enough. To finish, the greens were tossed with a little margarine and served at once.

Much of this information was teaching simple cookery as well as nutrition. The tone of the leaflets is patronising, but maybe the home economists were trying to reach even the least-educated women.

The Kitchen Front Broadcasts

Every morning, for five minutes usually from 8.15 to 8.20 a.m., the Home Service of the BBC broadcast to housewives, starting on Thursday, 13 June 1940. An announcer explained that the forthcoming series of short talks about food were to be timed before the housewife set out on her morning's shopping. The main speaker was the travel writer and broadcaster S.P.B. Mais: 'I'm here to save you money, to save you time, to save you trouble, to tell you of food that there's plenty of and of food that you've got to go slow on.'

Information and recipes originated with the Ministry of Food, or their home economists working in Portman Square. Some of the most frequent speakers were professional broadcasters, such as Freddie Grisewood, some were cookery writers, like Ambrose Heath. Both continued throughout the war. Others broadcast less often, but regularly, like the writers Helen Burke, Florence Greenberg and Mrs Arthur Webb. Sometimes there was a housewife, for example Mrs Florence Ingillson from Yorkshire. Listeners could readily identify themselves with her.

The Radio Doctor, Charles Hill, was another frequent contributor. His down-to-earth advice made him a popular figure, and he also gave many longer talks. He was the Secretary of the British Medical

Association, but because of the 'no advertising' rule for doctors he remained anonymous for a long time. After the war he became Chairman of the Independent Television Authority, and then of the BBC itself. At the time of the *Kitchen Front* though, he was a familiar voice giving easily understood advice about nutrition or health problems.

At first it was common for each speaker to continue for a week at a time. Later they often had a turn just once a week. They built up a following, and appeared to welcome the huge numbers of listeners' letters, often commenting or passing on tips and recipes. This helped to make the five-minute slot an informal one. It had the great advantage of speed from the point of view of the Ministry. If rhubarb was plentiful on Monday, for instance, a new recipe for rhubarb tart could be broadcast on Tuesday. If there was something you could do, like making use of a glut of fruit, you could be pointed gently in the direction of the nearest Women's Institute. This topicality was designed to be like a tip for the races. The Ministry would issue reminders about getting your new ration book or milk permit. There were friendly warnings about not hoarding things, or wasting food. You were taken behind the scenes to the local Food Office or Works Canteen.

The tone of the broadcasts was patronising, like very much of the propaganda of *Food Facts* and Ministry leaflets. Occasionally the effort to take an informal approach seems strained. For instance, Ambrose Heath acknowledged that he had been asked to promote the 'new' high extraction wheatmeal loaf by the Ministry, but had had a few doubts. Then, however (surprise!) he actually tasted some, and found it good. So that was all right, wasn't it? And no more expensive than the white bread you had been used to ...[11]

But a refreshing ironic note was sounded from time to time by using fictional characters. If Ambrose Heath had not convinced you of the virtues of the National Loaf, here are Grandma Buggins and her daughter:

Mrs. B:	Slice o'bread, Gran'ma?
G:	Is it that wheatmeal stuff?
Mrs. B:	Course it is.
G:	Because I met Louisa Nutbutton the other day, and she says it gives 'er indigestion somethink chronic. Goes straight to 'er arteries, she says, and sets on 'em.

Mrs. B: That's pure fancy, Gran'ma, and only shows up Mrs. Nutbutton's ignorance. Some of the 'ighest doctors in the land says it wouldn't 'arm yer, not even if you 'ad a gastric ulster, so now![12]

Criticism could be fairly pointed at times. Here is Grandma and her daughter Em'ly just after the war. Grandma wants to become a local Food Leader. What was that? asked Mrs Buggins:

G: Ladies, and so on, and is appointed to get the latest inflammation about food for 'er street.

Mrs. B: Sometimes I think we could do with a little less information and a bit more food …[13]

Perhaps the cockney accent and the malapropisms are not as funny as they seemed at the time, and are certainly no longer politically correct, but the broadcasts might have made sceptical people turn right off if there had been propaganda all the time.

Similarly, Elsie and Doris Waters, sisters of the actor Jack Warner, were well-known comediennes who took on the characters of two charladies, Gert and Daisy. Early in the war they could be heard chatting about using the Civic Canteen (later British Restaurant). Daisy points out that these could provide meals with less waste, less shipping:

Gert: If I don't cook me own dinner Hitler's going to lose the war.

Daisy: That's right – but that doesn't mean that if you have two dinners we shall win in half the time …[14]

The scope and purpose of the talks can clearly be seen by looking at a summary for a month of them.[15] March 1941 was one of the leanest times of the whole war. Lend Lease had not yet started. The ordinary ration of bacon and ham was 4oz per adult per week, cheese not yet rationed, but shortly to be only 1oz per person, sugar 8oz, tea, 2oz butter, margarine and cooking fat a total of 8oz and meat at its lowest level until the austerity years, at only 1/- worth per person. Milk and eggs were both in short supply.

The first of March was a Saturday, so there was a helpful chat about a meatless Sunday lunch with vegetarian recipes. On Monday Freddie Grisewood took over for the week. His subjects were marmalade made with carrots, how to keep preserved eggs, a trip behind the scenes at a Food Office, how to use plums that had been treated with Camden tablets and a visit to a Works Canteen. On Saturday he considered the problem of women workers who couldn't get to the shops.

The following week was taken over by a doctor – not Charles Hill, but an anonymous woman. She had the difficult task of explaining that most of the foods people were used to, and wanted, were not really essential to health, though the housewife had to produce nourishing meals. Manual workers needed extra energy foods, true, but not extra meat. Dairy products could be replaced. Vegetable protein could do the same job as animal protein. Besides, vegetables were in good supply. Salads could take the place of fruit, and wholemeal bread and oatmeal were 'protective foods'. Starchy foods could be used instead of sweet ones, and the Vitamins A and D added to margarine made butter redundant …

A French actress, Jeanne de Casalis, took over from Monday, 17 March. She gave simple directions for cooking basic dishes: meat hash from leftovers, the correct (French) way to make an omelette – still using fresh eggs – a Bath brown bread pudding, or *pain perdu* (without eggs), a simple brown stew with a bouquet garni to flavour it and a reminder of the virtues of several vegetable soups. Her method of cooking carrots by the conservative method was a real success. So was her way of making an apple pureé for puddings, where the apples were cooked unpeeled and uncored, with a little sugar and water, then rubbed through a sieve.

For the last week of the month Mrs Ingillson had a mixed menu. First there was a rather stodgy variation of bread and butter pudding with dates but no sugar or egg, and a steamed date pudding. She gave the National Wheatmeal bread a plug in passing. There was a reminder about National Milk permits, recipes for giblet and liver paste for sandwiches, and ox liver and kidney (offal was off the ration).

Another day was devoted to describing the new Queen's Messenger Convoys (see page 156), and Friday, probably just before Easter that year, had a recipe for hot cross buns. Saturday had a rhubarb and date tart and in a more sinister mode she said she had been asked whether people ought to be laying down stocks of food in case of invasion. The answer was No – but if you had something put by already, you should keep it. 'The Government has a plan ready …' This was indeed a time when there were justified fears of a German invasion.

Ambrose Heath was there for the end of the month and on into April. His Monday morning suggestion was for a substantial breakfast of a Yorkshire pudding with potatoes in it, topped perhaps with a rasher of bacon.

In this month several good points were put across. Freddie was helpful about preserved foods and some of the social aspects of rationing. Working women had real difficulties in getting their rations when shops closed early. The WVS helped, but they could not shop for everyone.

The doctor's contribution was probably the most important. She was trying to allay fears that rationed foods were not enough to keep people healthy. Jeanne de Casalis was giving a brief course in basic cookery. Mrs Ingillson filled in a few hungry gaps, and by describing the Queen's Messengers she showed that help was on the way for victims of bombing. The hot cross buns perhaps held a subtle message that no matter what, traditions would endure.

SUBSTITUTES AND STRETCHING

The Ministry home economists give the impression that they were quite desperately cheerful, assuring their audience that a little ingenuity and a lot of imagination could make good the direst shortage. The names of some recipes are revealing, – Mock Goose, for instance, Mock Duck, Mock Marzipan, Mock Cream. It is as if there was a psychological need to pretend that real goose, duck, marzipan and cream were not all that essential, really. And there had been a respectable precedent, after all, in Mock Turtle Soup.

Undoubtedly people felt there was not enough butter to go with the comparatively plentiful bread. Margarine could be used instead, but then there would be problems with baking, because you needed margarine for cakes and pastry. You needed cakes and pastry to plug the calorie hole. Subterfuge was therefore necessary to elasticate the butter ration.

There was a special leaflet *Making the Fat Ration Go Further.*[16] The first suggestion started with 8oz of butter (or margarine). Six ounces of this was creamed with a wooden spoon to make it soft. The other 2oz were used to make a white sauce with a tablespoon of flour, half a pint of milk and a little salt. It was cooled and mixed with the fat in the bowl before use. Magic! Where half a pound of spread had stood before, you now had more than double. Elizabeth Craig had a similar recipe, but with 1oz semolina cooked with ¼ pint milk and some salt. You then creamed 4oz butter or margarine and beat in the cooled semolina.

Or perhaps Potato Pete of Ministry propaganda would help out. Echoing advice from May Byron in the First World War[17] you could mix melted margarine (or butter) with an equal quantity of mashed potato, to be used cold. Maybe this would be all right for sandwiches, if the filling was well flavoured. The extended butter was intended as a spread, not for use in baking. Dripping from a roast was probably more acceptable, as it was not masquerading as something else, and was naturally savoury. It could be pepped up even more with pickle, meat extract, chopped onion or leek, bottled sauce, chutney, herbs, vinegar and grated cheese.

A different leaflet[18] suggests that if you are short of margarine for sandwiches you could try working dry household milk (that is, dried skimmed milk) into the fat, allowing one tablespoonful of powder to two of fat. The same powder could be sprinkled onto stewed fruit as a substitute for cream.

Every scrap of fat-bearing tissue that passed through the kitchen door had to be rendered down by heating, either in the oven (when it was already baking something else) or by boiling up with water. The resulting cooled fat could be strained from the 'scratchings' of the oven method, or taken off the top of the water and scraped clean. The crisp bits of scratchings weren't wasted either. They were put into pies, stews or rissoles. One good idea was to brush cut-up pieces of potato with fat, and then roast them. In this way you had a good alternative to chips with much less fat, and though this was not said at the time it would be better for you as well.

Another leaflet from the same series concerned *Making the most of the Sugar.*[19] If you had them, honey, golden syrup or treacle, jam and marmalade could be added for sweetness to baked goods, stewed fruit and sweet sauces. Sweetened condensed milk was acceptable for making custard-type sauces, and for tea, coffee or cocoa. Honey could be used for bottling fruit too, but the flavour was said to be noticeable – was this a disadvantage? Beekeepers especially might be grateful for honey ideas.

Otherwise honey, jam and marmalade were part of the preserves/sugar ration, so you might not save all that much by using them. Golden syrup and treacle, on the other hand, and sweetened condensed milk, were on points, so they might be worth getting. Honey or syrup could be used to make jam, using up to half the proportion of sugar to fruit.

The great and universal sugar substitute of the war years was of course saccharin. It is not absorbed by the body, but tastes several hundred times sweeter than sugar. The bad news is that it also has a slightly metallic aftertaste. But one of the standard little white tablets was the equivalent of a teaspoonful of sugar, so very many people put it into their cuppas. It has no nutritional value whatever, but was available during the war from chemists, and was an ingredient in soft drinks too – as it still is, though other sweeteners have been developed as well.

The MoF leaflet suggests using crushed tablets mixed with the dry ingredients for plain cakes, biscuits and steamed puddings, but only if there would have been a low proportion of sugar in the first place. It was useful for sweetening custard sauces, stewed fruit and starch-based puddings like cornflour mould. You were advised to crush the tablets and add at the end of boiling, because cooking brought out the bitter taste of the saccharin. Like the butter stretchers above, you could expand your sugar ration for tea by crushing thirty saccharin tablets with a rolling pin, and adding the powder to ½lb sugar, rather like the half-sugar you can buy today if you are slimming. You would use only half a teaspoonful in your tea or coffee.

Soya flour was a nutritious addition to many dishes, as it is a rich source of vegetable protein and minerals. In the absence of almonds, a reasonable imitation of marzipan consisted of 4oz each of soya flour and sugar, with 2oz margarine, a liberal quantity of almond essence and enough water to make a pliable paste. It was a bright yellow colour, and not quite as good as the real thing, but better than nothing at Christmas.

SOME POPULAR WARTIME COOKERY WRITERS

Many food writers had established a following before the war, and they kept going; though their books had to be published to conform to war economy standards on indifferent paper. They put their skill and popularity at the service of the Ministry. Cookery journalists too were employed. Recipe development was a growth industry.

Ambrose Heath

Ambrose Heath, already mentioned, was a good example of a well-known author. He was born in 1891 and had started to write about food in 1930. His journalism included work for *The Guardian*, *The Daily Mirror*, *The Morning Post* and *The Queen*. His first short cookery book was published in 1932 by Faber and Faber, *Good Food*. He went on to write about sixteen more before the war, most of them with 'Good' in the title, instantly recognisable: *Good Savouries*, *Good Potato Dishes*, *Good Sweets* … They drew on the tradition of simple French cuisine. He commented: 'What I had at heart was good food perfectly cooked and simply presented, without unnecessary trappings and superfluous garnishes …'[20] He had also been concerned with The National Mark of the 1930s, a government scheme to promote British agricultural produce guaranteed by quality control. When war came he used his skill to popularise innovative recipes and practical dishes in more than a dozen books, including *Kitchen Front Recipes*, *How to Cook in War Time*, *New Dishes for Old* and *Vegetables for Victory*. As the food situation eased, his recipes became less austere, *Good Food Again*, *Good Poultry and Game* and *Children's Party Fare* for instance. In all he wrote or translated at least seventy books before he died in 1969, and had contributed many airwave hours to the war effort. He was one of the most steadfast presenters of the *Kitchen Front* broadcasts, lasting all through the war from 1940 to 1946.

Elizabeth Craig

Elizabeth Craig was an experienced writer too. She produced comprehensive books of general cookery. Born in 1889, she was fully established by 1932 when her publisher Collins brought out her *Cooking with Elizabeth Craig*. It could have been called 'Everything the Middle-Class Housewife Needs to Know …', including nutritional advice, how to shop, and how to plan a kitchen, before she started on actual recipes which ranged through breakfast dishes, sauces, snacks, appetisers, soups, fish, game, poultry, meats, vegetables, salads, pastry, puddings, savouries, sandwiches, bread, biscuits and cakes, candies, preserving, beverages (including cocktails) and how to carve. In the early part of the war she produced a most helpful small book, *Cooking in War-Time*,[21] which included advice on how to feed cats and dogs too. With 120 pages it was based on the frugal part of pre-war cooking, making a virtue of rabbits, old fowls, toad-in-the-hole and soused mackerel for example. With peace, she was able to revert to comprehensive cookery again, with 922 pages of *Collins Family Cookery*, in 1957, when crab, venison, proper roasts, cream, chocolate and, above all, shell eggs made a celebratory come-back. To compare these three books by the same person is to be able to chart the disappearance of the *haute* in wartime cuisine, and to see the return of some French influence later on, while keeping some of the best of British regional dishes as well. Elizabeth Craig died in 1972.

Marguerite Patten

Marguerite Patten was originally a home economist working for an electricity undertaking. Early in 1942 she joined the Food Advice Division of the Ministry of Food. This was a special part of the Ministry, staffed by experienced home economists from industry and education, and a small number of dieticians and nutritionists. They worked throughout Britain teaching the public how to provide enjoyable and healthy meals based on the rations plus the limited range of unrationed foods. They gave talks and practical cookery demonstrations in markets, factory canteens, the waiting rooms in hospitals, large shops and stores, Welfare Clinics and any place where they could meet and help the public. Other experts checked on the nutritional value of school meals, rather as Jamie Oliver has recently done. At that time free or cheap school dinners were treated seriously as an important contribution to children's health.

Harrods of London had a Ministry of Food Advice Bureau and in 1943 Marguerite Patten took charge of this. In addition she contributed to the breakfast-time *Kitchen Front* broadcasts. A very prolific food writer, having produced 170 books, in the 1960s and 1970s she wrote many of the Hamlyn series of large paperbacks *500 Recipes* … These were for specific ingredients or types of dish, such as casserole dishes, soups and savouries, fish, or for groups – working wives, families and so on.

They gave accurate advice for nourishing and economical dishes. She is an expert on the recipes of rationing and austerity, with three collections still available: *We'll Eat Again*, *The Victory Cookbook* and *Post War Kitchen*. In 1991 she was awarded the OBE, and also holds four other awards, namely Lifetime Achievement Awards from the Guild of Food Writers, the BBC, the André Simon Fund and Wedgewood/Waterhouse.

CASE STUDY

The Jersey Experience

The Channel Islands were the only part of Britain to be occupied by German forces during the war. It had been agreed by the British Government that it was not possible to protect them against invasion in the summer of 1940, when so much of Europe had already fallen to the Nazi army. It was announced that the Channel Islands were to become a 'demilitarised zone' – that is, no resistance would be offered. Voluntary evacuation was for women, children, men of military age (who might be conscripted by the Germans) and any others who wanted to leave, if transport was still practical.

Some left, some stayed. The repatriation to Britain was hurried and took four days. Then the Germans moved in on 30 June/1 July 1940. White flags were hung out to signify there would be no battle for the Islands.

The story of the survival, suffering and daily life of the islanders is thus very different from that of the rest of the British Isles. It is a 'what if' example – what if Britain had fallen to a possible German invasion? Many people were convinced this invasion would be attempted. Indeed it had a German code-name, Operation Sealion, and it was mostly due to the heroism of Battle of Britain pilots that it was not tried. What would life have been like under the Nazis? The people of the Channel Islands had many responses – some maintained a dignified and aloof acceptance, but did not provoke the German authorities. Some complied with the regulations, some circumvented them whenever possible, keeping secret radio sets, for example, when these were forbidden. Some collaborated. At first the Islands were treated comparatively well, compared with the rest of overrun Europe, but the Occupation became much harsher as the war progressed, with imprisonment and deportations to concentration camps for some. Prisoners of war were brought in, and were treated with varying degrees of inhumanity. Everyone suffered severe shortages, especially of food, as the war lengthened. At the end it was found that children, for instance, were 2½in shorter than the norm, though because of the scarcity of sugar their teeth were in fair shape.

A British doctor, John Lewis, who had settled in Jersey just before the war, stayed on and wrote an account of his life and work there. He managed to get his pregnant wife safely back to England before returning. In his book, *A Doctor's Occupation,*[22] he tells many stories of heroism and tragedy, some humorous, like the disguise of a newly slaughtered pig. The German authorities were rigorous in keeping tallies of all livestock, as much of it was requisitioned. The pig in question was an 'illegal' one. When warning came that the Germans were on their way to make a check, it was deposited in the best bedroom, the bed and carcase covered with a white sheet, and Bible and candles disposed on a table in front of it. The search party had the decency to retreat in the face of family grief.[23]

The doctor was both ingenious and farsighted. He bought a baker's surplus stock and made rusks of it, which lasted for years. He bottled twenty cooked boned chickens in Kilner (preserving) jars successfully. (Bottling meat in this way was not recommended by the Ministry here, as there is a danger that the flesh might not be completely sterile.) The doctor kept bees and rabbits, as many people did on the mainland. But he had to risk his rabbits being stolen until he transferred the hutches into a loft with a barred window and padlocked door reached only by a ladder, which was of course kept in a safe place.

Alcoholic drinks were made from a variety of ingredients to eke out supplies that he had laid in or could obtain. At first there was a ration of one bottle of red wine a week, but the quality deteriorated. Many of his friends would not buy it then, until asked to do so by Dr Lewis. Using his scientific training, he was able to distil white spirit, which, flavoured with juniper and cardamom, turned into gin. (Again, this was a risky undertaking, because as he points out himself, poisonous methyl alcohol may be produced, instead of the usual ethyl alcohol which we know and love. This is partly why home distilling of alcohol is illegal today.) Cider was converted into a kind of dry Martini with bay leaf and quinine, but experiments with sugar beet were not successful.

The doctor survived the occupation to be reunited with his wife and son, and continued to serve the people of the Islands for many years.

★ ★ ★ ★ ★

The same spirit of invention and endurance was shown by Mrs Cecile Mallet.

She had been born in Britain but had married a Jerseyman and settled on the Island. She was in her thirties during the occupation, and wrote a description of her experiences. Her niece, Mrs Nancy Yates, showed it to me and has kindly given me permission to include it here.

MRS CECILE MALLET'S ACCOUNT OF FOOD SUBSTITUTIONS IN JERSEY DURING THE SECOND WORLD WAR

In writing this article I should first of all like to pay tribute to those thousands of women who were not so lucky as I and others like myself who lived on farms, and so had those extras which were unobtainable by the majority, and had our own crops to draw from.

They, in addition to the really hard work entailed in making the substitutes, had besides to stand for hours in queues for vegetables (which were in short supply owing to the incessant German demands), and for skim milk which was such a help when obtainable. People had to make trips backwards and forwards to the public ovens to have their meals cooked when the gas came to an end and fuel for cooking ceased to exist. In all weathers, on the go, this pluck and endurance should never be forgotten.

[Salt, absolutely necessary for adding flavour, was customarily made from sea water] and I wonder if anywhere else the public have had to buy sea water at [----] per quart as the residents in the town of St Helier did, as they were not able to go down to get it for themselves. [The beaches were mined.] Men had to be employed to fill containers and cart it to advertised points where the public could buy it.

Potato flour was made by practically all when potatoes were plentiful but during the last months of the war when the ration was reduced to 5lb. per head per week, it became a thing of the past, but it was a first rate substitute for cornflour and makes nourishing puddings and blancmanges. But what work all these substitutes entailed!

For instance, to make potato flour, first the potatoes were scrubbed or thinly peeled, then they were grated on a fine grater into large bowls of clean water and left until the following day, by which time the colour would have become a dirty brown. This water was carefully poured off so as not to disturb the pulp in the bottom, then fresh water was added and the whole lot was stirred up and passed through a fine strainer or muslin cloth and again allowed to stand until the water was clear; when it would be seen there was a fine white paste at the bottom. This water had to be poured off and fresh added and the process repeated until the flour was absolutely white. When the last water was poured off the paste was put in the sun or a warm place near the stove and left to dry, being occasionally stirred and turned. When quite dry the hard lumps were rolled out with the rolling pin and the finished product was as fine and white as the finest cornflour and used in the same way.

For sweetening drinks, puddings etc. we made from sugar beet a thick dark brown syrup, which if properly made was very good indeed, especially when spread on bread. The children loved it. It was very nourishing, but personally I found this the worst to prepare and make. One hundredweight [112lb] of beet root made 14–16 lb of good thick syrup. Usually we did half a hundredweight at a time and cooked it in the open on top of an oil drum which had been tightly packed with sawdust, a central space having been left clear down the centre and out at the side about one and a half inches in diameter. These sawdust tin 'cookers' were very popular and widely used until sawdust like other good and useful things came to an end. But I am digressing.

The sugar beet was first well scrubbed, then grated, a very hard job, especially if the beet was fibrous, then put to cook in a large preserving pan with just enough water to cover it. When it reached the boil it was allowed to simmer until tender, after which it was put into a home-made wooden press and left overnight for the juice to drain out. The second day the extracted juice was put to boil and reduce until it became thick and rich. At this stage care had to be taken to ensure an even heat, otherwise it was very readily inclined to boil over, and quite a surprising amount could be lost in a few seconds; so one just had to stick around and watch it, as it was no fun to lose a pound or more of syrup for the sake of running indoors for something. Several different methods for making the syrup were evolved, some of them very good, but I always used the foregoing method, which though tedious gave good results for certain.

As a substitute for yeast one pint of the strained liquid after the first boiling was set aside until fermentation began, when it was used in the same way as yeast, and though of course it was not as good, it worked and that was what was needed! Others used grated potato in water and allowed that to ferment to use as yeast.

In season we bottled all available fruit without sugar and found it to be a very successful method. Pears, in particular, were very good and a welcome addition to high teas during the winter months. One variety known as 'Pepper Pear' could be eaten without adding any sweetening at all, but to others we added saccharine. Bottled blackcurrants were very useful for colds; we strained the juice and added honey (from our own hives which we started keeping during the war) and a little brandy from a precious bottle which we made last for three years! A remedy for colds was obtained which was efficacious and soothing to throat and chest. The children loved it and at a time when medicines were almost non-existent it was a godsend. I wonder how many people know that if children and adults take a spoonful or two of honey through the winter months it is a preventative against colds and chills, that it gives energy and strengthens the action of the heart?

Well, so much for the cooking and preparation of substitutes, which with the meals took up so much time every single day; then there was the problem of clothes especially when there were children!

During the last years of occupation it was really awful; we had to make do, altering, repairing, patching and mending until some things had no resemblance to their former state. A few months of washing without soap will make even good clothing a trifle sad, but when it was sad before the soapless era, well, can you imagine it? There was no cotton or thread to be had. We had to unravel old wool garments to repair socks etc. and for cotton the only available thing was crocheted lace. Old drawers were turned out and countless 'relics', which had for ages not seen the light, came out and did their bit!

To the unobservant eye the population might have appeared neatly and even smartly dressed, but on looking close one could see the effects of constant wear and tear. Very few wore stockings, and shoes were in a very bad way. The children provided the worst problems because of their constant growth.

4

Dig for Victory and Vegetables

In 1939 Britain had 12.9 million acres of cultivated land, 18.8 million of permanent grassland[1] and produced only 40 per cent of its own food. By 1944 it had 19.4 million acres under the plough, just under 12 million acres of grassland, and was producing about 66 per cent of food consumed.[2] There were 649,000 farm horses at the beginning of conflict, and 55,000 tractors. By 1945 there were still 545,000 horses but 175,000 tractors.[3] The drastic change had to take place both because of the enemy onslaught on shipping and the national shortage of funds to pay for imports.

Like the propaganda campaign for housewives, there was a similar campaign for agricultural production – but in spades, so to speak. The government strategy had two strands. Firstly there were large-scale schemes and directives to encourage or force farmers to make their fields produce as much food as possible. The second strategy was aimed at householders, including those in towns, to grow as many vegetables as could be squeezed out of allotments, gardens, parks, golf courses and cricket pitches. Even the defensive moat of the Tower of London was turned over to production, defence against hunger this time.

AGRICULTURE – THE FIRST WINTER[4]

The Depression of the 1930s had affected not only industry, but agriculture as well. While scientific methods had been applied in Canada, Denmark and Holland for example, Britain had far fewer advanced farms between the wars. People had left the land for the towns too. There were only about a million families engaged in working the land out of the estimated population of 48 million.[5] Some effort had been made during the thirties to improve things – the National Mark was one such scheme. And in the spring of 1939, with war looming, a subsidy of £2 per acre had been offered to plough land that had been fallow for seven years or more.[6]

Since the First World War much marginal land had gone back to bramble, gorse and bracken. Land drainage had been neglected, so fields had reverted to bog and fen. The main thrust of agriculture was in meat production, and even then cattle were often fed on imported feeding stuffs as well as nibbling the native pasture. Yet even meat production was not enough for the urban population, which was supplied mainly with cheap imported meat. This had the blessing of some authorities, such as the Mottrams, quoted in Chapter 1. The shortfall between home-produced food and the quantities needed to feed the populace was estimated by anxious civil servants. The fields were producing less than a third of the sugar and cheese required, only a fifth of the fruit, 10 per cent of cereals and half of the meat eaten.[7] It was never going to be possible to be self-sufficient, but it must be possible to produce much more than in pre-war times. Cultivation became a cult.

For example, calculations (on Scottish yields) showed what needed to be grown. A hundred acres of land used to produce meat – beef or mutton – will feed nine people per year. The same acreage supporting dairy cattle will yield enough calories to feed forty people. If oats are sown, and the cereal fed directly to human beings instead of animals, the number of people nourished rises to 170 per annum. Finally, if you give the fields over to potatoes, you can produce calories to support 400.[8] Of course, nobody was going to live exclusively on potatoes – though it sometimes felt like it – but the statistics showed irresistibly that they would have to become one of the most important crops. Every farmer was in time given a quota that he had to fill. More than 6 million sheep and 2.5 million pigs had to make way for the arable crops. So too did 19 million poultry, which came to be regretted by the population at large when shell eggs became so scarce that they were treated as an alternative currency in some places.

First though, the land had to be cleared and ploughed in a hurry. Plans had been laid before 1939 for War Committees to implement the Minister of Agriculture's measures in each county. They convened immediately as war broke out, There were District Committees too, working on a local level to let all the farmers know what would be expected. The 'War Ags' were made up of generally successful farmers and others who knew their areas, and they had powers to dispossess men who were inefficient or not co-operative. (Given the importance attached to root vegetables, 'carrot and stick' was an apt description of their approach.)

As a start, any remaining crops had to be harvested in that fine, warm September. But an unprecedented amount of ploughing was still needed for the first sowing of the following spring. To make matters worse, many men had already been called up, so there was a shortage of skilled workers. There were not enough tractors, not enough horses even, not enough ploughs. Old machinery was heaved out of barns; the village blacksmith forged new friendships. The Committees organised maximum use of men and equipment, and contractors with machinery and crews were sent to help where they were most needed. The Women's Land Army had been set up and Land Girls started to make their mark, though ploughing was a specialist job and many had not yet had time to train properly.

The winter of 1940 was particularly cold. Frost made the hard surface even harder. A plough works by slicing into the ground and then turning it over, so that the grass – or weeds, old stubble and so on – are turned face downwards, with the cut surface on top. Later on more machinery chews up the earth until it is sufficiently fine for plants to grow in it. Different areas have different characteristics, naturally, so that clay is harder and stickier to work than a sandy soil.

The available tractors were kept going in continuous shifts as soon as the weather allowed. Horses had to have time to rest, but people worked seven days a week, from early morning until late at night, continuing to plough even in darkness. Moonlight helped, but you could put a lantern in the hedge to mark the end of the furrow, and aim for that, if there was no other way of steering. A light directed downwards showed where the plough was in relation to the furrow. Presumably the blackout restrictions did not apply here, but the lanterns were masked as much as possible.[9] During the day workers in the vulnerable country had to keep a lookout for the approach of bombers – if they were using noisy old machinery they were unlikely to hear sirens or the drone of aircraft until too late.

But by the spring of 1940, the ploughing target of an extra 1,700,000[10] acres was surpassed by 200,000.[11] The look of the land was transformed as the new acres stood ready for planting.

LATER DEVELOPMENTS OF LAND

Farming methods had to be reformed. The stereotype of the slow, backward-looking yokel, chewing a straw as he leant over his (broken) gate, was of course a slander on many, but there was not at that time any large-scale movement to send young people to Agricultural College to learn up-to-date methods. The deficiency was supplied reasonably tactfully by a posse of technical experts, teaching methods of making silage, for instance, the best use of fertilisers, pest control and care of animals. Soil could be analysed to find out which crops would do best in any particular locality, and what supplements needed to be added. Different rotations of crops were advised to keep the fields as fertile as possible. The co-operation of farmers was essential, so there had to be some horse-trading, so to speak, between immemorial knowledge and innovation. It was an interesting time. Change continued after the war until farming developed into agribusiness. Some might say it forced the land to over-produce, and opinion is now swinging back to older 'organic' methods of farming. In wartime though the priority was to get food onto plates in the short-term.

There was no question that land was regarded as a precious resource by the authorities, after the neglect of the inter-war years. But exactly how much land was available? What could be done to improve it scientifically? How many acres were growing crops, how many grass, how many were waste? Was there infestation by rabbits? Were rats a problem? What were the roads, lanes and cart tracks like? What was the condition of farm buildings and agricultural cottages? Ditches, drains and fences? Importantly, were electricity supplies and water available? An official Farm Survey was undertaken in 1940. It was compared with the Domesday Survey carried out by the inspectors of William the Conqueror in 1086. The object then had been to register the wealth of the land and assess what revenues could be raised. The Farm Survey was also authoritarian, to determine what could be expected to help the war effort. But like Domesday, it is a very interesting source of all kinds of information, giving a snapshot of the state of Britain at a turning point in her development, and now of great value to social and agricultural historians. On a family history level too you can look up your parents' or grandparents' birthplace perhaps, and see what conditions were like for them as they tried to defend their way of life.

Many farmers had had difficulty in making a living before the war, but when it became clear how much extra food would be needed, money was forthcoming. Subsidies were offered, as well as the ploughing incentive of £2 per acre. For sowing wheat or rye the farmer was paid £4 per acre, but £10 per acre for potato crops. Hill farms, which are generally much more suitable for sheep or cattle, had a subsidy of 6/- for a ewe, £10 per head of cattle, but this came later in 1943. Bonuses were paid for milk production too, which increased because of the emphasis on giving mothers and children enough. Farmers became relatively prosperous. Prices and markets were guaranteed. All agricultural wages rose, not before time.[12]

At the start of the war machinery had been pooled to some extent, to make the best use of it. This continued, but from 1941 more tractors, combine harvesters and so on started to come into the country. America supplied them under the Lend Lease scheme and so did Canada under Mutual Aid. Home production of farm equipment was difficult because of the priority given to war machines such as tanks and aircraft. Swords and ploughshares, traditionally considered to be mutually incompatible, were in competition with each other for scarce materials and labour.

The need to bring unproductive land into fertility was made more acute by the loss of farming land to war use. Aerodromes were built on the level fields of East Anglia for instance, and decoy dummy aerodromes spread out to tempt bombers to waste explosives harmlessly. Training grounds had to be supplied for soldiers. Real factories took up positions out in the country, where they were thought to be less at risk of bombing than in industrial towns, and shadow factories, like the dummy aerodromes, set up to mislead the enemy. When Britain was threatened with invasion after the fall of

France and the evacuation from Dunkirk, a lot of fields sprouted obstacles – old bicycles, concrete blocks, rusted cars – anything to discourage enemy landings, but which also discouraged cultivation. About 800,000 acres were taken over for war purposes.[13] But by the end of 1944 this loss had been made good many times over: 6,500,000 extra acres had come under the plough.[14]

New machines were used to reclaim neglected land, or to take wasteland that had hardly ever been worked. For example, the fens at Feltwell, Swaffham and Burwell, south of the Wash, were taken on by the Norfolk and Cambridgeshire War Agricultural Executive Committees. Concrete roads had to be built so that machinery could be taken into the marsh. Miles and miles of drains were cut and dykes constructed. Then you might say the work began. The site had once been a forest. Heavy, petrified trunks of bog-oak lay just beneath the surface, some 7ft thick and 100ft long. I expect that if the discovery were made today, a whole University Department of Archaeology would have taken it over for several years. But that was wartime, and wartime methods were used to clear the ground. The names of the machines speak of violence and power: prairie-busters, disc-harrows, and stump-jumpers which spring clear of obstacles instead of breaking. A hundred Land Girls dug to expose the ancient logs, and then Royal Engineers blew them up into shorter lengths, so that they could be pulled out of the mud. It was productive soil, worth the effort perhaps, giving large crops of wheat, sugar beet and – of course – potatoes.

In Montgomeryshire, hills that had been supporting only sheep and wild ponies began to be prepared – for potatoes. At first the ploughing was not deep enough, and after a first crop the bracken grew back as before. New machines, prairie-busters and more powerful discs broke and turned the ground. After applying fertiliser a crop of rape was sown, and sheep turned out to graze on it. A kind of animal ploughing with the sheep's hooves cut up the ground again, and their droppings improved fertility. Eventually the huge fields were producing enough potatoes (of course) to feed the whole of Manchester. All over the country the hills were farmed against traditional wisdom, proving that modern machinery could make an enormous difference to productivity. The Sussex Downs, moors in North Yorkshire, Cumberland and Wiltshire were turned into new fields. An exchange had taken place: war planes used the flat fields of peace, while potatoes climbed the mountains to make up for the loss.

THE WOMEN'S LAND ARMY[15]

There had been various organisations for women to help in agriculture during the First World War, including a Women's Land Army, so there was a precedent for the same in the Second World War. Countrywomen had, of course, been employed on farms for hundreds of years, in dairying for example.

To some, it was obvious that because of naval blockade and men's call-up, women would need to be recruited to do the work of agricultural labourers. But it was not so obvious to others. Lady Denman had been asked by the Minister of Agriculture to head a Women's Branch of the Ministry in 1938. She had been a successful pioneer and first Chairman of the National Federation of Women's Institutes, and Chairman, too of the Family Planning Association. She could organise and inspire. But she was up against an establishment wall of prejudice and apathy, which she had to dismantle brick by brick.

She managed to get a headquarters staff and start organising. Volunteers were recruited – but farmers were less than keen to employ them. Agricultural workers themselves were hostile, fearing that women would be used as cheap labour and so damage their struggle to improve their wages. To be fair, these were notoriously low already. There was a general feeling that women were physically unable to do the hard work of men. Again to be fair, some of the women recruits came from the towns, without much idea of what farm work was like, attracted by a recruiting campaign which would probably fail an advertising standards test today.

One recruiting poster shows a charming girl with a film-star figure, wearing brown jodhpur-like breeches, yellow shirt and a green jersey with the sleeves rolled up. Her hair looks as if she had just left the beauty salon, with a little bow on top. She has a pitchfork in her left hand, and is gazing pensively across sunlit acres of wheat. This romantic view contrasted with the reality of mucking out the pigs on a bitterly cold morning, milking stroppy cows, hoeing miles of young carrots, or lifting potatoes, either bent double or on her knees. She needed the advice in the *Land Army Manual*[16] on how to deal with rough or chapped hands and chilblains. She could be sent to do any of the thousands of different jobs that must be performed, summer or winter. She might well have to cope with sexist prejudice, as she struggled with an unfamiliar tractor for instance. Some Land Girls would not have started with any illusions, however, as they were countrywomen already used to this kind of work. But so many others came from the towns, from shops, offices and housework, that it is remarkable so many fitted in.

The war progressed. More home-grown food simply had to be harvested, with whatever labour could be found. The Land Girls learnt their jobs, and learnt fast. As far as the direction of labour was concerned, volunteering to become a Land Girl was an alternative to going into one of the auxiliary women's services if called up. She signed on for the duration of the war. There was a maximum of about 87,000 women employed in this way in 1943,[17] compared with 461,000 in the auxiliary services.

The hours were long. The standard was a forty-eight-hour week in winter, fifty in summer, plus overtime for peak jobs such as haymaking and harvesting. Double summer time meant that people could be working until eleven at night. The Land Girl was paid not less than 32/- a week, out of which she had to pay for her billet, which might be about a pound, but she was meant to have 16/- left over after paying for board and lodging. To start with, the minimum overtime pay was 8*d* per hour rising to 9½*d* an hour in 1943, when the standard wage also rose to £2 0*s* 6*d*. By comparison men were getting £3 5*s*. at the beginning of the war. Wages did continue to rise until the WLA was disbanded, but so did those of other workers. Nobody grew rich as a Land Girl. Eventually she had a right to a week's holiday with pay per year, and the occasional long weekend, though she might have to make up the time later.

It was difficult, in spite of Lady Denman's efforts, to secure standard wages and conditions for the women. They were not employed by the Government, but by the individual farmers, who were certainly individuals, ranging from totally mean to pleasingly enlightened. Girls were discouraged from moving around, and had to have permission and a good reason for leaving the farm to which they had been sent.

Many of these girls were young, away from home, often for the first time in their lives. If they came from large families they could be lonely, but the camaraderie among the girls may have helped a great deal. Joan Snelling, in her memoir *A Land Girl's War*,[18] describes how she started work with a group of six others. A month later she was joined by a Land Girl who had been working in the forestry division and who became a lifelong friend. But sometimes it was a lonely job. A woman could be out on a tractor in the middle of rolling country without another soul in sight. In the forestry division she could be alone for hours in remote woods selecting trees for felling, and might even be mistaken for a spy. (A lot of wood, like everything else, had been imported but now had to be produced from our own forests.)

Living conditions could be unpleasant too. The Depression of the thirties had resulted in many farmhouses lacking the most basic of mod. cons. Bathrooms were often absent. Less than 50 per cent of farmhouses had running water, and only 25 per cent electricity.[19] Peter Bumphrey remembered that there was no piped water in his house in Norfolk. The water came from a well and was hard, but his family kept several tanks for rainwater too. It took twenty turns of the handle to get the bucket down to water level in the well. There was compensation: 'It was always beautifully cold, even on the hottest days.' It was two or three years after the war before piped water arrived, and when it did the well water was condemned as unfit for human consumption.

At first, the Land Girls often lived on the farms to which they had been sent. There were stories of kindness, with the girls treated as part of the family, but there were also horror stories, of beds with a single thin blanket, of inedible and totally inadequate food, and of sexual harassment.[20] The Home Counties were the most comfortable, but remoter places might seem extraordinarily primitive to town girls. In time, and after complaints, many were housed in hostels, where they had company at least, and a basic living standard. On the down side of this they were subject to more rules. It was probably like living in a spartan boarding school. Here there might be system of working in gangs under the supervision of a more experienced girl – again rather like the school system of prefects. They were sent out to do specific jobs for different farmers.

Market gardens were usually nearer towns, and the women employed there might have a slightly easier time socially, though the emphasis was still on food production. A few worked in the gardens of stately homes too.

After VJ Day the Land Girls were told that they could leave the Army if they wished. Many wanted to stay on until it was finally disbanded in October 1950, when 8,000 still remained. It was expected that the women would receive gratuities and other benefits like the women's auxiliary services and Civil Defence workers. They had been called an army, and though not quite under military discipline they had agreed to stay where they were sent. They had worked in all weathers and conditions, and had made good the slogan that 'Food is a Munition of War.' However, the Government did not see it this way. With the war over, it was decided that the Land Army was like other industrial organisations, and its members were not eligible for help in resettlement. This even though the Land Army was still desperately needed to continue to work the land. There was a public outcry, as well as protests, even strikes, from the women themselves. Lady Denman resigned in justified anger. She was later made a Dame Grand Cross of the British Empire, when the king remarked that both he and the queen had thought that the Land Girls were not well treated. Queen Elizabeth had been a patron of the movement from the first.

Protests were met with a few concessions. In 1945 Land Girls were promised help if they wanted to train (further!) in agricultural work, and £150,000 was paid to the Land Army Benevolent Fund. In addition, the women were allowed to keep their shoes and coats (if they dyed them blue, so that they no longer looked like a uniform). That must have been a great comfort in the bitterly cold winter of 1947 …

In spite of all the hardships, comparative poverty, and final official ingratitude, many workers recalled their time on the land with affection and no regret. They knew they had done one of the jobs that had sustained the nation. They had the satisfaction, too, of knowing that the originally chauvinistic farmers recognised their effectiveness. They had not only dug for Victory, but shovelled a few spadesful of earth onto the coffin of prejudice against women.

MORE HELPERS NEEDED

Skilled male farm workers had been called up into the Services, especially at the start of the war. In time they were replaced by women in greater numbers. Though 98,000 men left, 117,000 women came in,[21] a large proportion from the Land Army described above. Even this was not enough. From the summer of 1941 Italian prisoners of war were employed too. Many of them had worked on the land in their own country, and made a useful contribution to our war effort. I can remember an Italian squad in the fields in Cornwall. They lived in a camp quite close to my home in the valley of Porthcurno, and were given to singing arias from Italian opera. There was an impression that they were relieved to be away from the front lines, doing constructive work.

Even so, at harvest time there was need for yet more labour. For instance *The Times* for 18 February 1943 carried an article 'HELPERS FOR THE HARVEST. 500,000 VOLUNTEERS WANTED. "A Major Emergency"'. The paper's Labour Correspondent reported on a speech given by the Minister of Agriculture, R.S. Hudson:

> Food production in this country has been increased by more than anyone believed possible before the war. The arable acreage is between 40 and 50 per cent greater than in 1939. More than double the 1939 acreage is under corn; the potato crop has nearly doubled, and the sugar beet acreage is over 20 per cent greater. This year another million acres are wanted. Several million tons of additional agricultural produce will be raised, and every bit of it at some stage will be lifted by hand. Some kinds of produce are man-handled several times.

The Minister went on to appeal for the 500,000 extra helpers, about 300,000 of whom would be school children from rural areas, and another 50,000 would attend school harvest camps run by public and secondary schools. People already living in the countryside were expected to provide 100,000 of the extra adult helpers required – they were especially useful as they knew the area already, and could live in their own homes and so did not need lodging or transport. Every village or parish had someone to organise the labour for the local farms where it was needed most.

Yet another 100,000 people were expected to volunteer from the towns. They would stay at one of 1,000 camps to be set up, mostly for men but some for women too, living mainly under canvas. They had to pay for their keep at 28/- a week, but could earn 1/- an hour, weather permitting. It was necessary to register two months in advance of the 'holiday'. Employers should arrange parties of their workers to be lent to farmers – some had already made arrangements to adopt individual farms. But the townspeople could not expect to be given board and lodging in farmhouses. Indeed, the farmer's wife probably needed help herself.

The tone of the article is appealing and demanding by turns. The townies were important. They were the 'third line' on the agricultural front, the first being the regular workers, Land Army and Italian prisoners, and the second rural reinforcements and country children. (The school leaving age was fourteen, so young adolescents were expected to take a full part.) But there was also a threat that if not enough volunteers rolled up their sleeves, 'it may be necessary to employ the Government's powers of direction'.

Another article in *The Times* two months later, on 22 April 1943, elaborates the scheme, again appealing for 500,000 volunteers, including schoolchildren.[22] A million extra acres had been ploughed since the previous year and the harvest was expected to be a bountiful one. Details of exact requirements of labour were being compiled. Voluntary land clubs were mentioned, where townspeople could spend weekends throughout the year. Employers had co-operated in releasing daily working parties when needed, and even the civil servants 'might be granted a few days' special leave'. On the other hand, perhaps the townspeople had not proved as useful as had been hoped. 'In some counties the help of the towns would only be called upon in the last resort …'

As a young woman I spent several weeks at farm camps run by the National Union of Students. This was in the fifties, but the idea was the same – to help get the harvest home, and perhaps to give students a bit of healthy exercise during the summer. The accommodation was basic, dormitories in a disused air base I think, with showers and loos in a separate block. Food was by then unrationed, and there was enough, but cooked in the institutional manner of school dinners. There was a lot of boiled cabbage as well as potatoes. The work was satisfying, appealing to a primitive instinct to gather food before the winter.

Lifting potatoes was a painful job though, as you had to keep ahead of the tractor travelling down the row behind you. Picking mulberries or currants for jam was fun, and harvesting apples led to unexpected ladder-climbing skills. I can still remember that you had to lift or twist the apples gently, not pull them roughly off the bough, and never, never, dig your fingernails into them. Perhaps it was a good thing that after a day on potatoes, fingernails had been pretty much worn down to the quick by the sandy earth.

ALLOTMENTS AND GARDENS: THE TOWN FARMERS

The 'Dig for Victory Campaign' took off in 1941. If the country farmer grew potatoes, wheat, barley and dairy fodder in quantity, it followed that there were no longer fields of cabbage or beans. You should use all daylight hours to grow your own (and double summer time was introduced in May 1941 to help the war effort.) In a Ministry of Agriculture advertisement women were told 'It is up to you to provide the vegetables that are so vital to your children's health – especially in winter. Turn your garden over to vegetables. Get the older children to help you. If you haven't a garden ask your council for an allotment. DO IT NOW'.[23]

Like the Ministry of Food, the Ministry of Agriculture created a steady crop of information designed to appeal both to patriotism and self-interest, encouraging do-it-yourself production of vegetables, pork and eggs.

Leaflets and advertisements amounted to a crash course in smallholding for beginners. The first *Dig for Victory* leaflet,[24] signed by R.S. Hudson, the Minister of Agriculture and Fisheries, set out the problems and challenges. It was published in the autumn of 1940 and entitled *Vegetable Production in private gardens and allotments.* It was addressed 'To everyone who has or can get an allotment or garden.' By then it was clear that the war was going to go on for a long time, and that imports of bulky commodities like fruit would have to be severely cut back to save shipping space. It was equally clear that a diet consisting of a great deal of bread and potatoes would need to be balanced by fresh vegetables all the year round. So the Minister pointed out:

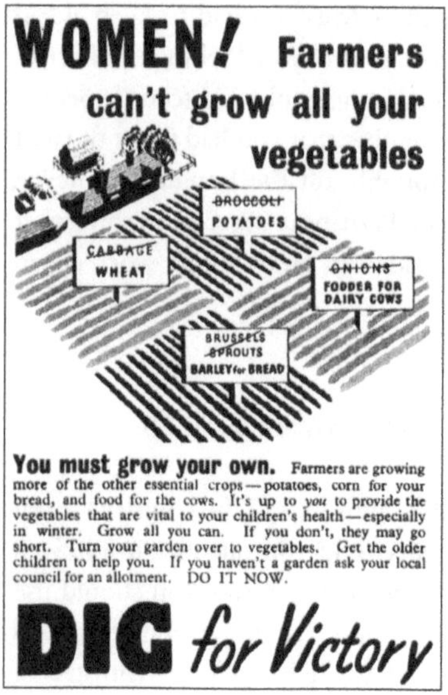

WOMEN! Farmers can't grow all your vegetables
BROCCOLI
POTATOES
CABBAGE
WHEAT
ONIONS
FODDER FOR DAIRY COWS
BRUSSELS SPROUTS
BARLEY for BREAD
You must grow your own. Farmers are growing more of the other essential crops — potatoes, corn for your bread, and food for the cows. It's up to *you* to provide the vegetables that are vital to your children's health — especially in winter. Grow all you can. If you don't, they may go short. Turn your garden over to vegetables. Get the older children to help you. If you haven't a garden ask your local council for an allotment. DO IT NOW.
DIG for Victory

'Women! Farmers can't grow all your vegetables.' Self-help was the rule. Vegetables were essential, especially when fruit was in short supply.

> Last summer many gardens had a surplus of perishable vegetables such as lettuce and cabbage. This winter these same gardens are getting short not only of keeping vegetables such as onions, carrots and other root crops, but also of fresh winter vegetables such as late cabbage, savoys and kale.
>
> We *must* try to prevent that happening this year. Next winter is going to be a critical period.
>
> This leaflet tells you how to crop your ground to the best advantage so as to get vegetables all the year round …

The schematic garden described was of the size of a ten-rod allotment, 30ft x 90ft,[25] a generous size for a town garden.

If you followed the advice and your fingers were sufficiently green, you would certainly enjoy a healthy amount of vitamin-packed produce. In January you would start on your savoy cabbages and kale, which would last until March or April. Shallots would keep going all year, and spinach beet or seakale beet would go on until October. In February, usually one of the bleakest months, you would still have the general winter crops of swedes, turnips, parsnips and brussels sprouts. Spring would bring the first lettuce and winter spinach. In May you could start on your leeks and summer lettuce, with radishes as a treat. June and July were times of plenty, with dwarf and broad and runner beans, beetroot which would keep going until the following spring, carrots, marrows, onions, peas, spinach – and of course potatoes, which progressed from new, to be boiled with mint, to the ones you stored in a clamp or otherwise to last all winter. August had a tomato crop, with careful planning.

Many of the summer vegetables could be kept or preserved for the leaner autumn and winter months. Onions and shallots needed 'an airy damp-proof building', carrots, turnips and beets lifted in October could be stored between layers of sand or soil, with a covering of straw or similar if left in the open. Potatoes, after drying for a few hours, went into boxes kept in the dark and protected from frost. Marrows could be hung up in nets if harvested when they were fully ripe. More advice was available from leaflet No.3. You needed quite a large shed, cellar or larder however to follow all the instructions and keep your harvest safe.

Fertility

Digging the ground was the first requirement. Like the emergency ploughing of the first winter, the gardener or allotment holder had to turn over the topsoil and break it up. Hence the slogan of 'Dig for Victory', the logo on the leaflet, and the posters displaying a boot on a spade to make the message quite clear. There was a right way to get your plot ready.[26] You should divide it in half lengthwise, then starting at one end, dig out a trench 1ft deep and 2ft wide across the end of one of the strips, shifting the first clumps of earth and turf to where the digging would end. Then you forked down and broke up the subsoil to about 10in deep. Moving to the next bit you dug out another chunk of the surface, turning the sods face down over the softened subsoil in the first trench. So you went on, digging, turning, forking, digging, turning, forking, until you had finished both strips, with the first sods turned face down onto the last bit of trench.

If you were using land already under cultivation, the technique was much the same, but instead of top grass you might add manure, compost or other plant material as a sandwich between the subsoil and the turned-over top slice.

Potato Scones. Mashed potatoes found their way into a lot of flour-based recipes.

The time-honoured and preferred method of manuring had been to recycle the dung of horses and other farm animals. Herbivores processed the eaten grass for the farmer, who had simply to collect it and return it to the land. However the home gardener or townsman had difficulty in getting this, so a compost heap was the answer – over time. 'How to Make a Compost Heap' came out as leaflet No.7:

> The process known as composting is based on the fact that if vegetable matter, air and water are brought together in suitable proportions, fermentation will ensue: this brings about a decompositon of the vegetable matter. Decompositon can be speeded up by means of an 'accelerator' which is either animal manure or a chemical substance. In this process of decomposition the vegetable waste is converted into the most suitable form for keeping up the humus supply of the soil, and at the same time some of the plant nutrients it contains are converted into available forms.[27]

Any garden waste such as grass cuttings, weeds, straw and vegetable peelings could be used if they were not obviously diseased, but not the roots of perennial weeds such as couch grass. The snag was that it could take several weeks if not months before it could be used. Heat from the fermentation process was good, as it killed weed seeds.

Crops suggested by the Minister of Agriculture were those favoured by the Minister of Food as well. There are very many potato varieties, some of which continue in an unbroken line from before the war to the present day. King Edward's are one such. The recommended ones were Epicure, Arran Pilot, Sharpe's Express, and May Queen, all early varieties, followed by Great Scot, and then the late or main crop Majestic, King Edward VII, Arran Banner, Gladstone, Kerr's Pink, Redskin, Up-to-Date, Arran Victory, Arran Peak and Dunbar Standard.[28] (The Arran varieties may give a clue as to their place of origin!)

Detailed instructions for growing peas, beans, cabbage and its relations, root vegetables and tomatoes were all covered by leaflets. Leaflets about jam making and bottling, even canning, were available too. Canning vegetables could be dangerous however, due to the presence of heat-resistant bacteria in soil, unless you had an autoclave or pressure cooker that could be kept at 10lb pressure. Probably it was better to dry those vegetables that could not be stored in clamps and so on.

People who had no gardens, nor access to allotments – or perhaps no time or energy available for heavy work – were still not excused. They could grow things in window boxes or on flat roofs. With a roof, a few planks to make boxes, or old buckets, or a Dutch frame securely fastened down you could produce various saladings and root vegetables, as well as marrows, squash and dwarf beans. You had to remember that it was colder up on a windy roof than on the ground, and make sure the soil you used was fresh each time. The plants had to be watered of course, and drainage considered carefully.[29] (People living in the rooms just below the roof would not welcome soggy ceilings.)

Window boxes also provided salads, but more especially herbs, which were a really good idea. The possible range was wide and they made a surprising difference to monotonous ingredients. Parsley was an excellent choice, being high in Vitamin C content as well as cheering up the appearance of a bland dish. It was added, chopped, to soups, stews and sauces and to many rissole or meat cake recipes. Dried and shell egg dishes were the better for it. But parsley was not the only herb. Others were recommended too. Thyme was good in fishcakes, tarragon flavoured vinegar, chicken and rabbit. Chervil went with potatoes and fish. Chives were especially useful in the absence of onions, while sage and mint were already well known. You needed a patch of garden for a bay tree, rosemary bush or horseradish roots, but any odd bit of earth would do for nasturtiums, whose seeds, pickled, were capers. Even if you had no access at all to garden or window box, mustard and cress could be produced by sowing the seeds on a bit of damp flannel or blotting paper on a plate.

Yet however much attention you gave to your personal plot, you had to remember too that there were subversive elements at work. Slugs, snails, black fly, flea beetles, Cabbage White caterpillars, potato blight. They could chomp their way through stem and leaf, or murder the crops where they stood, invalidating all the painful hours of digging, planning and planting. They had to go. Another *Dig for Victory* leaflet[30] elaborated on the basic advice of leaflet No. 1, describing further horrors: wireworms, which damaged potatoes, leather jackets and cutworms, black aphids on beans. The cabbage was particularly vulnerable. It was subject to attack when very young, first from flea beetles, then cabbage root fly. Next came the ubiquitous caterpillars, followed by cabbage aphids and cabbage white fly. Carrots had their carrot fly, celery a leaf miner. Onions were attacked by another fly, peas by beetles and weevils as well as greenfly. The precious potatoes had to be watched not only for wireworms and slugs, but eelworms. They could spread easily, and rotation of potatoes with other crops was recommended.

The insecticides available for routine use were derris powder, to protect cabbages, pyrethrum for greenfly and nicotine in solution. This last is poisonous, and if you bought it you had to sign the Poison Book as a deterrent to misuse, to put it mildly. Metaldehyde was sold as slug bait, and could be mixed with bran and left around in little heaps for them to discover. Other creative ways with slug trapping included smearing syrup or old jam over a bit of wood. Once a week you could turn it over and dispose of the pests that had gathered there. Children were sometimes given the job of stripping the caterpillars and eggs from cabbages by hand. They needed to learn not to be squeamish about such matters.

It was said that a form of biological warfare was used towards the end of the war. Colorado beetles, which destroy potato plants, were dropped on the Isle of Wight and Kent in boxes of fifty or a hundred.[31] Schoolchildren were employed to find them, counting carefully. Maybe some did get away, because there was a scare about this serious pest in the late 1940s. In 1950 there were twenty-three outbreaks, many of which were dealt with by remaining members of the dwindling Land Army.[32]

Fungicides charmingly called Bordeaux or Burgundy Mixture could be prepared at home in small quantities from copper sulphate and hydrated lime from the horticultural shop, added to water, or from copper sulphate and washing soda and water as before. They were used against potato blight, leaf spot in celery and leaf curl of some stone fruits.

Other insecticides used (definitely NOT recommended today) included cyanide and sulphuric acid, and sterilising the soil with steam applied by a special machine.[33]

How seriously people took all this advice is difficult to estimate at this length of time after the event, but very many people undoubtedly did their best.

Several of my friends mention that their parents had taken the advice to heart. Cliff Townsend remembers that his family's allotment was quite large, but covered at first in couch grass which had to be removed. They grew kale (but not cabbage), carrots and sprouts but not potatoes, which took up too much room. His wife Dot's family had a large garden, where potatoes and cabbage were grown. Cliff explained too:

> The other thing about allotments was that a lot of runner beans were grown. This of course was not only because they were heavy croppers, if there was a decent rainy period, but also because they went up rather than out and so they conserved space tremendously, and you could spread out with your other things like kale that gave a lot of leaf and didn't have to bear fruit.

Dot added that beans were often cut up and salted and so preserved for the winter. This too was in line with MoF recommendations.[34] Even children away at school used to help. My friend Mary Rowe remembers days at a convent near Bridgenorth where, in distinguished company, she planted potatoes on the farm.[35] Ronald Knox was the chaplain, and, dressed in a shabby black cassock, he too lent a hand. 'The distance between the potatoes was a subject of discussion,' she says. Perhaps neither of them had read the relevant *Potato Growing* leaflet.

5

Country Life

The experience of civilians clearly differed depending on where they lived. Cities were perceived to be far more dangerous, with essential industries and concentrations of population making them obvious targets. The expected instant bombardment of London had led to the mass evacuation of schoolchildren and vulnerable adults to the safer country. Many people went of their own accord to stay with relations out of bombs' way.

As events unfolded, these perceptions changed several times over. London was not attacked – until the Blitz. Before that happened, many children returned to their families in the familiar streets. Then, when the bombs and, later, doodle-bugs fell, there were movements away from danger again.

The countryside was not under threat – until after the fall of France, when South Coast towns were relabelled as risky, some inhabitants evacuated. Factories were shifted to the country, and of course there were military camps, both British and Allied, dotted all over the rural scene. There was, in other words, a huge shift of population with many individuals becoming exposed to country life for the first time in several generations. Rural people who had hung on to their traditions were challenged by the newcomers, but war affected daily life far less in the country than in the towns.

As far as food was concerned, people were meant to have equal shares of what was available, no matter where they lived. It was recognised, though, that 'agricultural workers [were] probably in a better position than townsmen to take advantage of the various privileges enjoyed by producers.' They had opportunities for 'rabbiting, fishing, collecting fruit and the neighbourly exchange of goods,' and were better able to grow vegetables. On the other hand, there were fewer catering facilities and 'Fish, cakes, and cooked meats are some of the foods of which the lack is most felt by country workers.'[1]

If there had been absolute equality, the family of a successful farmer should have had the same as the family of an absent serviceman, whose wife was working full-time in a munitions factory, hardly able to get to the shops. Of course this was not the case. It is more surprising that shares were even approximately fair.

PACKED LUNCHES: A TALE OF COUNTRY FOLK

The Ministry of Food recognised at least one essential difference between town and country food customs. Lunch. Many agricultural workers, including Land Girls and a host of others, had to eat outside at midday. For them, the nearest canteen or British Restaurant was miles over the horizon. There was, therefore, a special ration of cheese. In place of the ordinary ration, they were entitled to a larger one. This varied from 8oz in May 1941, to 12oz in December of the same year, and then a high of 16oz (1lb) in July 1942, which was double the domestic ration. It dropped back to 12oz in January 1943.[2]

It might be thought that cheese was dependent on the domestic supply of milk, but in fact there was very little liquid milk left when priority groups had been supplied. Therefore most cheese continued to be imported, and the percentage actually rose from 76 per cent pre-war to 93 per cent in 1944.[3] For many people cheddar was a synonym for cheese. This kind is a good traveller. It is compact and keeps well. Most of it came from America, Canada, Australia and New Zealand. The basic ration was usually about 2 or 3oz per person per week, except for the high spike in summer 1942.

The list of workers entitled to the larger ration is worth quoting in full, as it evokes the busy countryside of sixty years ago. It was a landscape of figures toiling in all weathers to keep the nation functioning. The most obvious were all the field and forestry workers, but there were many others such as electrical linesmen restoring supply after a storm, men laying gas mains and canal boatmen. There were also a surprising number of industrial workers. Various industries had grown up in the countryside, such as modest flour mills. Men followed coal wherever it

Country people who might have a few eggs to spare sometimes sent them to their friends. They needed very strong packaging to get through the post safely.

was to be found, either underground or in open-cast mines. Another example was the tin-mining area of Cornwall.

Cliff Townsend worked in one of these mines. Aged seventeen he volunteered to work in the South Crofty tin mine at Camborne, later on the last to shut down. Every tenth man called up at the end of 1943 was directed to become a so-called Bevin Boy, a conscripted miner, but Cliff volunteered as he did not want to join the Army on grounds of Christian conscience, though not formally a Conscientious Objector. He did this since many lads were more scared of the mines than the army. He lived in a hostel, and worked permanently on the night shift, which he preferred.

His job was to break up the mined ore-bearing rock with a sledgehammer before it went through a 'grizzly' or grill and then to the surface in a skip. A shift lasted for eight hours, but at night you could work hard to get the job done and then come up in perhaps five hours. Then in daylight, after he had slept, he could cycle in the country to study wild plants.

The mine was 2,000ft deep, or 315 fathoms, approximately. It was very hot and thirsty work – water was the liquid he drank. He ate enormous pasties, mostly filled with potato and onion, with a little meat. Water ran down the rocks, so hot that an egg left in the gutters soon became hard-boiled. Tin was needed to make solder, and was therefore a vital raw material for industry.[4]

This is the list of workers. They are a varied lot, but all share the myth of the cheese sandwich:[5]

Agricultural workers employed under contract of service in agriculture and horticulture including ancillary workers, e.g. threshing machine workers, tractor workers travelling blacksmiths and agricultural maintenance engineers, dry-stone dykers, hay pressers, trussers and cutters.
Brick and tile workers in small units in isolated areas.
Canal boatmen.
Canal maintenance workers.
Charcoal burners working in forests.
Civilian employees of Services Departments in eligible categories.
Coal borers.
Coal distributive workers.
County and rural roadmen and scavengers.
Dry-stone dykers.
Electrical linesmen and workers employed with them in rural areas.
Electrical sub-station staff on continuous shifts of 8 hours in small isolated sub-stations.
Fishermen (excluding holders of the weekly seamen's book and fishermen for whom other special provision has been made).
Forestry workers, including hauliers, fellers and saw millers in or connected with forestry who actually work in forests, timber workers employed at saw mills, in country districts and lorry drivers exclusively employed in the transport of timber between the forest and railway stations.
Gas-main layers working full-time in country areas.
Hay pressers, cutters and trussers.
Land drainage workers (including Catchment Board Workers).
Miners working underground.
Ministry of Transport trunk road workers employed in experimental road-surfacing in isolated districts.
Ordnance Survey Field Revisers.

Permanent water bailiffs paid by Fishery Boards.
Post Office engineers (external).
Quarrymen – roadstone, limestone and slate, including chalk diggers and slag workers procuring slag for road construction purposes.
Railway manual workers employed on continuous shifts of not less than six hours with no rostered meal break or at a place where no canteen or catering facilities are available.
Rural building and civil engineering workers.
Sand and gravel pit workers.
Scale repairers included under the description 'Service Adjusters engaged on repairs and/or contracts'.
Sewage farms and works' employees.
Surface workers at iron-ore mines.
Surface workers at coal mines where there are no canteens.
Threshing machine workers.
Tractor workers (including owner-drivers not employed on own farms).
Travelling blacksmiths and agricultural machinery maintenance engineers.
Trainees and members of the Women's Land Army.
Trainees in agriculture and forestry under Government schemes not residing in hostels.
Wagon repairers working on railway and colliery sidings.
Waterworks undertakings employees.
Workers employed within the confines of iron stone quarries.
Workers employed at small country flour and provender mills in remote areas.

Apart from the larger cheese ration, there were no extras as such for workers doing heavy manual jobs. What they really needed was copious carbohydrate and fat for energy, supplied by plentiful potatoes and bread, and the adequate fat ration. Yet the aim of the Ministry was to supply 'at least one hot nutritious meal every day at a reasonable price' to workers everywhere. British Restaurants fulfilled the need in towns, but in the country there was the alternative of a pie scheme. In the spring of 1942 Pie Centres were organised for the supply of prepared meals, snacks and sandwiches – even pies.[6] They were run by a typically British mixture of local authorities, voluntary organisations such as the Women's Institutes, individuals approved by the War Ag. Committees, and local traders. The actual cooking was done by village bakers (such as Bexon's described below), in British Restaurants or anywhere where a large kitchen could be found.

Food was supplied on the catering scale for packed meals according to the number of pies sold. By the end of May 1945, 5,000 villages were chewing their way through nearly a million pies a week.[7] They must have made a welcome change from cheese sandwiches.

The seasonal workers were not forgotten either. The organisers of volunteer groups who took time to help with the harvest were licensed as catering establishments in Category A, with authority to buy priority scheme foods too. The aim was to allow for breakfast, packed lunch, dinner or high tea, a lighter tea-type snack and five hot drinks a day per person.

An earnest civil servant somewhere worked out precisely what was meant by breakfast, lunch, dinner and tea.[8] (This will be a valuable reference for food historians of the future.) Breakfast was a substantial meal, served, in case you were wondering, 'during the normal breakfast period'. You could put away 'porridge or breakfast cereal, fish, bacon, egg or sausage', but if you had only bread/toast, butter/margarine or preserves, it counted as a tea meal.

A main meal had to consist of a portion of meat, fish, poultry, game or eggs, or 'a correspondingly substantial dish' plus potatoes (of course) and other vegetables, and one or two other courses. (Soup and pudding?)

Sandwiches, meat pies or other snacks without any other courses counted as 'subsidiary meals', and for the sake of logic, so did 'any other meal which is more substantial than a tea meal, but does not contain any course which would make it a main meal.'

A 'tea meal' did not necessarily include tea, but was made up of bread, buns, rolls etc. plus butter, or more likely margarine, jam, cakes or biscuits.

Finally a 'hot beverage' meant 'a hot beverage in which added sugar is customarily consumed, whether served alone or with a meal, but it does not include any spirituous beverage.' Bring your own warm beer folks. At least the sugar allowance for hot beverages was included.

Farmers were also entitled to extra rations of tea, sugar and milk for their workers.[9] The tea had to be 'brewed communally and consumed at work', and there was in theory enough for two hot drinks a day. The precious tea break then did not depend on the worker's individual ration, though many no doubt took a thermos with them from home.

At seasonal times when the workload was at its peak, such as during 'haymaking, harvesting, threshing, hoeing and singling of root crops, sheep shearing and lambing', there was a bonus – four hot drinks were allowed per day. The supplier and farmer must have needed a letter balance to make sure they were selling or receiving the correct amounts. The daily allowance was worked out per person – possibly by the same bureaucrat that had defined the meals – as 9/32oz of tea (yes, really) and 4/5oz of sugar. These amounts were not on top of the ordinary couple of drinks, but were in place of them. In addition there were two snacks a day, with an allowance per person of ¾oz margarine, 2/5oz cheese, ¾ oz of preserves, and half a point coupon to splash out on something like sardines or Spam. It is to be hoped that the hungry haymakers were careful not to exceed their three teaspoons of jam each. At least the bread was not weighed out for them. However, this bounty was not available if they were able to get a meal from an ordinary or mobile canteen or Pie Centre.

THE WOMEN'S INSTITUTE[10]

In Britain, the first Women's Institute was inspired by a Canadian organisation founded in 1897. In 1915 an inaugural meeting took place in a fairly small Welsh village with an exceedingly long name: Llanfairpwllgwyngyllgogerychwynrndrobwll-Llantysiliogogogoch, which translates as the Church of St Mary, in a white hazel wood near a rapid whirlpool close to St Tysilio's cave near a red cave. The first subject for official discussion was *The Food Supply of the Country*, a prophetic title in view of the help the Women's Institutes were to give in both World Wars. Not, of course, that food was the only preoccupation of the organisation. From the start they had a fairly radical agenda, devoted to self-improvement and the raising of all kinds of living standards in the country. They encouraged women to take a full part in society, and were non-sectarian and democratic. More Institutes were opened in the country districts of Wales. It was a matter of policy to keep the Institutes in villages only – if any were set up in town they became centres with a role of helping country areas. By 1917 a National Federation was formed, with Lady Denman as its first chairman. The Board of Agriculture's Food Production department became involved, but allowed the Institutes to remain self-governing. Many more were set up. From the first there were many areas of interest, by no means just the domestic ones that the 'jam and Jerusalem' gibe suggested.

Under the umbrella target of making society better in practical ways, the WIs aimed to improve skills in food production, and in craftwork to provide income for village women. Cultural pursuits were encouraged, and the women increasingly took an interest in social problems and public affairs generally. Markets sold local produce, perhaps the forerunners of the farmers' markets we have today. In 1920 the NFWI broke away financially from the Board of Agriculture. Over the following years a Rural Community Council linked the WI, YMCA, Village Clubs Association and Workers' Educational Association to prevent duplication of effort. Training and education were increasingly stressed, libraries in rural areas organised. Music was added as an important strand of the work, and so were community projects. Resolutions were debated concerning maternal mortality and child health, a part of an increasing general concern about social welfare.

This trend continued in the 1930s, with the Depression and unemployment making domestic skills doubly important. Food growing and produce markets continued to be promoted – and this was of course at a time when, nationally, agriculture was in a bad way. In 1934 a resolution welcomed the supply of milk to school children in both town and country, and in 1939 LEAs were urged to improve school dinners in elementary schools. The Institutes were also far-seeing. They raised matters that concern us today, such as wearing furs where cruelty to animals was involved, and (in 1936) the pollution of rivers by effluent, suggesting that legislation was needed. By 1943 there was a call for equal pay for equal work for women, one of the key demands of Women's Lib.

Back in 1938 Lady Denman, the first National Chairman, was asked to become the designated honorary director of the Women's Land Army, then being set up. Her work for the country-based Women's Institutes had of course fitted her for this new responsibility. Although she hesitated in case her work with the WI might be compromised, in the end she took it on in addition to her previous job. She remained

Chairman until 1946. In a sense the WLA grew out of the Women's Institutes, though the women who worked the land were paid, while WI members worked voluntarily.

At the outbreak of war, there were about 291,000 members spread throughout the country, experts in growing food and marketing it, in handicrafts of all kinds and what was then called domestic science. This covered all aspects of home management, cooking, child care, home nursing and budgeting. Added to these skills were wider concerns of national child welfare, conservation of the countryside, and cultural pursuits such as music and drama. The women were organised and able to voice creative criticism of government policies as they affected the lives of ordinary people.

Their first job in the war was to help with the settlement of evacuees. They published a report, *Town Children through Country Eyes*, in 1941. It drew attention to the problems of child poverty. Concern about this eventually led to the payment of Family Allowances.

As far as food was concerned, the next job was to help preserve the fruit harvest. This was not only commercially grown but came from the surplus of gardens, allotments and blackberrying expeditions. The fruit was paid for, but prices varied regionally. When it was not possible to import fruit, it was in the public interest to save the home-grown harvest.

The Ministry of Food asked the NFWI to look after the National Fruit Preservation Scheme. This covered canning as well as jam making. America supplied a lot of equipment, and 1,000 cans in the first year grew to 10,000 in the second. Bottling and canning were alternative ways of keeping fruit, but jam seems to have held a special place in the planners' hearts. There was not enough butter for bread-and-butter, but bread-and-jam was a good standby.

Centres were organised in any institutions with enough kitchen space, such as schools, where local volunteers went along to make preserves from Ministry recipes. The Ministry also supplied the sugar. The idea was to standardise the product, so that it contained enough sugar to make it keep well (60 per cent) and to be of high enough quality to use for rations.[11]

It is interesting to see what home-produced jams arrived on the grocers' shelves. (Not all of it of course from the amateur factories.) According to *Shaw's Monthly Food List*[12] which was published to give information to retailers about current prices, there were six price groups. Jam was sold in 1lb, 2lb and 7lb jars, this last probably for catering establishments and institutions. The first group was the most expensive, with prices of 1/1½*d*, 2/2*d* and 7/1*d* according to size. You could choose from apricot, apricot and peach, bilberry, blackberry (seedless or jelly), cherry, elderberry jelly and elderberry seedless, greengage or pineapple. (The pineapples might possibly have been grown in the hothouses of stately homes.) All these were comparatively scarce.

Coming down a bit, costing 1/1*d*, 2/0½*d* or 6/7½*d*, were blackberry or bramble, blackcurrant and blackcurrant jelly, peach and mixtures with citrus fruit, plum and strawberry, or plain strawberry.

Then enter the apple. Comparatively cheap and comparatively plentiful – though all fruit was scarce at times – apples contain a lot of the pectin which combines with sugar in solution to make a gel. So in group three at a halfpenny a pound less, there is apple and blackcurrant, apple and strawberry, damson, loganberry and loganberry seedless, plum and blackcurrant, plum and raspberry, raspberry or raspberry seedless or jelly, and redcurrant jelly. There must have been a good crop of raspberries that year, as well as apples.

Group four is again only a halfpenny less per pound, with apple jelly plain, apple and raspberry and/or loganberry, plum and plum jelly, quince jelly, raspberry and redcurrant, rhubarb and raspberry, strawberry and gooseberry, and special standard marmalade. Quince jelly is interesting here – perhaps there was not a great demand for it, though quinces have an interesting taste and were once widely used. (The original marmalade was made from quinces, not oranges, in the fourteenth and fifteenth centuries.) Rhubarb and gooseberries, both quite humble produce grown in many gardens, appear for the first time.

Cheaper still in group five, at only 11½*d* per lb, were apple and blackberry, apple and damson, apple and plum, raspberry and gooseberry, rhubarb and blackberry and marmalade other than the special standard.

Finally at 11*d* per pound come gooseberry, rhubarb and 'all other jams'. By this time one wonders what other jams there could possibly be. The price differential for the pound size was only 2½*d* between the most expensive and the cheapest, but there was probably a big difference in desirability between more costly cherry and cheaper rhubarb jams for instance. (If you made your own jam for domestic use the cost of preserving sugar was 4½*d* a pound. The price was controlled, and of course the sugar was also rationed.)

After the war the WI continued to develop as a pressure group on rural and family matters. Perhaps Jerusalem is within their sights still. They certainly made a success of the jam!

SHOPS IN THE COUNTRY

The number of shops available depended on the size of the village or small town. Some had just a general store, often doubling as a post office, where people bought their basic rations. In that case it was necessary to go to town every now and then to buy essential clothes and household goods. You usually went by bus or bicycle, because petrol was rationed. On such trips the housewife might be lucky and find a queue with some fish still available at the other end of it. Or she might be in line – literally – for a treat of some prized item like canned peaches, on points.

A Village Business

In many slightly larger places the village bakery was luckily available for the supply of bread, when shopping elsewhere was difficult. One of my correspondents, David Bexon, grew up in Awsworth, Nottinghamshire, where his father ran a business as baker and confectioner. David's account starts with a family reminiscence of 1919 and follows the development of the business through the war and after, up to 1972 when his father retired. The account also describes the customers, and aspects of village life. It illustrates very well that though innovation did take place – the introduction of machinery for instance, and motor vans for deliveries – there was also continuity in spite of war. Very hard work was the key to success, and also earned respect from the whole community.

David Bexon's Account[13]

> Oddly, baking was never Dad's choice; he'd always fancied being a motor mechanic, but Grandad hauled him out of Ilkeston Grammar School at the age of 12 in 1919 to help run the business. He soon had him driving,

having lied about his tall son's age, and Dad never took a driving test. Soon Dad was practically running the business himself, having learned his trade at Nottingham Technical College (now Trent Poly) where he later taught baking for a few years, with considerable success. Grandad had been a good reliable worker at Giltbrook Brickyard, but was soon happy to rely on Dad, so that he could slope off to the racecourse with his cronies in the afternoon. He died the year before I was born, but many years later some of our oldest customers who remembered Grandad's skill at picking winners used to beg me for tips for the Derby or the St. Leger, hoping I'd inherited his nose!

Before the war Dad had used a horse-drawn wagon for local deliveries, and as a lad he'd had to catch the reluctant horse in its often foggy field down by the Erewash canal, bridle it and lead it back up the lane to the bakehouse. All before setting off for Ilkeston Grammar School on foot, carrying a large wicker basket full of bread for outlying farms.

My most vivid childhood memory is the arrival in about 1943 of the huge mixer for Dad's bakehouse. The idea that he and his men could heave that great monstrous machine off the lorry and haul it into position into the far corner of the bakehouse was exhilarating. Someone reckoned it must weigh at least a ton, but after much straining and grunting, much sweating and cussing, they managed it.

By the next morning it was taking much of the hard labour out of the daily chore of mixing the dough, as its twin stainless steel arms plunged down into the sticky mix of flour, yeast, salt and water, work previously done by human muscle. Until Dad could afford, a few years later, to buy a divider, and later, a moulder, the mixed dough still had to be heaved, in floppy slabs, out of the bowl onto a floured table, sliced into chunks, slapped onto a scale pan, flopped onto the table to be moulded by hand (two at a time) and finally dropped into greased tins to prove while waiting their turn in the oven. After the war a second oven was built and both were converted from coke to oil.

Dad never complained about being pressganged into the trade and came to enjoy his work, taking pride in his products. He enjoyed working alongside his men, paying them above the union rate and keeping his prices down for his customers. For a quiet, mild-mannered man, he was a driven worker, and no-one could keep up with him in the bakehouse or on the round. While they all took their turn at the heaviest tasks, humping one hundredweight sacks of flour down from the loft, loading trays of tinned dough into the proving cabinets, Dad generally worked the ovens. He was braced like an ancient Greek hoplite to spear the heavy tins of dough two at a time into the fierce heat on the broad blade of his long-handled peel (compare French pelle = shovel), and later retrieving them, swivelling round to crash them down onto an aluminium bench so as to loosen the loaves from the tins. Then two of us with barm-bagged hands would have to knock them out, stack them on slatted trays and cart them out to cool in racks in the yard.

After the war, competition from the big new plant bakeries became so intense that many small bakers went out of business. The daily routine was punishing enough already, requiring a weekday start around five, a 2 a.m. start on Saturdays and for Bank Holidays and Christmas, a 9 p.m. start on Friday nights, to bake enough bread to last several days. We also made barm bread (fruited loaf), milk bread (soft textured batch/small loaf), Hovis of course and steamed loaves (baked in tins to steam the dough, making it interestingly chewy). We made sausage rolls all year round and pork pies in conjunction with the butcher round the corner. All the bread had to be out of the oven and cooled enough in the yard for some of it to be sliced and wrapped in time for it to reach the shops by 8 a.m. Only then could the men relax over their breakfast sandwiches for half an hour, sprawled on sacks of flour in the loft. The rest of their day's work had a more relaxed tempo, working on the cakes and pastries.

As for the cakes, before and after the war there were ginger parkins (flat circles with an almond on top), brandy snaps (until the war), Eccles cakes, fruited scones baked in rounds of four, iced buns, cream buns, fruit cakes, sponges with various fillings, crumpets (known as pikelets in Derbyshire and Nottingham), flaky pastry (cream horns were my favourite!) and madeleines.

Specific seasons and occasions required extra effort: hot cross buns by the thousand, finger rolls for weddings and receptions, and the birthday and tiered wedding cakes that Dad made to order, iced Christmas cakes and logs, and loads of mince pies.

As the business thrived and even expanded after the war, Dad employed up to eight men, and a woman to run the shop, where we sold groceries, twists of yeast (barm) in paper bags, salt and sugar in navy-blue paper bags, weighed in pounds, scooped out of sacks.

I was about nine when I first worked in the bakehouse just for half an hour on Friday nights when the need to operate several machines

JOAN BULL takes the BISCUIT!
—and needs it too. Biscuits help her to carry on her countless jobs, whether in the Services or on the land, in factories, in hospitals, or keeping the home going.
Biscuits are concentrated energy-food, and the finest ingredients obtainable—wheat, sugar and fats—are used by Weston, the largest makers of biscuits in the Empire.
(The distribution of Weston Biscuits is made by zones according to Ministry of Food instructions, and as supplies are allocated in exact proportion to individual quotas, every Weston stockist receives exactly similar treatment.)
Weston BISCUITS
FOR CHOICE

'Joan Bull takes the Biscuit'. Although for much of the war biscuits were on points, manufacturers were keen to keep brand names going in anticipation of post-war demand.

simultaneously required an extra pair of hands. I also started going on the rounds on Saturdays and most days during the holidays from school, and later from university. Doors were usually unlocked and often open, so we usually entered with our baskets, sometimes finding the correct money on the table in an empty house. Life was harsher then, but people were generally more trusting: it was a time before mass marketing and TV ads, so few people had any of the consumer durables that invite today's burglars.

Over the years we roundsmen developed a very happy relationship with our customers and at Christmas I had a job to fend off their Christmas boxes, feeling that as a member of the firm, I shouldn't expect any.

Some of our customers were eccentric, like Miss L., who made her staff call her Sir, and dressed in layers of long skirts, which she hoisted up without ceremony to retrieve wads of banknotes when paying her bills. Then there was Herbert W., another shopkeeper, a real scatterbrain. Whenever we asked him how many loaves he needed that day, he would smile ruefully, scratch the back of his head and admit: 'Buggered if I know!' One house I hated to call at belonged to an old lady with ulcerated legs. Her son, an Old Contemptible, used to like to buttonhole me with the same old tale of how Lord Kitchener himself had paused in his inspection of the ranks to congratulate him on his smart appearance. And all I could think about was escaping from the stench of the poor woman's varicose sores!

Deliveries to the village often came by horse and cart, especially during the war, and long after it in some cases. Barrels of beer, for instance, came on drays drawn by those huge Shire horses all the way from Hanson's Brewery in Kimberley, and were lowered on thick ropes down into the off-licensee's cellar through a trap-door in the pavement. Coal was delivered by lorry from the nearest pit at Cossall, made famous by D.H. Lawrence, who renamed it Cossethay and used Marsh Farm, where I went potato-picking, as the venue for *Women in Love.* Coke and oil for the bakehouse ovens came by lorry, as did the butcher's deliveries of meat and huge cubes of ice, until fridges became a commonplace. Other regular visitors to Awsworth were the rag and bone man, on his pony-cart, hollering 'Any old iron?' and the knife-grinder on his bike, with its very useful grindstone. He also mended pots and kettles.

Since Dad was born and bred in the village, everyone knew him and called him Bill or Mr Bexon. He'd played goal for the local football team, Awsworth Rovers, alongside the young miners who were his contemporaries. Many remembered his parents too, and everybody knew me. As the only businessman in Awsworth, he had a certain status. He could always be relied upon to donate groceries for village fêtes, chapel festivals and a huge bread wheatsheaf for the Harvest Festival. He was remarkably indulgent towards some longstanding customers whose bills dated from the Depression, allowing them to pay off a few coppers when they could.

As everyone knew everybody else, you always greeted people in the street; men either touched or raised their hats to women, and called them by their married names, as in 'Mornin' Missus –'. Women always called men by their surnames, or simply said: 'Mornin' Mester.' Everybody wore a hat, the men usually a flat cap, the women usually a felt hat, unadorned. The more familiar greeting was 'Ey up, mi' duck', the title of a local booklet about Derbyshire dialect. A probably apocryphal incident has a local woman say of a bride: 'Ee, she lewked luvvely, cummin dahn th'izzle wi' a bucket in 'er hand'.

After the war we owned four or five green vans, all bearing the logo *J. W. Bexon, Baker & Confectioner.* As well as the shops which were his best customers, Dad had developed three extensive rounds in the village itself and in the nearby hosiery towns of Eastwood and Kimberley. The shops were supplied daily, and the houses either three or four times a week. Frosty weather often caused starting problems, cold engines had to be cranked into life with a starting handle, vans had to be pushed to the nearest hill and jump-started.

When I was fourteen we moved to the pleasant western Nottingham suburb of Wollaton, so I had a five-mile bike-ride each way from then on over very hilly country! I worked almost every day and finished the day before my wedding, when I was twenty-two, and moved to my first job in Yorkshire. I had only one minor accident in all that time: pushing loaves down the bread-slicing chute into its whizzing blades, I left my thumb there too long, but had the presence of mind to see it bandaged before I passed out.

Although I only received pocket money, Dad kept me on at school, at a time when many brighter pupils were made to leave. He also supported me through four years of university, so I never felt aggrieved. [David became a language specialist in a secondary school, teaching French and Spanish.] I really admired my father's fairness towards his men and his determination to stay afloat, but the nervous tension of his punishing routine gave him dreadful migraines on Sundays. His early starts and long hours in the over-heated floury atmosphere meant he often fell asleep during the evening, and of course he had to be in bed by nine or ten. I know he never read a book after leaving school; just the *Nottingham Evening Post*. He loved to read out adverts for stuff he didn't need, just to show what amazing bargains were on sale, much to Mother's annoyance, because it was all entirely irrelevant to their lives.

At sixty-five my father finally agreed to Mother's long-standing plea and sold the business as a going concern. Typically, he agreed to carry on working for six weeks without pay to train the new owner in the basic routines. A few years later, Mother and Dad moved to Norwich to be near my brother, and had a long and happy retirement there. Dad died aged 90 in 1997.

THE FARM IN THE BACKYARD

Agriculture on a large scale has been described in Chapter 4, as well as the production of vegetables wherever they could be tucked in. But there was another group of food producers, who might loosely be called smallholders. They existed in towns too, but their work fitted in better with existing countryside patterns.

Restrictions on keeping livestock were lifted in the summer of 1940. The RSPCA offered helpful leaflets on the proper care and treatment of pigs, poultry, rabbits etc. for beginners.

Hens[14]

To keep a few hens was part of the country economy before the war, so that it was natural to keep a few more in wartime. In the end the numbers had doubled, and the habit had spread into the towns where there was any space that could be used. Henhouses and runs were ad hoc affairs, knocked up very often from bits of old timber, corrugated iron and any netting you could find.

Household scraps were part of their food, though with the Ministry propaganda about wasting nothing there might not be much left for them. If you gave up your shell-egg allocation you could get balancer poultry meal instead – 5lb per month by 1945. This was made from wheat leftovers from flour milling, whole ground grain, town waste (as for pigs) and fish meal. With the same quantity of household or garden waste it was said to be enough for one hen. It wasn't really worth keeping one hen at a time though, so you could co-operate with the wider family and neighbours, and get more balancer meal (and scraps) in return for each shell-egg allocation given up. Then of course you shared the eggs.

There was a cap on the number of hens that could be kept, however. More than twenty-five and you became a commercial poultry keeper, and had to sell the eggs to a packing station.

The birds were useful as a source of meat, too. You could not afford to keep bad layers or old hens, but they were perfectly good for the pot. There might have been, however, some difficulty (as with rabbits) in despatching and eating them. It is always problematic to kill and cook any creature that has become part of your household circle.

Rabbits

Rabbits were introduced by the Romans and after a short period of acclimatisation have continued to flourish until their numbers were reduced by the viral disease myxomatosis after the war. They breed prolifically in the wild – like rabbits, in fact – and have been kept in captivity for several purposes, partly for their fur, partly for their meat, and partly as pets for children.

Backyard rabbits were a source of protein however. Rabbit clubs could get bran rations for up to four breeding does. More than eight counted as a commercial enterprise, and you then had to sell on your young rabbits for breeding or meat, though you could sell them to whom you liked.[15] Rabbit skins were used for making such things as gloves, but you had to know what you were doing to preserve and cure the skins in the first place. An alternative for some people was to keep angora rabbits, and to spin and knit the hair which you obtained from carefully combing the animals.

Pigs

Pigs also have a very long history in country economy. Cottagers kept them long before either World War. Peter Bumphrey remembers how his father and almost all his neighbours had one:

> The pig was kept in the garden. There was a pigsty 300 yards from the house. When the pig was fattened up with household scraps the local butcher came and dealt with it. (You ate everything except the squeal, as many people remarked.) Seven or eight people – neighbours – all kept pigs, but they were killed at different times. There was a swapping arrangement, which meant that fresh meat was available over a long time. You got a licence to kill one pig, but you had to forfeit one person's bacon ration for a year.

The pig had an anomalous position as far as the Ministry of Food was concerned. Imported meal for porkers was reduced, so pig farm production was halved. But the invasion of the Netherlands and other European countries that had formerly supplied us with a lot of bacon and ham left us short. Individual backyard animals made up for some of this. The pig is not a fussy eater, and household scraps can be turned into pig swill. Pigkeeping was organised by the Small Pig Keepers' Council,[16] a name which does not mean that the pigs were tiny, but that they were kept in small numbers. The favoured breed was not particularly large, on the other hand. A docile Middle White would grow to 13 stone and could be slaughtered at twenty weeks. The pig manure was valuable as a fertiliser.

In towns there was a pig bin in almost every street, where you were expected to put food waste – though a keen-eyed inspector checked that there was nothing that could have been consumed by humans. One hopes that his sense of smell was less acute than his eyesight. The local councils collected and treated the food and sold on the product. The contents of the pig bins had to be boiled to sterilise it. Pig clubs – more formally set up than the informal one described above by Peter Bumphrey – arranged to share the meat fairly. They were so successful, and absorbed so much of the available pig meal, that the Ministry of Food had to cut back in 1942. This was when the ordinary bacon ration had to be given up, or half the pig handed over to the Ministry.

Many people had not had any experience of butchering or preserving meat, so they had to learn. Ministry ladies went round to advise, and the mysteries of curing pig-meat were revealed. Some of the processing involved rubbing salt and saltpetre into the joints, and leaving them to cure buried in salt for up to three weeks. A bath was said to be a good place to leave them. Perhaps the spirit of co-operation meant you offered your neighbours a hot bath if their own was otherwise engaged, or maybe they made do with a galvanised iron one in front of the kitchen fire, as had been the custom in the past.

Once the meat had been converted by curing into ham or bacon, it was rinsed, dried and hung up in wood smoke if possible, to give it an authentic smoky flavour. Any parts of the animal that were unsuitable for preserving were made into sausages, brawn, black puddings, faggots or raised pork pies.

Goats and Cows

These animals were also kept by some, but in much smaller numbers than poultry, rabbits or pigs. You really needed a proper field to be successful.

Beekeeping

I can remember standing in a shed in my grandfather's garden when I was about ten, watching as he sliced down the sides of a honeycomb with a sharp carving knife. The comb was resting on a meat dish on a bench, and immediately the wax that covered the cells was removed it started to ooze. The oblong frame holding the comb was about 15in by 12in, I think, and heavy to lift. It was slotted into a kind of drum, the extractor, with others similarly prepared. Then he pressed a switch, the drum picked up speed and started to whirl – rather like the drum of a modern washing machine, but with a vertical axis rather than a horizontal one. The sound of spattering honey was interesting, but not as attractive as the sticky bits of honeycomb that I managed to scrape off the dish. I was told to go indoors to get a bowl, and we would then have some of the crunchy wax and honey debris for tea.

My grandfather was a countryman. He had been apprenticed to an engineering firm making boilers for steam trains, but in the First World War served in France organising fodder for army horses. When peace came he returned to his farming roots in Berkshire. In nominal retirement in the Second World War he had a small poultry farm with a large vegetable garden, an orchard and several hives of bees.

Getting the honey out of the hives involved his wearing a beekeeper's veil – a piece of fine-meshed netting which covered his face and neck down to the chest. On top of that he put his ordinary trilby hat. He had thick gloves and tied string round his trouser legs and the cuffs of his jersey. I didn't know about science fiction then, but if I had I would have recognised him immediately as an alien. He took great care to puff smoke gently into the hive from a small machine, explaining that it was to quieten the insects, not to kill them. Then he lifted off the roof, and piled the honeycombs onto a tray in a wheelbarrow, shaking or brushing off any worker bees still clinging to them. He put back new frames for more honey, then shut the hive again, and off we went to the shed, where he removed his gloves and veil and started puffing on his own pipe, perhaps needing to quieten himself after a successful mission.

He told me about the dangers of swarming bees, and kept a spare hive empty in case this happened. If a rival queen was allowed to grow up in the hive she would attract some of the workers to support her instead of the old queen, and a whole ball of bees would fly off to start a new colony. 'You can shake 'em off a tree branch into a box', he assured me, but I never saw him do it – I was only visiting, after all. He was a kind man, and never seemed to get stung because the insects trusted him, I think.

Valor paraffin heater. The oil was held in a reservoir at the base, and burnt through a circular wick. Paraffin was cheap, but there were tragedies if the heaters were knocked over accidentally.

Beekeeping is one of the most ancient and primitive forms of farming there is, and during the war it came back into fashion. Honey was the main sweetener for food for centuries before sugar began to be imported during the Middle Ages. The only drawback from the rationing point of view was that if you take all the honey away from the bees you have to supply them with a sugar solution to feed on in winter and spring. Beekeepers were allowed 10lb of sugar in the autumn and 5lb in the spring, though with more in a bad season. In a poor year there might not be very much of a net gain. Honey was part of the preserves ration, but is sweeter than sugar, and so you could use half a spoonful to sweeten your tea, for instance instead of a whole spoonful of sugar. If you kept bees you could try making jam with honey, and in puddings and cakes it was certainly a welcome and nutritious alternative to ordinary sugar.

The cottage farming of the war was really just an extension of what country people would have been doing anyway. Tradition can be a comfort, and to be in touch with old methods was a steadying influence for many people. You could forget the war for a time while feeding the hens or watching the bees come home laden with pollen and nectar.

6

The Wild Harvest and Preserving

Country people, especially during the Depression, were used to growing their own vegetables, and poaching the odd pheasant was surely not unknown … Then of course country people have always used the resources of field, woodland, heath and seashore to provide many of their foods and medicines perfectly legitimately. Traditional knowledge would be passed through the generations, and methods of trapping wild animals, catching fish and gathering berries, nuts and herbal plants would be part of the country child's birthright, even though their families might be poor. With the coming of the industrial revolution, when many rural people migrated to the towns, the knowledge became less widespread, but nevertheless was never entirely lost. The Scout and Guide movements, which started in the early part of the twentieth century, also helped to keep young people interested in Nature.

The self-help aspects of food policy in wartime favoured the country, however much the allotment holder in the city might try to keep up. Pressure on food supplies meant that traditional wisdom became even more useful. County Herb Committees, organised by the Ministry of Agriculture,[1] gave advice to the cautious citizen about what could be eaten safely, including some fungi.

Children were involved as a matter of principle in helping to gather fruit and herbs. Their contribution was really helpful. Blackberries were the favourite country fruit, as they can be made into pies or jam, or bottled for winter. But going blackberrying, or nutting in autumn, was fun as well as useful. It was a kind of initiation for some children too – you put up with the scratches in order to get hold of the harvest. Learning about natural history and working responsibly were educational. It never hurt anyone to know the difference between poisonous berries such as deadly nightshade, and edible ones such as wortleberries.

The Ministry of Food, of course, was there with simple advice on getting the best out of the autumn. Using wild foods was a recurrent theme, appearing every year in the early part of the war in leaflets and *Food Facts*. For example the advertisement for September/October 1941[2] in women's magazines has varied suggestions. It advertises a helpful book, *Preserves from the Garden*, 'price 4d. from your paper shop'. There are details of hedgerow fruits – blackberries, rose-hips, elderberries, rowanberries, crab apples.

There was, too, sunshine itself, which enabled the body to make Vitamin D under the skin, the 'sunshine vitamin'. Women were advised to let children 'wear their sun-suits as long as it is warm enough. Go bare-armed and bare-legged whenever you can, and store up health for the winter.'

The advertisement gives a recipe for rose-hip jam, rich in Vitamin C, explaining (for the benefit of the evacuated townie perhaps) that the hips are the 'seed-pods which form when the wild rose blooms have died off. Don't confuse them with haws, which are smaller and are the fruit of the hawthorn (may)'. In fact rose-hip jam was not generally a success, as it is very difficult, even with careful sieving of the cooked hips, to remove all the irritant hairs which they contain along with the seeds. In the following year the equivalent recipe was for rose-hip syrup, which was strained through a jelly-bag.

But in 1941 it was back to the hedgerows. There were more of them at that time, as many hedges were grubbed up after the war to make bigger fields more convenient for machinery. Elderberries were 'excellent' when combined with apples, '1lb elderberries to ½lb apples for stewed fruit, pies or tarts. Elderberry-and-apple jam is delicious. Rowanberry conserve is a great favourite in Scotland. It is rather like cranberry. Both elderberries and billberries [sic] can be dried and used instead of currants in cakes and puddings'. The true countrywoman would have smiled, perhaps. Another 'excellent' use for elderberries, as well as elderflowers, was and still is to make a potent wine.

Like the squirrel that illustrated the *Food Facts* advertisement, you could collect nuts and bury them in the ground, 2 or 3ft deep. Unlike the squirrel though, you needed to put the dry nuts into a tin with a tightly fitting lid. 'Hazel nuts sprinkled with salt and baked until crisp are a good substitute for salted almonds, as too are the kernels of beech nuts.' They are pretty good in their own right too, not merely as a substitute.

Alternative marmalade, made with apple purée and sweet orange peel.

By August 1942 the *Food Facts* authors were expanding their horizons. Again children could be included in the harvesting expedition. 'Be sure, however, that in their excitement they do not damage bushes or hedges, or walk through growing crops, or gather mushrooms, for instance, in fields without getting the farmer's permission'. Elderberries are there, but now sloes make an appearance. They look 'like tiny damsons', and though too sour to use as stewed fruit 'they make a delightful preserve with marrow'. I haven't tried this, but I rather doubt it. The cliché 'a bitter disappointment' probably originated with the first human to taste them. Sloe gin *is* a way to use them, but in wartime gin was difficult to obtain.

Crab apple juice could be used as a substitute for lemon juice, a neat historical inversion, as crab apples were one of the things used to make verjuice in the Middle Ages, later superseded by lemon. Rowanberries, or mountain ash, were still around to make a conserve 'admirable to serve with cold meats'.

In the previous year you had learned to differentiate between hips and haws, but in 1942 you could use the haws as well, to make 'a brown jelly that is very like guava jelly'.

Nuts are no longer buried – perhaps the location of the hoard had been forgotten, as squirrels do? Cobnuts, walnuts, chestnuts (that is, sweet chestnuts, not conkers) and filberts should be of good quality. They were removed from their husks and spread out to dry overnight. Cobnuts and filberts were put into jars or crocks and covered with crushed block salt an inch thick. Walnuts and chestnuts were covered with an inch of sand instead of salt. Lids were then put on, if you had them, and the nuts were said to keep until Christmas.

Mushrooms, as everyone knows, should be gathered in the early morning 'before the mushroom fly has had time to attack them', (and before other mushroom collectors had got there first, in my experience). Several of my friends mentioned the pleasure of gathering mushrooms. Local knowledge helped. Peter Bumphrey's father 'knew where to find them. We often went out early on Sundays …'[3]

A helpful leaflet, *Hedgerow Harvest*[4] would be sent to anyone who asked for it from the Ministry of Food. It went into several editions, still being distributed after the war. As well as many jam recipes it included directions for bottling wild fruits and making pickles; instructions for storing nuts, as above; a recipe for mushroom ketchup; hints for drying mushrooms, and various puddings. The fruits mentioned were blackberries, elderberries and elderflowers, rosehips, sloes, crab apples and rowanberries.

All this, though presented as novel, goes back hundreds of years into the traditional gathering traditions of the countryside. For the more adventurous (or hungrier) new country dweller there was a book published in 1940, specifically written for wartime conditions: *They Can't Ration These.*[5] The author was a Free Frenchman, the Vicomte de Mauduit, who had already written several cookery books – *The Vicomte in the Kitchen, The Vicomte in the Kitchenette* and others. David Lloyd George, the former Prime Minister, wrote the foreword to the 1940 book.

He provides an example of the 'back to nature' sentiment which is an inevitable counterweight to industrial urbanisation. He deplored the change from rural to town life, writing of:

> … the tough sturdy health of country life, the infinite interest and variety of natural surroundings, the urge to resource, craftsmanship, and self-reliance, the homely and frugal but nourishing country fare. Our people have grown more sophisticated, but less wise; intellectually more elaborately taught, but practically less widely competent.

> It has long been one of my ambitions to help in restoring a juster balance between town and country; to bring back to the empty fields and villages of Britain some part at least of the exiles of the towns, and to establish them in that healthiest and most satisfying of all tasks – the winning of food from the soil …
>
> But what reason and peaceful persuasion have been unable in long years to accomplish, war is now bringing to pass …

The evacuation of children, would, he hoped, bring knowledge and love of the countryside into their lives, so that some would settle there permanently. This is similar to the many attempts by individuals in recent times to 'downsize' jobs and stress, and become self-sufficient in the healthy outdoors – the TV series *The Good Life* was a friendly satire on the idea. There have been many distinguished books since the war too, describing the joys of traditional foods, such as Dorothy Hartley's *Food in England*,[6] or Richard Mabey's *Food for Free*.[7] But unfortunately the countryside is simply not big enough to supply enough wild foods for the population at large.

Back in 1940, however, the Vicomte was certainly doing his bit to persuade people already living close to Nature to make the most of whatever was around. For instance, the Ministry of Food suggested nettle soup, but the Vicomte goes further with nettle cake, purée and toast. Nettles are good for you, being a traditional 'blood purifier' in the spring, and may help to reduce blood pressure levels.[8] They grow readily on waste ground, but they pack a painful sting, so you need gloves to gather the young tops. (If you are stung, the traditional antidote is to rub the place with a dock leaf, usually growing close by.) They were once used to make cloth, as the stems are fibrous.

The Vicomte goes on with further vegetable suggestions with dishes of sorrel, yarrow, clover, corn salad, wild fennel, cardoons, hop tips, pickled broom buds and mushrooms, of course, among others. You *might* even have found truffles, as they grow under beech trees. (You would have needed a friendly pig to go with you, as in France, or have had a specially trained dog to sniff them out.)

An intriguing suggestion, which the Ministry of Food did not seem to be aware of, was that grass or hay might be included in the human diet. The Vicomte referred to a BBC broadcast given by a Mr J.R.B. Branson early in 1939. Mr Branson claimed to have eaten a diet of grass, rolled oats, currants, sugar, lettuce or yarrow or dandelion or fruit, and maybe a little cheese. The Vicomte also quotes an article from *The Evening News* of 25 April 25 1940, which in turn cites evidence from three Kansas City chemists to the American Chemical Society. The claim was that 12lb of grass, dried, contained more vitamins than 340lb of fruit and vegetables, that is all the vitamins except D.[9]

It is certainly possible that grass *might* be eaten as a vegetable, though if so it has not so far caught on. It contains cellulose which the human digestive system cannot break down as herbivores can, but this is like many a vegetable where the cellulose is referred to as plant fibre. Maybe the Ministry missed an opportunity here? But eating grass was thought to be the ultimate desperate fallback and sign of madness, like Nebuchadnezzar in the Old Testament, so perhaps they dared not suggest it.

The tea ration was not particularly generous, so many people turned to herbal infusions to supplement it. The point about tea as a beverage is that it contains caffeine, like coffee, and is therefore a mild stimulant or pick-me-up. Many people find it acts both as an energiser and a soother, according to their mood. Herbal teas do not have any caffeine, but are pleasant to drink and some have other desirable qualities. Peppermint tea, for example, helps digestion. Camomile tea is a mild sedative. Hyssop tea was thought to be good for chesty coughs. You poured a quart of boiling water over a handful of flowers and leaves and left it to infuse for twenty minutes. Adding honey helped to make it more palatable.[10]

Currants and berries and their leaves were often used. Blackcurrant tea, made from the fruit, was like hot Ribena. But you could make tea with the leaves as well, as you could with raspberry leaves and blackberry leaves. This was a recommendation of the Ministry of Food, to extend the ordinary ration, from a leaflet of August 1943, *How to Make Use of the Hedgerow Harvest*:

> Blackberry Leaf Tea
>
> Pick the leaves on a dry day, choosing the best on the bushes. Spread them on sheets of paper in a warm room turning them every four hours. After 24 hours, roll the dried ones gently between the palms of the hands. This must be done while the leaves are still pliable or they

> will be reduced to dust. Continue the rolling as the leaves dry, then finish drying in a warm oven until crisp. The drying must be gradual or the delicate flavour will be lost.
>
> This tea may be infused like ordinary tea (sufferers from indigestion will like it because it contains no tannin) or it may be used half and half with ordinary tea to eke out the ration.[11]

But plant foods were not the only ones. Hunting, even if only knocking down rabbits when the last corn was cut in the middle of a field, has equally been part of the supply chain through long years of nostalgia.

The best game birds had been protected for hundreds of years, with penalties more or less severe for those caught poaching. But in wartime, as Peter Bumphrey said, 'the gamekeeper was probably called up, but if not, country people knew where he was. Consequently pheasants were sometimes "available". There were thousands of pigeons too. You've got to find ways of replacing what you can't get.'[12]

In fact, 'game' is an elastic term, covering most edible wild birds and animals such as hares and deer. Wild rabbits are not so much game as fair game for anyone who can catch them. The most esteemed birds are grouse, partridge, pheasant, snipe, teal, widgeon and woodcock, but there are many more. Even swans are edible – just – though protected, and peacocks were once served up roasted and wrapped again in their plumage as a status symbol in the Middle Ages. You might have to be rather desperately hungry to eat them, however.

Rooks, like pigeons, are very common, and can be made into pies, though there is very little meat worth eating on them, and you need a lot of young birds, perhaps if you have been clearing out a rookery in spring.

Wild bird's eggs were valuable too. The Vicomte assured his readers that it would not destroy wild stocks too much to eat them, particularly the eggs of lapwings and black-headed and herring gulls. Nowadays conservationists would be horrified at the suggestion of raiding birds' nests at will, though gulls' eggs have been part of the economy of some coastal communities for hundreds of years.

Rabbits and hares can be cooked in very many ways, and rabbits were never rationed. Probably they were one of the most useful animals to be caught. (Rabbits were also raised in back gardens as

I have said, though it might be difficult to enjoy eating the bunny you had been treating as a pet.) But other mammals are edible too. Even hedgehogs can be baked covered in clay, as gipsies were said to do. The clay is cracked off, bringing the spines and skin with it. Squirrels (grey or red not specified) are also delicious, according to the Vicomte, though in Britain they are considered to be inedible. I can't say how many people broke the taboo during the war.

It is interesting to consider how our food habits are conditioned by custom and sentiment. Horse flesh, for example is eaten in some European countries, but not usually by people in Britain, though it may have been consumed in the war or just afterwards. It may be used in dog food, however. Edible snails are appreciated by many, especially in a context of garlic butter, but I have never been able to bring myself to touch them. I am sure that if one is actually starving a disgusted response would weaken, but most British people were lucky enough not to have to find out.

The sea also provided a bountiful larder for those living close to it. I can remember, for example, how people used to go fishing from the rocks near the Minack Theatre, close to where I lived in Cornwall. Mackerel came home to be fried or baked immediately for supper. In a tiny bay just round the coast, Porthgwarra, lived a few fishermen who laid down baited lobster pots, catching both lobsters and crabs. They were of course luxuries, and very good.

Seaweed is another resource. There are several edible kinds, rich in minerals extracted from seawater, particularly iodine. The best known of these is laver, a delicacy in South Wales, where it is cooked to make a thick purée and then frequently rolled in oatmeal and fried in bacon fat for breakfast. Alternatively it is a sauce for mutton. Carrageen, or Irish moss, can be used like gelatine to set jellies and has industrial uses too. It grows on Atlantic coasts of the British Isles, and in spite of the name is not confined to Ireland.

MEDICINAL HERBS

Drugs were in short supply as well as food, and there was a campaign to gather useful plants from the country. Under the guidance of the National Herb Committees, with the Ministry of Health at the top of the tree, pickers were trained in plant recognition. The WI was helpful in this work too. People then went out to gather essential supplies of such things as foxgloves, deadly nightshade and henbane, for the extraction of digitalis for heart complaints, atropine, hyoscyamine and hyoscine. These have been superseded today, but were of value in wartime. Also important were seaweeds to make agar jelly (which was used in the development of penicillin),[13] and sphagnum moss for dressing wounds. Before the war about 90 per cent of the herbs used in making medicinal drugs came from abroad, so these stocks were profoundly important.

On other days wild rose hips were gathered to make rose-hip syrup for babies, and 2*d* per pound was paid for them.

PRESERVING

People have always made an effort to preserve food from harvest or hunt to keep alive during the hungry months of winter. Drying and smoking, salting and preserving with honey are really ancient technologies. Many root vegetables will remain in good condition in earth-clamps or boxes in a cool place. Vinegar has long been used to prevent spoilage of vegetables and fish, and is the basis of innumerable pickles. Alcohol is a preservative too, but expensive. Fruit conserves and syrups took up an increasing amount of space on the larder shelf from the sixteenth century onwards, when sugar was imported in fair quantities, until jam became one of the staple foods of the poor. Bottling in glass jars had an antecedent in potted meats, sealed with fat, and the discoveries of Nicholas Appert, who vacuum-packed foods for Napoleon's army. Canning uses the same process of sterilisation and exclusion of air. It was undertaken by the intrepid Women's Institutes, when cans and machinery were supplied under Lend Lease agreements. (See page 112.)

Long before the start of the Second World War, economical housewives practised all these methods of preserving, though canning was more often a commercial enterprise. The only really new development since then has been the supply of frozen foods, though the idea itself is not new. Freezing in icehouses on country estates was possible (for a very few) by the eighteenth century in this country. Ice cream followed.[14] It was a treat by Victorian times (frozen in a container plunged into crushed ice and saltpetre), and a lucrative business by the twentieth century. Its manufacture was stopped in early 1943. Frozen foods only took off for the home consumer after the war, when vegetables, meat, and fish were sold in the new supermarkets. Refrigerators became widely available, with small deep-freezing compartments. Then separate freezers took over. Their success has led to a decline in bottling and to a large extent in the use of canned goods, though these are hanging on still.

With the need to conserve food stocks in wartime, there was official encouragement and information to make all kinds of preserving a national duty. If you dug for victory, you could bottle and jam for it too. Indeed a leaflet about drying, salting, pickles and chutney was published under the spade-and-boot logo of the *Dig for Victory* campaign.[15] More detailed instructions appeared in *Domestic Preservation of Fruit and Vegetables.*[16] Bottling was a topic for the Ministry of Food, and there was more advice from them about other preserves.

Drying is a simple technique, which needs very little equipment. One leaflet suggests making a tray from four wooden laths nailed into a square. Canvas or wire gauze is fixed to this to make the bottom of the tray, and you needed a bit of muslin to line it.

This method was good for fruits. Apple rings are suggested frequently, but you could try grapes, plums and pears, though berries were unsuitable. Runner beans could be dried or salted, marrowfat peas and broad beans dried. You spread out the clean food on the tray and put it into a very cool oven – not more than 140°F. To save fuel you could use the heat remaining after you had baked something else. Or you could use an airing cupboard or warm place over a kitchen range. You might have to have several goes if you were using the oven. Fruits were dried until they were leathery but not hard, and needed to be soaked for twenty-four hours before cooking. Sugar should be added at the end of this time, as it would make the fruit tough if put in too soon.

Herbs were dried successfully too. They were gathered just before flowering, rinsed and shaken dry. Then, tied loosely into bunches, covered with muslin if you liked, they were hung up somewhere airy. When they were dry the leaves were rubbed off the stalks and stored in airtight jars. If powdered herbs were preferred the crisp leaves could be crushed with a rolling pin. Parsley was the exception to air drying; it could be put into a fairly hot oven for a few minutes until crisp.

Jam uses a combination of heating, to cook the fruit and kill off any bacteria, and sugar (or honey) which forms a gel with pectin if present, making the jam set. It also inhibits the growth of bacteria during storage. If you had any to spare, you could use up to a half-and-half mix of honey to sugar. The general proportion of sugar to finished jam is 60 per cent. You should therefore get 10lb of jam out of 6lb of sugar. When it was rationed you certainly needed the extra allowed in the jamming season. Sometimes you could swap your preserves ration for sugar. As described in Chapter 5 the Women's Institutes came to the rescue of the National Loaf, making tons of jam for the Ministry of Food

Fruit syrups are similar to jam in some ways. The juice from the fruit, sometimes obtained by stewing it, is mixed with sugar, boiled, bottled and sealed. Rose-hip syrup was made for babies on account of its Vitamin C content. However, many private bottles of blackcurrant syrup too found their way down sore throats in every age-group.

Bottling was popular for keeping gluts of fruit under control. The principle was that you stopped enzyme action and sterilised the food by heating it, and then made a vacuum as the space under a tight lid filled with water-vapour. If no air could get back in as the food and vapour cooled, there was literally nothing there – a vacuum! Air pressure then kept the lid on until you opened it deliberately. Apples or apple pulp, plums, greengages, gooseberries, pears, blackberries, apricots, peaches and tomatoes were the most successful and popular fruits, and were comparable to commercially canned fruit in quality. The usual method was to use a patent Kilner jar or a jam jar with a special lid and clip.

The firm fruit was packed into the jar as closely as possible without bruising. There were several methods which could be used to sterilise the contents. You could use a slow water-bath, such as a fish-kettle or preserving pan. Cold water or syrup was poured over the fruit to cover it, and then the lids were put on and screwed down loosely. A rubber ring between the jar and lid ensured a good seal later. The jars went into the large pan, with a wooden board on the bottom and with water up to their necks. The whole thing was then heated slowly for about an hour and a half to simmering point and kept there for about fifteen minutes. The Kilner screw band was quickly tightened to keep the lid on while a vacuum was formed after heating. The next day you could unscrew the band and lift the jar up by the lid. If the vacuum was satisfactory the lid stayed firmly in place. If it was not, you either had some stewed fruit to eat as soon as possible, a re-boiling job to do, or a wasteful mess on the kitchen floor.

The second method was similar, but quicker. The syrup was poured in hot, the fish-kettle filled with hot water, raised to simmering in about thirty minutes, and held for ten to twenty minutes. Screwing down the lids was as before.

The third way used a pressure cooker, following the directions on your particular pan. It was much faster but usually you could process only one jar at a time because the pan was smaller.

Another method was to heat the fruit in the oven, adding the syrup either before or after the fruit was thoroughly heated through.

It was possible to do without the special jars though. An article in *Woman's Own* for 1 June 1940 gave the method. You put your fruit into large jars – 3lb size if possible. Then they were filled with water or syrup and put into the large pan (as above) padded on the bottom with newspaper. The jars were also packed round with paper to prevent them banging into each other. The outer pan was filled with water as above, and brought slowly to boiling point. When you thought that the liquid over the fruit was also near boiling, you took out a jar at a time, ran a dessertspoonful of salad oil over the contents, followed by melted mutton fat or paraffin wax to a depth of one-third of an inch. (Later in the war you would probably use mutton fat in cooking, not for preserving.) When the jars were cold you added a little more fat or wax to make sure the edges were well sealed, and smoothed them with a matchstick.

Camden tablets used a different principle. The sulphur dioxide contained in the tablets was dissolved in water and poured over the raw fruit. The jar was then sealed with a tight cork painted with paraffin wax, or a firmly woven material dipped in melted wax and tied on before it hardened. The sulphur dioxide bleached the fruit, and when you turned it out it smelt unappetisingly of sulphur too. You had to boil it for several minutes to get rid of the smell, and the method wasn't suitable for soft fruits or vegetables.

Pickling in vinegar is a more appealing way of preserving both vegetables and fruit. The acetic acid in vinegar inhibits the growth of bacteria and is of course edible in its own right, unlike sulphur dioxide. At its simplest, vegetables are soaked in brine or sprinkled with salt and left for a day or so, then covered with vinegar and put up in jars with lids, not necessarily airtight. You can – indeed, you should – flavour the vinegar with spices, bay leaves, chillis and so on to make quite delicious additions to a monotonous diet. Sometimes it is necessary to cook the vegetables first, like beetroot for example. The pickle could be sweetened if you liked.

Chutneys were more elaborate, like jam with vinegar in it. In wartime windfalls could be turned into apple chutney, and the cherished tomato plants on the allotment were useful to the last unripened fruit, as in green tomato chutney.

* * * * *

Many people enjoyed the challenge of finding natural foods and taking them home without using money or coupons. It was a return to a primitive hunter-gatherer existence. The found mushroom tasted far better than a bought one. There is undeniable satisfaction too in preserving food, with a full store-cupboard giving security against the want of winter. Traditional knowledge was honoured, at least for a time.

7

Towns

The greatest difference between living in town and country during the war was the increased risk of bombing in the towns, especially if you lived near factories or obvious targets like docks or mainline railway stations. Another difference arose as a consequence. Evacuation diminished numbers in cities, increased the population of the country. The movement of people caused disruption of the careful large-scale planning of food distribution, while destruction of homes, shops and food depots upset local arrangements. Volunteers, especially from the WVS, helped to give emergency cover after raids and comfort snacks to those in public shelters. The need to nourish workers properly meant that towns were the focus of industrial feeding and British Restaurants.

SHOPS AND QUEUES

'Whether the town worker or the country worker is the better fed under rationing has been the subject of some controversy,' said the Ministry of Food.[1] The countryman had the advantages of being close to food production, with access to wild foods and considerably more experience of hunting and gathering than the townsman. His wife knew, or could be taught, the skills of preparing unprocessed food. On the other hand, shopping in towns was undeniably better, even if many goods were in short supply and you had to queue to get them. What the Ministry called 'semi-luxuries and less essential foods' were, maybe, just around the corner, in the little shop there. With problems of distribution it was simply not possible to get out to all the rural areas with full and varied quotas of points goods, or fish for instance.

Shopkeeper's scales.

However, even if some things were more available in urban shops, not everyone could get there. Many women worked long hours in factories, as well as doing housework, and in addition often had fire-watching duties and volunteered for outfits like the WVS. Sleeping in the grim conditions of public or Underground shelters meant that there simply was not enough energy to line up in the hope of getting a couple of oranges, for example. Some had to be absent from work just to get the rations home. In places the WVS helped out, and later on shops were opened in factories.

Even for those women who were full-time housewives, shopping took up a lot of time. In those days few ordinary households had refrigerators, and perishables had to be bought little and often.

Retail shops of seventy years ago were organised differently from today. The self-service supermarket was a post-war development. There were a few large establishments in cities, such as Selfridges and Harrods Food Halls in London, which had many different counters. At the opposite pole there were general stores or corner shops which often combined groceries with a few miscellaneous and chemist's items for instance:

> 'Half a pound of broken biscuits please – they don't look too bad.'
> 'They're good value. They broke because the tin fell off the counter when the land mine went off down the street. They're half points too. Anything else, madam?'
> 'Yes, please. I'll have a big tin of black shoe polish, 25 aspirin tablets and a quarter-pound packet of cocoa powder.'
> 'Thank you. That'll be – let me see – eightpence for the biscuits, sixpence for the polish, cocoa fivepence and the aspirins one-and-a-penny ha'penny. Two and eightpence ha'penny please.[2] And one point coupon.'

But before the supermarket arrived there was usually a string of different establishments. In many places high streets spread out with the butcher, the baker and cake shop, grocer, fishmonger, greengrocer, newsagent, tobacconist and confectioner, wine merchant and occasionally specialist cheesemonger and game purveyor. The non-food shops included chemists, drapers and ironmongers. They all had counters, a waist-high shelf dividing the customers' space from the back of the shop. Shelves behind generally held the stock, though sometimes there were shelves in the front as well. Lighting was much dimmer than today – no fluorescent tubes – and this was made worse by blacked-out windows. The main difference though, was the presence of the shopkeeper or shop assistant standing behind the counter. You asked for what you wanted, often checking out the price too, and the goods were piled up on the counter before they were packed into your basket or bag when you had paid for them.

As the shops were scattered, you had to walk or cycle around a lot even to get basic foodstuffs. If you had to queue for bread, then again for cabbage and potatoes, then for your weekly meat ration, and double back to the grocer because someone in the last queue said there was a consignment of sardines on points, you spent much time thinking about your aching legs and what you could possibly prepare for supper. If the air-raid siren went off when you were near the head of the queue you had to decide if it was worth the risk of staying where you were, or taking cover and losing your chance of the sardines.

You were limited to what you could carry in your string bag, or shove into your bicycle basket, or pile round the baby in the pram. Pre-war, many shops in at least middle-class districts had had a delivery boy or two, who would bring round your meat order, for example, but the supply of boys dried up, and there was certainly no petrol to spare for a van to deliver things except in rural areas. The only tradesman you could expect at your door was the milkman, with his cart often pulled by a horse. You could rely on him, though, as the distribution was zoned, and one street equalled one milkman, no choice of dairy.

BUFFETS ON STATIONS

If you needed to get out of town on business, or because you had been directed to another part of the country for war work for example, you faced a hungry, long journey. Food on the move was hard to come by. Travelling by rail was difficult, uncomfortable and very slow, as train services were frequently disrupted.

There were a few buffet cars on trains still, but most people had to get what they could from the station cafés – *if* they could, might be a better way of putting it. They were sorry places with cracked cups and spoons chained to the counters, and very little to offer.[3] Buffets for the Forces were marginally better, run mainly by voluntary workers, but they frequently refused to serve civilians.

Because food was scarce on these journeys most people took their own. Even this might be hazardous. Mrs Betty Neil who was nineteen when war broke out, and married in 1943, remembers a journey during the blackout, not knowing which station she had arrived at. (The names of towns were frequently painted out, to confuse potential invaders.) She had a bar of chocolate, which she tried to cut with a knife on her knee. The knife slipped and gashed her leg, so that she had to have it patched up at the first-aid post when she finally arrived.[4]

BRITISH RESTAURANTS[5]

A British Restaurant was a modest self-service concern, with plain food in simple but pleasing surroundings. In 1940 Lord Woolton had had an idea for publicly run, non-profit making restaurants open to everybody. By 1943, 630,000 midday meals were being served in 2,160 restaurants. Some also provided breakfasts and evening meals, or a takeaway service.

They might make snacks for the pie scheme described in a previous chapter. The experience of a Londoners' Meals Service, supplying air-raid victims with food, was one part of their development.

The cooking was done by volunteers, organised by paid supervisors. They were good value for money. A course of meat or fish and two vegetables could be bought for *6d*, with pudding at 3*d* and soup, tea, coffee or cocoa only a penny. For example, on one day the Byrom Restaurant in Liverpool offered a choice of fish pie or beef with dumpling, followed by currant pudding or a milk pudding.

Their customers were a good social mix, not only of manual and office workers, but of professional people and students, who presumably even then appreciated a good meal at a bargain price. According to a survey, 60 per cent thought they were very good, only 15 per cent considered them bad, with the rest cautiously approving, considering the price and locality in which they were to be found.

Commercial caterers were less happy with them, especially towards the end of the war. They pointed out that the restaurants were feeding not only essential workers, but were being used for private parties and even wedding receptions. Their allocations of unrationed foods, subsidised prices and volunteer labour meant they could undercut the business sector, which was, in their opinion, unfair.

They were thought to have been a success by the Labour Government of 1945, however, and even after the war they continued to operate, though the number declined. In 1947 they were renamed 'Civic Restaurants' and there were still 678 of them in 1949. It was an interesting experiment, for they were run directly as a public service. They had made a good contribution to national life and nutrition.

INDUSTRIAL CANTEENS

The planners were faced with a difficult problem. On one hand it had been established, partly because of the pressure of Trade Unions, that there should be equality of rationing. No special cases. On the other hand, it was obvious that there had to be differentials. For example, dockers unloading essential supplies under pressure, or people turning out Spitfires, had to be properly fed or they could not work. The whole war effort depended on the sum of individual efforts.

Canteens were the answer. The food served was extra to the domestic ration. There was control over what was served, so that it could be made as nutritious as possible, suitable for the kind of work done. Factories with more than 250 workers were required by the Ministry of Labour to establish canteens, as were docks and some building sites.[6] Colliery canteens were the responsibility of the Ministry of Fuel and Power. Factories with fewer than 250 employees were encouraged, but not forced, to provide canteens too, though smaller groups of workers had the alternative of taking meals at British Restaurants, where they had priority over the non-industrial customer. It must have been a bit difficult to jump the queue sometimes:

'My job is more important than yours.'
'No it isn't.'
''Tis.'
''Tisn't.'

Industrial canteens were supplied through permits – like mass ration-books – for the controlled foods they could buy. There were two categories, A and B Industrial Group. A was entitled to more than B, but both got more than ordinary catering establishments such as restaurants or hotels.

The heavy industries covered by Category A are listed,[7] and like the country trades detailed in Chapter 5 provide a snapshot of the kind of work essential to our wellbeing in the war years. Not all of them, of course, were exclusive to towns:

1. Brick, tile and cement manufacture.
2. Building, constructional and excavational work.
3. Mining and quarrying.
4. Docks.
5. Gas works and coke ovens.
6. Heavy engineering and steel constructional works.
7. Iron and steel works, and metal extraction.
8. Rolling and tube mills.
9. Shipbuilding and repairing.
10. Tinplate works.
11. Agriculture and forestry.

12. Cold stores operated as part of the Ministry's Cold Storage Control Scheme.
13. Coal distributive trades.
14. Light metal foundries.
15. Tanning of hides.
16. Manufacture of sanitary ware, sanitary fireclay and salt glazed pipes.
17. Sections of plywood manufacture industry handling heavy logs.
18. Abrasive industries.

Category B covered other industrial works canteens and (a confusing bit here) commercial catering establishments, but these were special ones which had more than 60 per cent of industrial workers as customers. Presumably if you were one of the 39 per cent of ordinary customers you would eat a bit better than in the plain café down the street.

Both categories had extra meat allowances, which were worth having when the domestic ration was sparse. Category A had 2*d* worth per main meal served, B had 1½*d*, compared with 1*d* for ordinary eateries. Today this seems absurd, but one must remember the effect of sixty years' inflation. The basic meat ration for domestic consumers was around a shilling's worth, sometimes with some corned beef too. So canteen meals approximately doubled the amount of meat available to workers in heavy industries. Extra fat as well as cheese was allowed, so that it was possible to make a good deal of pastry for pies and so on.

They also had priority for extra sugar for making 'Flour Confectionery', that is cakes and such, and extra soft drinks, 'starch food powders' (probably custard, gravy powder and cornflour), and coffee essence.

The influence of J.C. Drummond, the Scientific Advisor to the Ministry of Food, introduced in Chapter 2, can easily be traced in the kind of meals served in industrial canteens. He wrote the foreword to an official Ministry of Food booklet, *Canteen Catering.* The advice given to managers and cooks is a concentrated version of the dietary advice given to housewives in the various Ministry of Food leaflets. It is clear that food education was being promoted here too.

The problem with feeding the workers was that many people were not yet accustomed to a good diet. They suffered from a lack of the 'protective foods' – milk and milk products, margarine, vegetables, fruit, wholemeal bread and oatmeal. Home conditions might be disrupted by war. The aim had to be to provide a main meal with 'a substantial proportion of all the essential nutrients required by the body.' Then other meals were less important.

In planning meals, national wheatmeal bread was given hearty endorsement. Breadcrumbs could be put into steamed puddings, soups and coatings, and stuffed into stuffings so to speak. Sliced, the bread could share a charlotte with fruit, or be the staple of other bread puddings. It followed that the flour used in baking should be wheatmeal too, unless it was oatmeal.

It should come as no surprise that potatoes formed the essential roots of wartime catering, not merely as an accompaniment of a main dish. Echoing one of the household leaflets, you should serve potatoes at *every* meal, and in large quantities. They could go into pastry, scones and cakes, make flan cases and pie coverings (as in shepherd's pie), and be found in soup of all kinds. Mashed potatoes could extend fish and minced meat and turn up in fish cakes. A baked potato with a filling made a nutritious snack, and grated raw potato could replace half the suet in steamed pudding and suet pastry. (So it was said.) And finally, instead of cakes or buns for tea, you could serve up potato fadge (fried potato cakes), potato pancakes or scones. (That would be fine if there was enough butter or even margarine to eat with them.)

The next thing was to use more vegetables, two portions of them as well as potatoes with a main dish. Even fish and chips could have an accompanying vegetable to go with them. You should put them into soups, hotpots, stews, curries, pies and puddings. Grated carrot in steamed pudding and cake helped to sweeten them, so you could use less sugar. Cooked mashed vegetables could be used as sandwich fillings too. And because fruit was in short supply it was important to compensate with raw vegetables and fresh salads. If you had no lettuce, shredded cabbage was a replacement. Parsley (rich in Vitamin C) was more than a garnish for savoury dishes, and watercress or grated carrot could also be used to add vitamins and colour.

The canteen was meant to supply a third of a pint per head per day of milk, especially if adolescents were among the workers.

But would the workers eat this nourishing (and inexpensive) food? Well, they might. You had to be tactful and introduce unfamiliar ingredients and new dishes gradually, with no sudden changes. You could enhance an old recipe by quietly adding something, oatmeal to a meat pie for instance. (Perhaps they won't notice …) A new dish could be partially disguised with popular gravy or custard. As in the Ministry advice to the housewife[8] you should never have a new main dish plus an unfamiliar pudding: one at a time, please. (The technique is similar to what mothers do to persuade suspicious toddlers that they really will enjoy this peculiar new taste …) When stepping up the veg., you could use it first as a garnish, and then as a salad. Above all, you had to make sure your staff knew what was going on, so that they could help with public relations.

The booklet included two-dozen menus for midday meals. The meals were substantial. All main dishes except three contained meat or fish – lamb, beef, rabbit, and frequently liver, with or without bacon. The fish is often anonymous, 'fish and potato pie' or 'baked stuffed fish', though the workers sometimes got herrings and even salmon, possibly canned, with salad. The three vegetable main dishes were vegetable cutlets, brown vegetable pie and vegetable curry, spaced out at nos 11, 18 and 23 of the twenty-four suggestions. 'Potatoes' came with all meals, though sometimes they were jacket or mashed, or part of the main dish – sausage and potato pie for instance. Nowadays there would be chips, but not then, not in this canteen anyway. Wheatmeal bread was always available in addition to the potatoes.

Puddings were frankly stodgy. There were seven boiled and steamed puddings, several based on pastry, and six on milk. Custard or sauce is included with most of the starchy ones. Fruit puddings were served five times, being apple charlotte on one occasion, otherwise unspecified. To end your meal you could have tea on seven days, coffee on sixteen occasions, and cocoa once. This was probably to get the required milk into the meal. The coffee was, I suspect, made from coffee essence, available, as we have seen above, as a priority to industrial canteens. Real coffee would have been too expensive and anyway not imported in sufficient quantity. Instant coffee had been invented before the war, but did not make much impression in Britain until the 1960s.

Here are a few of the suggested menus:

Roast joint and stuffing with swedes, watercress and potatoes. Wheatmeal bread. Rolled oats Bakewell tart with chocolate sauce. Coffee.

Vegetable cutlets, raw cabbage and beetroot salad, jacket potatoes. Wheatmeal bread. Steamed pudding and custard. Coffee.

Grilled red herrings, parsley sauce, carrots, mashed potatoes. Wheatmeal bread. Summer pudding and custard. Tea.

Rissoles, watercress and raw vegetable salad, jacket potatoes. Wheatmeal bread. Flaked oats milk pudding. Tea

Liver and bacon hot pot, spinach, potatoes. Wheatmeal bread. Baked curd flan. Coffee.[9]

SCHOOL MEALS[10]

These canteen menus remind me of my own school dinners during the late 1940s, but by then the Welfare State was in action.

During the early part of the war, provision of meals for children was patchy. For school meals, you need a school in the first place, but there were often no premises for evacuated children, or pint-pot buildings which had to accommodate quart or gallon numbers. Back in town many schools had been taken over as rest centres or closed for other reasons, so as children drifted back after the first months of evacuation there was sometimes nowhere for them to go, even if they had wanted to.

The position did improve. The voluntary services plugged some of the gaps at first. Schools reopened to some extent in the cities. School meals were paid for by local education authorities, but cost was an issue. In 1941 Lord Woolton got together with R.A. Butler, who was president of the Board of Education. They agreed to co-operate, with school meals forming part of the general communal feeding policy. Cooking depots sent out large numbers of meals to schools. In September 1943 4.5 million meals were supplied, but after that local education authorities gradually took over depots or opened their own.

By 1945 a third of all schoolchildren were being fed at school, with one in seven meals being supplied free to the most needy, the rest at a subsidised price. There was an effort to provide plenty of meat or other protein, as it was suspected that in some families the child's meat ration did not quite get past father's plate. But there was a further disadvantage to the disadvantaged: the dinner register was indiscreet. The children were known as the recipients of 'charity', and sometimes teased by others who turned up with their righteous 5*d* to pay for the mince and rice pudding.

Boarding schools were classed as institutions, as were residential nurseries and orphanages, and they received their proper quotas of milk, eggs (and no doubt cod liver oil), as for children living at home.

FOOD AND BOMBING

There were air raids which affected the countryside of course, as for example when airfields were targeted, or when enemy planes ditched their bombs to get away more easily when intercepted. However, it was the towns, particularly the docks and industrial areas, which had to endure the heaviest bombardments. Everyone thinks of the London Blitz of 1940, or the devastation of Coventry in November of the same year, of raids on Liverpool, Birmingham, Plymouth and Portsmouth … People sometimes left the towns at night altogether, and went out into the country for a night's sleep in comparative safety and quiet.

The anxiety caused by danger could sometimes be reduced by having something to eat. 'Comfort eating' is a well-known concept. It was important, therefore, that people in shelters should have access to snacks – sweet and starchy for preference. And drinks, particularly hot drinks, would help dry mouths caused by tension.

Muriel Gibson remembers sheltering in the cellar of a Teachers' Training College, wrapped in an eiderdown because it was so cold and damp down there. Afterwards the girls were revived by their tutor giving them comforting hot Oxo.

One *Food Facts* advertisement gave this advice:

> *FOOD FOR YOUR AIR-RAID SHELTER.* If possible hot drinks should be taken into the shelter. If you have a vacuum flask, fill it with hot soup, tea or coffee. Plain biscuits with a handful of sultanas or a piece of chocolate are most sustaining. So are sandwiches made with cheese, sardine or canned salmon. Children need plenty of water to drink. Barley sugar is excellent for them.[11]

A mother had to remember in advance to pack a box or basket with the things that her baby might need during a long wait in the shelter. Even if she were feeding the baby herself, it was wise to take boiled

'Siren Meals for the Smiths Again'. Mrs Peek came to the rescue once more. Air raids often disrupted the preparation of meals.

water and infant formula to make up a bottle, as her milk might dry up under stress.

The spread of air-raid shelters was patchy, the planning inadequate, even though it had been thought that bombs would fall within hours of the outbreak of war. There were several approaches to the problem of keeping civilians safe. Firstly, people who lived in well-built houses, especially those with basements or cellars, could make them reasonably comfortable with camp beds, blankets, torches and a supply of food in a biscuit tin. Advice was given on how to make a room in the house proof from gas attack as well, though gas masks were quickly supplied.

My friend Mary Rowe described where, as a child, her family sheltered in Solihull, near Birmingham. They had a cellar converted; that is a room two steps down from the kitchen and scullery. The place had a stone floor and was formerly used to store coal. It was strengthened, and had bunks put in. There was also a space between four doors, where the family sat at first, as being the safest place in the house.

Mrs Betty Neil remembers incendiary bombs right round the station in Newcastle. Her father-in-law was an Air Raid Warden.

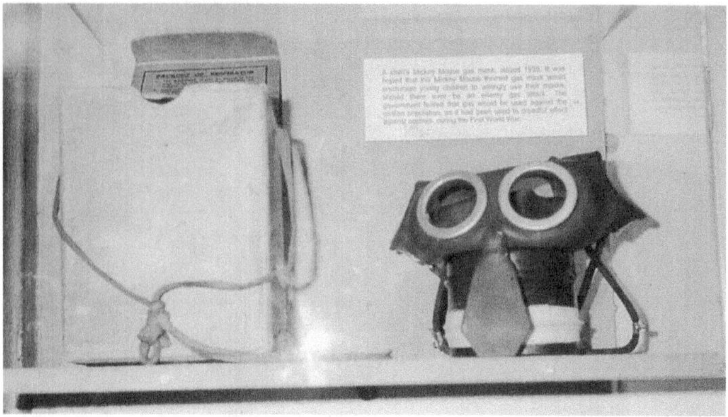

Gas mask for a child, intended to look like Mickey Mouse.

The bombing followed the river. When there was a raid they went into a deep cupboard under the stairs, though they had a shelter in the garden. Indoors felt safer. They had a torch for light. There was gas lighting in the house, but no electricity. They took anything available to eat – such as bread and jam or marmalade and a flask of tea. They stayed there until the all-clear sounded. 'Sometimes it was a long, long sit.'

The garden shelter was probably an Anderson one. These were issued widely to people without safe rooms in their own houses in both town and country. They were a do-it-yourself assembly job. First you dug a hole in the garden, and then erected the curved corrugated iron roof/walls to make a cave-like hut, mostly below ground level. There was a flat back wall and a strong door. Over the top you heaped the earth which you had dug out, and many people then camouflaged it with vegetables, particularly marrows. Marrows were often grown on a raised bed anyway, so it would look natural to low-flying bombers!

I can recall one in my own garden, hastily put up in a waste patch. Steps led down from ground level into the shelter, which was about 7ft long by 6ft wide. Two rough bunks had been built against the back wall. I can remember being carried there at night on several occasions. This was a scary experience for a child of six, but once inside it was like an adventure. My mother had stocked it with blankets, torches, candles, non-perishable food in biscuit tins and bottles of water and carbonated drinks. I can recall one called *Kia-Ora*, orange flavour. I also had a few toys. The disadvantage of this shelter was that it rapidly became damp inside, and in rainy weather the floor flooded. Many people, my family included, came to prefer the alternative of a Morrison shelter.

This was a large steel table, designed to withstand the collapse of a house on top of it. It was used as a dining table in many households. It almost filled a small room, as it was about 7ft wide by 6ft long, meant for a whole family to bundle up together at night. There was a bolted-on mesh close to the floor to support a mattress. Removable metal mesh panels surrounded the sides as well. Inside, it was like being in a cage. It was probably the most uninviting bed I shall ever sleep in. The mattress was very hard and inclined to lumps. Because it was only an inch or two off the floor there were cold draughts at neck level. The dark underside of the table above one's face was depressing and claustrophobic. The rest of my family soon made unarguable cases to risk sleeping in their proper beds, but I had to stay there, uncomfortable but safe, for several months. The great advantage of this shelter for families was, of course, that it was in one's own house, and it was comparatively easy to collect a thermos and sandwich as the siren sounded.

PUBLIC SHELTERS

Under really heavy bombing, like the Blitz, ordinary houses even with Morrison shelters did not feel safe, and in any case there was a psychological need to be with others in times of great danger.

Public shelters came in many guises. They might be in substantial buildings such as Town Halls, or in the basements of department stores. Purpose-built deep shelters were not constructed in London until quite late in the war.[12] Some public shelters had been built at surface level, originally just to be safe places for people caught outside during a raid. They were constructed of brick and concrete, often in the middle of the street. They had no bunks, no lighting and poor ventilation,[13] and easily became overcrowded. There were occasional scandals when it was found (too late) that inferior materials had been used, and people were killed when they collapsed.[14]

In London, the station platforms of the Underground were an obvious magnet for people wanting to shelter from bombs.

The authorities, however, were very unwilling to allow access to anyone who was not a traveller. Weight of numbers brushed aside the objections, and in any case people could buy the cheapest ticket simply to get through the barriers, and then stay below ground. In October 1940 Herbert Morrison, the new Home Secretary, had to make the best of the people's common-sense occupation of stations. The platforms became dormitories, with families bagging their places, if they could, early in the evening, just in order to be able to get a night's sleep.

Somebody had to take action to render all public shelters not only more comfortable, but also less of a health hazard for the thousands who used them. Without proper sanitation, heating, lighting, bedding or refreshments, the public shelters whether above or below ground could easily become filthy. Masses crowded together could pass on infections that might become epidemics. The conditions were a little like those of recent times, where (to our national shame), homeless people sleep under railway arches, or in shop doorways, huddled together, wrapped in dirty blankets. But in war conditions these groups were multiplied a thousand-fold.

The Salvation Army was among the first of the voluntary bodies to help, before any official government action. The police had asked them to supply shelters in the East End of London with food as early as September 1940. The Ministry then assigned shelters among other voluntary agencies to prevent overlapping. The WVS, YMCA, Church Army and the Women's Legion were soon doing their bit in any emergency. Commercial firms were not particularly helpful, as shelter feeding was not profitable.

Conditions were improved in the Underground. Disused lines were boarded over, bunks built, lavatories installed (instead of buckets), and there were even lectures, concerts and books to borrow.[15] Areas to the back of the platforms were designated for shelterers, leaving just about enough space for travellers to get on and off the trains. Numbers were controlled by issuing tickets to regular users. In fact only one in seven people were sleeping in public shelters or Underground stations in October 1940. But that was still a lot of people: perhaps 120,000 in the Underground, and another 220,000 in other public shelters. Another survey by the Ministry of Health estimated that 13 per cent of people in Metropolitan London slept in communal shelters and 27 per cent in Anderson shelters or those in their own homes.[16] The numbers declined as the Blitz did, but rose again with the flying bombs at the end of the war.

It was obvious that these people needed canteens. Some might have gone straight to their pitch on the platform after work, for instance. The London Passenger Transport Board ran a distribution service, using its women workers. The food came on trains, six of them, setting out from depots in the afternoon.

The Times of 15 November 1940 ran an article about the inaugural food train: 'A new kind of Underground train ran beneath London last night. Instead of business people or theatre-goers, it carried food, nocturnal snacks for the shelterers in the Tubes.'

The authorities were climbing on the bandwagon, too. After the initial attempt to prevent the Underground being used for shelter, on this occasion:

> Among those who cheered this food train on its way were the Lord Mayor (Sir George Wilkinson) and the Minister of Food, Lord Woolton, who is keen to do all that his Department can achieve to ensure that those Londoners who use the Tubes shall shelter in comfort.
>
> The City concurs, and so last night, while outside the barrage boomed, the Lord Mayor took part in a pleasing ceremony, and this again was something quite new of its kind.
>
> For this City function, not Guildhall nor the Mansion House was the setting, but somewhere well below ground – the Bank Station – and here the Lord Mayor handed to Lord Woolton a cheque which will help to provide those amenities for the Tube shelterers which the Minister has in mind ... The cheque handed to the Minister was for £20,000, and the sum came from the Lord Mayor's Air Raid Distress Fund.[17]

Thereafter every night LPTB staff walked among the shelterers carrying huge 2-gallon cans of tea or cocoa at 1*d* a cup. (Bring your own cup.) Some carried baskets or trays of refreshments such as buns, apples, meat pies at 1½*d*, chocolate (not rationed until 1942) and packets of biscuits at 2*d*. Cooking on the station was not allowed – no naked flames and no flues. Water was heated by electricity however for the drinks. There was milk for children and a bottle-warming service for babies.[18]

The London Passenger Transport Board was owed £17,500 at the end of the war for running the refreshment service, but this was considered a 'reasonable figure' by the Ministry of Food.

EMERGENCY FEEDING AFTER BOMBING RAIDS

The forward planning for rationing, distribution and control of food stocks in straightforward circumstances had been well thought out, generally speaking, and it was agreed that it had been a success. However, the vision needed to provide for people after large-scale bombing was inadequate, at least in the early months after it began. After a major air raid there were of course many dead and wounded. Coping with these front-line casualties was mostly well organised. The rescue services removed the corpses and took the injured to hospital or first-aid posts as appropriate. But who should look after the shocked but uninjured survivors immediately after a raid? Their first necessity was for a hot drink and a snack of some sort. For example, my husband was only twelve when a landmine exploded close to his family home. All the tiles were ripped off the roof. If his mother had stepped out of doors to see what was happening she would have been killed. He remembers spending the night at a neighbour's house, and all his parents wanted then was cup after cup of hot tea.

Even before the war it was recognised that a supply of boiling water would be required to make hot drinks. 'With this, tinned food and bread and margarine will provide a meal for adults … boiled potatoes can be added … for children, bread and margarine, jam and biscuits should be provided.'[19] This does not show over-much compassion or exercise of imagination on the part of the planners. However, they had to learn on the job:

> First aid at 'incidents'
>
> Experience of raiding soon revealed other groups of people needing attention. Most victims of bombs were the better for a snack or at least a drink of hot, sweet tea, administered on the spot, as quoted by every First Aid manual as an elementary treatment for shock. There was need for some service to bridge the gap between the rescue and the transfer to the rest centres as well as to cater for those involved who were not

'and Fireman Fred meets an old friend ...' Men in the rescue services needed hot drinks and snacks as much as the victims of raids. The WVS often supplied them, as well as colleagues on the job.

technically rest centre clients. Mobile canteens, operated by voluntary organisations, could and did prove effective in this type of work, but inadequacies of food supply and complete lack of co-ordination in their operation lessened their value. The ineffective management of mobile canteens became a serious problem later in the year and their inclusion within the framework of the emergency feeding scheme was to prove one of the most intractable problems of the Minister's communal feeding Division.

War is not tidy, and frameworks are apt to crumble when stressed. Experience did show that the Salvation Army, the WVS, the neighbour with a working cooker and so on were there helping the victims as best they could.

But many shocked and homeless people had literally lost all their possessions, including their documents. There were many who, although not quite as desperate, could not go back home. Their houses might be too damaged to be usable. There might be no gas or electricity available for heating and lighting, including cooking. The presence of unexploded bombs could prevent a whole street from being occupied for days on end, until the experts came along to make it safe. Sometimes family members had been killed or injured so that dependents had to be looked after elsewhere. Sometimes the food in the pantry had simply been rendered unfit for use, as described in Chapter 7.

Rest centres had been set up, but the planners had thought that they would be used mostly by the really very poor, and that their clients would be similar to those who had come under old Poor Law arrangements. But it turned out they were the only refuge for anyone who could not stay with friends when made homeless. There simply had to be proper meals and even beds available. All this cost money, of course, and there were unseemly wrangles about who should pay for what. Someone had to accept responsibility for operating losses on food, for instance, and the capital investment needed for building and equipping even minimally comfortable refuges. People who were bombed out felt they had a right to be re-housed and properly looked after. It was difficult to argue with this point of view.

Static kitchens were found to be less useful than mobile ones. Cooking centres might be put out of action themselves by bombing, as happened in Sheffield in December 1940. That particular crisis was overcome by using old coke-fired ovens in a public assistance institution – a former workhouse.[20]

Local authorities were responsible for emergency meals centres, feeding about 4 million people throughout the country. Mobile canteens, on the other hand, were often paid for and run by voluntary organisations, but collaborated with officialdom.

The Queen's Messenger Convoys[21] exemplified this. They were meant to be run by a new women's corps to supplement existing mobile canteens, and be sent to disaster areas. The vehicles were to be paid for partly from gifts made by the United States British War Relief Fund. Queen Elizabeth also made a donation, and agreed that the new organisation should be named The Queen's Messengers. However, the WVS was already in the field, and so it was agreed that their members should become Queen's Messengers on the job, and came under the direction of the Wartime Meals Division which sent convoys through the country wherever they were needed. They were of great use in Bootle and Liverpool after raids in May 1941, almost the only emergency feeding service for several days. They were not, however, called on to operate very much, being held in reserve in case of disasters.

Part of the problem was financial. Nobody really wanted to hand out free food, so a compromise was reached – food was free for the first two days after an 'incident', but after that users were expected to pay for their meals.

The convoys themselves were self-contained. The main vehicle was the canteen, which was equipped with urns for soup and tea, mugs and bowls, spoons and trays. Fluid intake was expected to be high, as the mugs and bowls were half-pint capacity. Washing up was provided for by an 8-gallon urn of hot water. There was a serving hatch at the side of the vehicle from which the food would be handed out to the queue. Store lorries held the actual food – enough for 6,000 meals, including canned soup, baked beans, meat roll, biscuits, margarine and tea, cocoa and condensed milk. Because water was needed immediately the canteen swung into action, a water tanker with 300 gallons on board was included, and a kitchen lorry with ten soyer boilers and other equipment followed for use by voluntary organisations. (The 'soyer' boiler is a link with the Victorian chef and reformer, Alexis Soyer, who helped to reorganise army catering in the Crimean War.) Later on a utility van and welfare van were added to complete the convoy, the utility van to bring in relief crews and supplies, and the welfare van a place for the crew to sleep, wash and prepare their own meals.

In spite of being comparatively under-used in Britain, the convoys were not wasted, but were handed over as complete units for relief work in Europe after the war.

THE WOMEN'S VOLUNTARY SERVICE[22]

References to the WVS have run like a stream throughout this chapter. This is a fair comparison, as the women who made up the organisation constantly bubbled up where they were most needed, taking on a huge number of different tasks.

In the 1930s many women's organisations existed already. The National Federation of Women's Institutes was one example, the Girl Guide Movement another. When it was almost certain that war was coming, the planners set up a service to deal with air-raid precautions. It was realised that women could play an important part in civil defence, and in 1938 the then Home Secretary, Sir Samuel Hoare, invited Stella, Lady Reading, to become the chairman of a new organisation for this purpose. Lady Reading was the second wife, and widow, of the Marquess of Reading, who had been a Viceroy of India. She had also been involved with an organisation called the Personal Service League, helping the families of the unemployed during the Depression of the 1930s, and had a network of contacts throughout the country.

The Women's Voluntary Service very soon drew upon the goodwill of these influential ladies. In a way the birth of the organisation was typically British. It was an ad hoc arrangement to meet a perceived need, with a dedicated woman appointed to run it. Recruiting volunteers would be of prime importance, but training was also needed: in air-raid precautions, obviously, but also in child care, driving ambulances and such, and also to undertake the hands-on work of organising stores and cooking. Think of an ideal housewife, with all her different skills and ability to do several things at once, to improvise, to perceive a need and to supply the remedy. Acknowledge that all this is work of national importance, and then you have the basis that was developed in the work of the WVS.

A uniform helped to give a collective identity, though it was not obligatory to wear it, and it had to be paid for. Indeed when clothes rationing was introduced coupons had to be given up as well as money. It was designed by a London couturier, Digby Morton – basically a grey-green suit with dark red blouse and a respectable hat that could be worn at various angles. The uniform was an outward sign of the relationship the WVS held with the local authorities. The volunteers themselves were not under official control, but because they were so helpful, indispensable in many ways, they achieved quasi-official status. The local authorities were meant to provide premises and back-up, the women were to do the actual work on the ground. They were in effect unpaid social workers, though some key organisers were offered expenses.

The organisation was intended to be non-political, non-hierarchical and socially inclusive, but we are talking about pre-war attitudes too, when these ideals were much less prominent than they became later. Middle-class women were inclined to take charge – to be bossier perhaps – than the equally able women who happened to be worse off and less well educated. Nevertheless, the war had a smoothing effect. It must have been difficult to put on airs when you are wiping the nose (or any other part of the anatomy) of a distressed evacuee.

Before the Munich Crisis of 1938, which brought a false hope of peace and a year in which some preparation could be made for war, the WVS made plans to help with the mass evacuation of 2 million vulnerable civilians from London. At that time the plan came to nothing, but it was to be a rehearsal for the real evacuation the following year.

The WVS had helped to check the accommodation available to receive the thousands of children and mothers expected to leave London and other cities. When the day came they helped to marshal the children and teachers onto trains, they went on the trains themselves in many cases, and at the other end more volunteers were there to help, first to refresh and then to disperse the tired, hungry and distressed or excited travellers to their billets. It was a huge job, and though there were flaws in the organisation it was done without any major casualties.

Willing helpers attracted work. The children who came from inner cities were very often in need of clothing as well as health care, and canteens had to be provided for schools which would otherwise have been unable to cope with the newcomers. The WVS helped to set up nurseries, too, for children who were homeless or without parents. The American Red Cross assisted in this work as well.

The WVS was at hand to help not only the victims of bombing, but to provide hot drinks and snacks for rescue services and police. Some members volunteered for duty at NAAFI canteens for the Services as well. Their role also included the collection of salvage, especially aluminium, already described in Chapter 3. They were to be found throughout the war wherever practical help was needed, and especially where food had to be distributed to sustain the wretched, the tired, and the dispossessed.

8

The Black Market and Grey Areas

'What us? We'd never do anything like that!' Most citizens prided themselves on their patriotism. They did not often question the idea of fair play and fair shares, which was the constant theme of home front propaganda, especially during the earlier part of the war. But there was nothing wrong, surely, with getting a little bit extra from the grocer if he happened to have a larger allocation of sugar than he needed. Perhaps the butcher had a friend a mile or two away in the country who had just slaughtered a pig which had somehow slipped out of the official figures. It would have been terrible to have let these things go to waste. The bureaucrats probably had enough to do without worrying about a tiny screw of sugar or rasher of bacon.

The people I have talked to, mostly children during the war, have almost all told me about the small supplements their parents managed to acquire, and they would not have been good parents if they had not done their best for their children:

> 'We never had anything extra – except sugar. Don't quite know where it came from, but my mother kept it in the airing cupboard.'
>
> 'My father came back from the farm with a big bit of butter about once a fortnight.'
>
> 'My father was a Church Warden, but we once had a whole side of bacon from his cousin in the country.'
>
> 'A farmer I knew was in the habit of letting his men have some unofficial chicken feed for their backyard hens. Then one evening the village constable called on him. "Hear you've been giving out some grain without authorization …" The farmer nodded very slowly, thinking of the magistrate. "Well, I keep hens too," said the policeman.'[1]

Such informal infringements were crimes only because the Government said they were. Before the war of course there had been absolutely nothing wrong with buying whatever a shop or producer had to offer. The present of some food from the country was a kindness, a gesture of family solidarity. The farmer who looked after his men was praiseworthy, and received loyal service in return. To have some bureaucrat telling you that this was now not only unpatriotic but also criminal seemed to many people to be impertinent and silly. The little bit on the side did not count in the public mind as part of the black market.

What did count were the actions of criminals who stole from docks and railways, who looted bombed buildings and ran rackets and frauds to supply scarce goods for large profits. Those who, in other words, exploited shortage and greed to get rich at the expense of the country as a whole. If it had been really successful the black market could have undermined the whole system. It was the shadow side of control, brought into being by shortages and regulations. It was a barometer of how much the public would support restrictions, because of course without the public paying to use it, the black market would not have existed.

Lord Woolton was aware of the potential problems. At least two of the *Food Facts* advertisements issued by his Ministry in the summer and autumn of 1941 appealed directly to patriotic fervour. The first is about the connection between the customers and the black market. It stated that there had been 22,356 convictions for rationing and price control offences since the beginning of the war. Efficient rationing was part of the war effort, and crooked dealers would have their licences revoked. 'Black markets exist for black sheep,' so the customer was guilty along with the profiteers.

The second advertisement was published from 14 September 1941 in the 'National Dailies, Sundays, London Evenings, Provincial Mornings and Evenings, English and Welsh Weeklies.' Complete with an illustration of a spyglass it tried to evoke fighting spirit by reversing Lord Nelson's famous action. 'Not with the blind eye, please. Let's face the facts squarely – especially FOOD facts. Ask yourself these 5 questions …'

> Do you ever try to get more than your ration? Or accept more if offered?

> Do you ever shop-crawl? That is, go from shop to shop trying to buy a little here and a little there of some food which is scarce?
>
> Do you ever pay more than control prices, or pay unfairly high prices for foods that are not price controlled?
>
> Do you ever waste food of any description?
>
> Do you neglect to produce all the food you can or to preserve foods whilst they are plentiful?

Only the first and third of these transgressions were black-market related, but all carried black marks. The point was that individual selfishness made a great deal of difference if it was repeated by many people. Even 'a bread crust, and outside cabbage leaf … multiplied by the entire population – 45,000,000 [sic] – [amounts to] many thousands of tons of wasted food.' And this involved not only money and shipping space, but seamen's lives as well.

However, maybe he had overstated his case a little. Probably not many people spent sleepless nights over a discarded cabbage leaf, particularly if they had donated it to the pig bin or put it on a compost heap.

There was a graduation of public condemnation. The spiv, who could find you a pair of nylons, was disapproved of but often tolerated. He was on the criminal fringe, and though you knew you ought not to deal with him, the temptation was often strong. He was only a small operator after all. But the large-scale racketeer making a lot of money out of shortages was widely censured. When asked their opinion, the public strongly disapproved of the illicit market, according to the surveys. A Gallup Poll of January 1942 found that 85 per cent of the people questioned would approve if everyone convicted of such dealing were sent to prison without the option of a fine.[2] Extreme opinion was in favour of flogging the culprits, or even the death penalty, because evasion of regulations was seen as a kind of treason. (At this time treason and murder were both capital offences.) However, these penalties were never actually applied, whatever *Letters to the Editor* might say.

In June 1943, 72 per cent of the people taking part in the poll thought that Lord Woolton had been mistaken to deny the existence of a significant black market. Perhaps hoping that appeals to the national conscience had been effective, or for propaganda reasons, he had claimed that a combination of public hostility and heavy penalties had meant very little illicit trading.[3]

The punishments certainly became severe. At the end of 1941 fines had been set at the rate of three times the value of the black-market goods. In June 1942 there was widespread concern about thefts from docks and even from reserves which had been set up in case of German invasion. A fine of £500 and/or several years' imprisonment could follow conviction. A maximum term of fourteen years was proposed. Non-payment of the fine led to bankruptcy and the closure of the defaulter's business. At this time £500 was a great deal of money, compared with an average wage (in 1944) of £6 4*s* 2*d* per week for adult men.[4] (Adult women were earning on average about half this amount.) But the serious racketeers had plenty of money.

Food was not the only, nor perhaps the main, commodity. Petrol and clothing coupons were subject to theft and forgery. (Clothes were rationed in June 1941.) Stolen cigarettes were highly profitable, and so were bulk robberies of ration books themselves.

Ration books were issued for a year at a time, and were delivered to local Food Offices, which were not always secure. The books might be diverted in transit, or taken by entering the premises. Sometimes a corrupt employee might co-operate with the thieves. In 1944 a total of 114,000 ration books were stolen in Ware and Romford. The 14,000 from Ware were simply removed by a couple of men with a lorry in the early morning. Passers-by assumed that they were just making a delivery of new books. Sometimes a guard was placed on the premises, and one such was the victim of an armed robbery in May 1943 at Tulse Hill. This was also the work of two men, who got away with 2,000 new books.[5] Such books were not stamped, but the stamping could be counterfeited.

An amnesty for black marketeers was offered in June 1942 at the same time that penalties were increased. However, the criminals were not impressed and the amnesty was a failure.[6]

MINISTRY RELATIONS WITH SHOPKEEPERS

The prosecution of those involved in large-scale thefts and rackets was of course justified. Not only did the crooks siphon off goods to the unfair advantage of the unscrupulous rich, but it meant that honest people actually had a smaller share of the available stocks.

Smoking was widespread, as the dangers were not then understood. Players was a leading brand. Some people rolled their own cigarettes, using papers such as the Rizla ones here. Cigarettes were often part of the Black Market.

As stated, there was widespread anger and resentment among the public. The Ministry could defend its clampdown on all infringements of the law on the grounds that even a small amount of goods that escaped the official system ultimately benefitted the black marketeer.

Retailers though could easily feel persecuted by all the regulations and checking that went on. Directions and prohibitions poured out of Government Departments, it seemed in inverse proportion to the volume of goods available. It was sometimes impossible to comply with the system no matter how much goodwill there was. Counting cut-out coupons was an example. With young Johnny away at the wars, the wretched shopkeeper had to stay up half the night trying to make his returns, sometimes by the light of a candle in the blackout. When the parcel arrived at the Food Office, Big Johnny was also away at the wars, so checking was impossible.

The numbers had to be taken at face value, more or less, and this inevitably led to some abuses, though the system was changed quite quickly to one based on registrations.

There was no shortage, apparently, of Ministry 'snoopers'. An innocent-looking customer, often a young woman, would go into a shop with a plausible sob story and ask if she could buy something like sugar or butter without coupons. Sometimes extra money would be offered. If the shop assistant took pity on her, and such a transaction took place, the next thing would be a visit from a Food Inspector, followed by prosecution.

It was illegal for the shopkeeper to sell, but also illegal to ask for extra. However, because the entreating 'customers' were engaged in enforcement they got away with using these tactics for some time.[7] After the first three years of war 57,794 people were convicted of infringing Food Regulations,[8] more than double the numbers cited in the *Food Facts* advertisement of 1941. The bad feeling that existed between the authorities and this branch of the retail trade was due, partly at least, to petty prosecutions of offenders.

Small retailers were often family businesses without large reserves of capital. Their profits were already hit by shortages, and even unrationed goods were controlled by quotas or fixed prices. Often the goods were simply unobtainable. It was extremely tempting for the small shopkeeper to make some kind of profit if he could. But a conviction could result in losing the licence to trade. Even those who had nothing alleged against them could be closed if they had too few registered customers. Many little shops went out of business altogether, a trend which continued after the war.

Buying black market goods was not only illegal, but could be disappointing, even dangerous. If you bought a pair of nylons at a street corner, for instance, and then found they were laddered when you unwrapped them, well, that was just tough. Even if you felt like going back to complain, the nylon vendor had vanished, replaced perhaps by someone selling perfume and cosmetics at bargain prices. The perfume probably came from a spiv's basement factory, complete with forged labels. The cosmetics could actually be harmful.

A hunger for meat could lead you into buying some strange commodities too. There have always been jokes about sausages for example (not rationed) and some meat intended as dog food may have found its way onto the human dinner-dish.

Another story – perhaps an urban legend – concerned the meat from animals sold legally, including a crocodile, ex-inhabitants of London Zoo.[9]

WAR ON WASTE

There was a constant theme in the Ministry's advertisements that waste was offensive. In fact wasting food became an actual offence in August 1940, with penalties including imprisonment for three months to two years. If you threw away a crust of bread, or failed to scrape the last trace of margarine from its wrapping, or disposed of the odd cabbage leaf, as above, you were guilty of putting merchant seamen in mortal danger.

Feeding unnecessary mouths was dicey too. A large number of pets had been put down at the beginning of the war, but many cats and dogs as well as canaries, budgerigars and so on remained. You were not supposed to give milk to pet animals, but could feed them on the scraps supplied by a butcher or from your own table. Sometimes the animals took a hungry view of this and helped themselves before the scraps could reach the table. One incident made a strong impression on Cliff Townsend:

> When the war broke out I was 13 so I don't remember too much about it but one very vivid memory is when my mother put down in the cellar of our house, on a shelf probably four or five feet from the ground, a full leg of lamb. This was our ration for I don't know how long, probably about three weeks for the three of us. Somehow or other this little terrier contrived to reach this shelf right up there. He was only tiny, probably only about nine inches off the ground. For some reason my mother, finding him with very little but the bone left, thought this highly hilarious. Well that was her privilege. She had to find the food to make up for what he'd noshed.[10]

Working animals were another matter. Horses could replace motor vehicles for deliveries for instance, and there were great numbers on the land still. Cats were valuable mousers, as well as comforting pets. They were generally well looked after. A tonic for cats, 'Tibs', was extensively advertised. I can remember giving it to my own family companions, Sooty and Fluffy. They were spoilt by comparison with the hardworking farm cats in the district. They spent the war years, as I remember, on a production line of their own dedicated to more mousers. They had been 'evacuated' to our house by their mother, a semi-feral animal, who turned up at the back door one day carrying Fluffy in her mouth. Having seen her baby welcomed, she went away and returned the next day with Sooty. She made a few more visits to make sure they were well and happy, and then went off on her own cat business. We used to feed them on table-scraps, but they were not as well trained as they might have been. They used to jump onto our laps to make sure that the next mouthful went to them.

SALVAGED FOOD

As the housewife was constantly told not to waste a crust, the Ministry was expected to set a good example in salvaging all possible foods after bombing raids. This was not always done. Sometimes the food even found its way to the Black Market.

After the Dockland raids in September 1940 a Special Commissioner was asked to deal with saving stocks from damaged warehouses and cold stores. But the docks were in the jurisdiction of the Port of London Authority. By the time the red tape had been untangled, much of the meat in Nelson's Wharf had been removed, but there was still 2,500 tons, which could not be used. The cold store owners passed the buck to the Ministry – it was their meat after all – and so the Divisional Food Officer had the job of clearing it up. After that things were better organised, and there was even a system for drying out foods such as grain that had been soaked by water after a fire. It was found that up to 75 per cent of food could usually be salvaged after a raid. The destruction of processing plants such as mills and sugar refineries turned out to be more serious than the loss of the stock itself.[11]

BOMBED FOOD IN THE HOME

Filthy dust was one of the squalid effects of bombing. Of course it was not to be compared with your house being demolished around you, or of finding a heap of broken beams and rubble when you came out of shelter in the morning. But unless you had taken precautions, you might find your stored goods were too filthy to eat. Many houses in inner cities were old. Coal had been the main fuel for heating for several centuries, with its attendant soot, so that the even the most house-proud woman probably had a good weight of dust under the floorboards, in the attic and in the coal cellar itself. The blast from a bomb would disturb all this, as well as produce its own direct quota of pulverised plaster, brick and shattered glass.[12] This was even mentioned in a *Food Facts* advertisement, probably at the time of the Blitz:

> PROTECTION FROM BOMB DUST. Never leave food uncovered. The thick dust which settles after blast due to a bomb explosion frequently renders food unfit to be eaten. This dust even penetrates cartons and wrapping. Cover any food which is not in boxes or tins with a thick cloth or dust-sheet. This will also keep out fine splinters of glass.[13]

It would probably have been difficult to persuade the authorities that you needed replacement rations because you had carelessly rushed off to the shelter before tucking the dust sheet into place.

FOOD HAZARDS

Death by epidemic diseases is as much to be feared in war as death due to armed combat. Famine and pestilence have always been seen as the buddies of the sword-carrying skeleton on the horse. The influenza pandemic which followed the First World War killed more people than the war itself.

The authorities therefore kept a very close medical eye on infectious diseases. Dr Charles Hill, introduced in Chapter 3, was The Radio Doctor, a kindly chap with popular appeal and a sense of humour. In his talks about all kinds of physical and emotional ills he could be relied on for common sense. He was the propagandist for good health of all kinds, and as might be expected had much to say about food, nutrition and food hygiene.

He pointed out that typhoid was a killer disease. Typhoid carriers were a particular risk. Infective bacteria could persist in their guts even after they had apparently recovered from the illness. If they were careless about washing their hands and handled food intended for others, the others could be in real peril. 'In these days of canteens and communal cooking, everyone preparing food should take the precaution of washing after using the W.C.' said The Radio Doctor firmly.[14] Even after the war I can remember the notices in public toilets, in schools, hospitals, even cinemas – 'Now Wash Your Hands'. Sometimes it was 'Now Wash Your Hands Please'. Even today there are occasional public reminders of this social duty.

Dysentery was another very nasty possibility, spread in the same way, or by flies. Most of what I have said of typhoid applies to dysentery, a much more common disease. Both are diseases of war. In fact in the wars before 1914 far more soldiers died of typhoid and dysentery than as a result of gunshot wounds.[15]

Pork needed to be properly cooked as it was occasionally infected by a parasite which caused trichiniasis (or trichinosis) when the muscles were invaded by the trichina worm. This was a time of course when backyard pigs were popular, but standards for keeping them not stringent. A lot of pork meat emerged in sausages, so it was a good rule to make sure that they, too, were thoroughly cooked. It remains a sensible precaution even today.

Milk for children was one of the themes of the Ministry of Food, but it too could be hazardous. Cows can suffer from tuberculosis and pass on the bacillus in their milk. Bovine tuberculosis affects the bones and joints, particularly of children. It was recognised long ago, and herds of tuberculin-tested cows produced milk for which people were willing to pay a little more. Boiling milk was also a way to make it safe, and pasteurisation is now almost universal – but it was not in the war. Much milk sold in towns was treated, but out in the country it was often unpasteurised on grounds of cost.[16] *The Times* reported in February 1943 that a deputation of doctors' representatives spoke to the Minister of Food.

Professor Picken, who introduced the deputation for the British Medical Association, said the profession was satisfied that pasteurisation was the only practical safeguard and that it had no serious disadvantage.

Professor Garrod said that bovine tuberculosis was a widespread menace and from 5 to 10 per cent of churn samples of raw milk were infected. Milk-borne tuberculosis chiefly affected young children and was estimated to cause 2,000 deaths a year, with many more cases of serious and sometimes crippling illnesses.[17]

However, the Minister, the same Lord Woolton who had said that the proper feeding of children was one of the priorities of his Ministry, was non-committal on this occasion. He merely said that he and the Parliamentary Secretary to the Ministry of Health (Florence Horsbrugh) would report the matter to his Government colleagues. In fact it was not until the 1960s that pasteurisation was applied everywhere.[18] In the meantime The Radio Doctor advised his listeners on many occasions to boil milk before drinking it, not only to kill the micro-organisms that caused tuberculosis but also other infections, such as those carried by flies.

ACCIDENTAL POISONING

At a time when people were being urged to try out novel foods, and make the most of everything, there were not enough warnings perhaps about potentially harmful ingredients. In the very first *Kitchen Front* broadcast, for example, it was suggested that young bracken shoots could be eaten like asparagus. This was accepted as country knowledge, but a later writer, Richard Mabey, was more cautious, saying that bracken contained small quantities of a carcinogen, and was best left alone.[19]

The tops of many vegetables were recommended – turnip and carrot tops for instance. These are fine. However, the unwary might also have tried potato foliage and the green leaves of tomato plants, both of which belong to the same family as the deadly nightshade. These greens are poisonous. (It is interesting that when first introduced into this country, the bright red tomato fruits were themselves thought to be poisonous, though now highly valued as food.) Potatoes which have been stored incorrectly and have turned green are also toxic. Rhubarb leaves have been known to kill people, as they contain a high proportion of oxalic acid. The stems too have a little of this acid, and may disagree with some individuals, though they are classed as edible.

Field mushrooms, and many other fungi are delicious, but it was certainly wise to make sure you knew which ones were harmless and which were not. The County Herb Committees, mentioned in Chapter 6, must have saved several lives. For instance the death cap has an accurate name, and the fly agaric is hallucinogenic as well as possibly fatal.

FLIES

Flies were a hazard to public health. There has long been a campaign against them, and it is well known that their life-cycle begins in filth and often progresses onto exposed foodstuffs. They wipe their feet, true, but only after landing, especially on meat and sugary foods. They cannot bite, only suck, so they regurgitate liquid onto the food they are about to consume. They are carriers of all manner of diseases, some mild, some deadly, including typhoid and dysentery. Infantile diarrhoea and vomiting too can be fatal.

Bluebottles or greenbottles lay their eggs on meat if they can find it, and the resulting maggots mean waste at the very least.

To keep flies and food separate called for constant care. All food needed to be covered, kept in gauze meat-safes for instance. Today we think far less about them. Refrigerators keep out flies as well as slowing the growth of bacteria. Food hygiene laws are more stringent and most food is pre-wrapped anyway. This is not good news for the campaign for greener policies however.

It was obviously important – still is – to cover garbage and dispose of excreta. In wartime if there were flies in the house there were some measures to get rid of them. Fly papers were long strips of paper with a sticky substance on both sides. They were hung up to attract and trap the insects. Another expedient was the fly swatter, an oblong bit of mesh attached to a handle. If you were quick enough you could squash a fly as it rested on the wall or table, but your targets were often quicker. Aerosol sprays were a post-war development of course.

RATS

Both mice and rats eat stores of human food, and spoil more than they actually devour. Rats in particular were a real hazard. An advertisement issued by the Ministry in the later stages of the war had the large headline, 'RAT MENACE IN MARYLEBONE.' Then came a photograph of several dozen attacking stored sacks.

> *Every man, woman, and child is asked to be a 'Rat-Reporter'*
>
> Rats are a growing danger! 'Every year rats and mice together are

> either destroying or fouling 2,000,000 tons of food,' said the Minister of Food recently.
>
> At this moment there are probably 40 million rats in this country – almost as many rats as people. They are at an alarming level right here in this area.
>
> A country-wide effort is being made to destroy [them]. The campaign starts this week in the Greater London area.[20]

It was said that rats bred in huge colonies, which could be traced from notification of foraging animals. Expert rat catchers were waiting for your telephone call, postcard or completed coupon, but if the rats were on your own property it was your responsibility to get rid of them.

This rat, eating like a fifth columnist aiding and abetting the enemy, was the brown rat, *Rattus novegicus*, unfairly named for Norway. Other aliases are town rat and sewer rat. They are not confined to town though, but are country dwellers too. These rodents are clever opportunists. They eat more or less anything, and live in large or small social groups close to humans, whose careless habits ensure they have plenty of food. They breed prolifically, a female having about eight young to a litter, and typically three to six litters a year, though not all survive. In warm weather and favourable environments they can breed even in winter, but usually live for only a couple of years or so. They each eat about an ounce of food a day, and foul much more with urine, droppings and hair.

The Minister of Food was concerned with the amount of spoilage, but the Minister of Health should also have been concerned with the diseases that rats can carry. One of these, we now know, is Leptospirosis, another name for Weil's disease, spread by contaminated water. They also damage property by gnawing through wood and plaster and chewing electrical cables with resultant risk of fire. It was the black rat, *Rattus rattus*, which carried the fleas that spread bubonic plague, conjectured to have been the Black Death. However, the black rat was not common in Britain during the war, nor is it now. This is the only good rat news I can think of.

The rat population explosion of the war could have been connected with the bombing. Damaged houses, shops with food stocks scattered and spoilt, the blackout that would have favoured nocturnal animals, would all have helped rats to thrive. If they were bombed out themselves, when for instance a grain store took a direct hit, they simply moved along to the next suitable site and set up home again, because they will shift territories if required. (It is said, incidentally, that they are doing very well today under the timber decking which is currently fashionable in gardens.)[21]

SHOP CRAWLING

Going from shop to shop, buying whatever you could, was regarded as anti-social, but became necessary as shortages increased. In fact joining a queue if you saw one was often the only way of getting something that had just arrived, and which would be sold out in a few hours. The general scarcity of such essentials as matches, candles, torch batteries, hairpins and lipstick meant that if you saw anything that might be useful you bought it, carried it home triumphantly and stashed it away, whether you really needed it or not. It would come in handy later …

It may be that we who grew up during the war acquired the habit of collecting everything, never throwing away any object remotely likely to be useful, with the result that our garages and attics were full of bits of string and empty jam jars until recycling schemes absolved our houses and consciences.

HOARDING

Anxiety at the prospect of a shortage leads to panic buying too, and this was a problem immediately after the announcement that Britain was at war. There were stories of rich people touring the East End to buy up sugar for instance.[22] Indignant shopkeepers might have refused to sell, but undoubtedly some people managed to find stocks of tinned goods and things which would keep well, such as dried fruit, and squirrelled them away against the dark empty cupboards to come. It was simply prudent to keep a supply of emergency food if you could. Nobody knew at the beginning of war, or when invasion seemed likely, how long the national food supplies would last. The government itself had stockpiles for the same reason. My family certainly kept a few tins of meat and condensed milk, and packets of biscuits. The biscuits were eaten before they went stale, but the tinned goods were sacrosanct for several years.

The Ministry was itself ambivalent. 'See that your emergency store is always in order', was one piece of advice from *Food Facts* during the Blitz – the same which gave advice on what to take into the air-raid shelter, described in Chapter 6.

A booklet produced by the Canned Foods Advisory Bureau, founded in 1937 and then in Regent Street, W.1., had advised on reserve stores.[23] Sixty-four cans of food were considered necessary for a family of four consisting of two adults and two children. Besides the cans, there should be a supply of dry goods – flour, tea, sugar and cereals. The canned stash should consist of six thick soups, six of fish, five of meat, twenty of vegetables, five of fruit and five puddings, eight evaporated milk, two of cream, one of coffee, two of jam or marmalade, two cans of butter, one of cheese and one of suet. It was noted that canned butter did not keep very well. There was no mention of margarine.

It is not clear how long this ought to keep the family fed in the complete absence of supplies coming in, but it would certainly enable them to continue to live in pre-war comfort for several weeks. There would even be some cream for the coffee, or for the fruit. However, though canned fruit and vegetables do contain some Vitamin C, the most pressing need would be for fresh vegetables. It is interesting that such a family thought suet pudding or pastry was essential. You could make jam or marmalade roly-poly for days when you didn't want to open the fruit, or use it for a pie using one of the cans of meat.

Once points rationing came into force it would have been very difficult indeed to build up such a stock. From the start hoarding was regarded as anti-social, and by 1942 it had become an offence. It was wasteful to try to keep food for a long time. Even cans might deteriorate before they could be used. Moderation was the key here, as in so many circumstances. You were allowed to keep a week's supply of food, but no more. Still, most families would hang on to something for when Johnny came home on leave, or for the longed-for Victory celebration.

9

Let's Have a Party

If you believed the propaganda, Britain had a cheerful civilian population, which, having enjoyed a social evening in the shelters, woke in the morning to hurry to 'do their bit' in the factories. They might relieve their feelings by mocking Hitler or the enemy in general, or singing the patriotic songs of the time.

Most people did try to keep hopeful, so there was a bit of truth in the idea, but it was certainly not the whole truth. For some, war brought almost intolerable stress and grief. Sons and husbands were away, often in unknown parts of the world, with no clue if they were in battle areas or not. At home, particularly in towns, as we have seen, there was a constant danger of bombs or other attack. Your evacuated children far away might be unhappy, or you might feel guilty if you had brought them back. You could have lost your home and all your possessions. Friends and relations were dead, injured or missing. The future had a blank face.

BEER

The pub was a refuge where you could get away from the war until the sirens sounded, and allay anxiety with a pint, or a nip of something stronger. It was a meeting place for your surviving friends and neighbours. The idea that you might not be there tomorrow could lead to an *enjoy life now* attitude, or 'eat, drink and be merry'. (As might be expected, there was also a rise both in venereal disease and in children born or conceived outside marriage.) During a time of very heavy bombing, people did keep away from the Red Lion to some extent. Many pubs were on street corners, and so might suffer blast damage from several directions. There was a suspicion that pubs were specially singled out for destruction. However, when the worst bombing was over, the convivial atmosphere drew people in, many as part of a group, as off-duty ARP workers for instance.[1] Service men on leave, or allies stationed in Britain, were also part of the gathering.

Beer was not rationed, but was weaker than it had been pre-war. Using valuable barley to make it was controversial. Beer has some food value: alcohol is a source of calories, but Lord Arnold argued in the House of Lords that it would be better to feed much of the barley to hens instead, and so increase the egg ration.[2] The Government did not agree, possibly because beer could be taxed, as eggs could not, or, in a more charitable interpretation, because it was valuable for keeping up morale.

In fact more beer was made than before the war, though the strength was reduced by 15 per cent. The price of a draught pint more that doubled, from about 5*d* in 1939 to 1/- in 1945. Consumption rose from 20.3 gallons to 25.6 gallons per head per year. The country was split into zones to supply local thirsts, with each pub having to deal with the nearest brewery in order to save transport.[3] Cider continued to be produced, but was mainly consumed locally. It did not become a fashionable drink until after the war.

WINES AND SPIRITS

Beer was the drink mainly of the working man – and during the war, of women too, to some extent. Wine had tended to be the choice of the middle and upper class because it was expensive. But in wartime, wine-drinking people had to rely on existing stocks. (If their cellars were doubling as shelters, perhaps they had some consolation in air raids.) Most wines had been imported from France, Germany or other European countries, and naturally the trade stopped. If a consignment of Empire wine came in, it was also heavily taxed.

Spirits had had an interesting history. Cheap gin had been the means by which the poor of the eighteenth century could blot out their poverty for a few hours: think of Hogarth's painting *Gin Lane*. Brandy, made from French wine, invented during the 1620s, had been imported or smuggled into Britain ever since, a luxury for the elite, or for 'medicinal purposes' in more modest households. Like wine, it became very scarce. Whisky, distilled in Scotland, was a little more available, but much of it was kept for export to the United States in return for food and arms[4] or appeared on the Black Market at high prices and of dubious quality.

HOME-MADE WINES AND BEERS

These country drinks came into their own for those people who could spare a bit of their sugar ration or could get hold of some honey. Wine is not difficult to make, though it needs attention to detail as well as good corks or stoppers. A fat glass gallon container could sometimes be begged from a chemist. You could use a clean bucket if you had to.

Juice of berries, or water flavoured with leaves, roots or flower petals, is mixed with sugar. Yeast is added, the container fitted, if possible, with a device such as a fermentation lock (or plug of cotton wool) which will allow carbon dioxide to escape but keep out bacteria. Failing this, just a lid will do. The liquid (known as wort) is left in a moderately warm place to ferment. When the yeast had turned most of the sugar to alcohol, which can be judged because the bubbling has stopped, the wine is strained and bottled. Suitable corks are needed in case the fermentation has not quite finished, when the bottle may either fizz over or, in a bad case, explode as pressure builds up. If fermentation continues in the bottle you have either a sparkling wine or a disaster. Most wines improve by being kept in a cool, dark place for a while.

Some classic country wines were and are made from elderberries, elderflowers, dandelion leaves or flowers, blackberries, mulberries and parsnips. It is an improvement to add chopped raisins and sometimes lemons to the wort, though in a war you might not think it worth using them for this purpose. Nettle beer can be made in much the same way with nettle tops, and ginger beer with bruised root ginger.

The resulting liquor was often rather sweet, but certainly much better than nothing at all. Elderflower champagne and parsnip wine are really very good indeed. These drinks were not for sale, but were consumed at home. Cheers! We needed them.

SOFT DRINKS

There had been a flourishing soft drinks industry pre-war, but with the shortage of fruit, manufacture became limited. Carbonated drinks continued to some extent, and I can remember, quite fondly, hanging out with my friends in the local village shop, where we could buy bottles of 'pop' and get a free straw to drink it through. This treat came in two flavours – or perhaps two colours would be a better description: lemon/yellow and raspberry/red. Any similarity to fruit depended on a vivid imagination. For a little while at the beginning of the war one could still buy large bottles of fizzy lemonade or orangeade, the tops held down with a lever-controlled stopper to control the gas.

Ministry of Food recipes and cookery books recommended boiling apple peelings and cores to make a drink for children. Rose-hip or blackcurrant syrup was diluted to make a healthy thirst-quencher for infants. Later in the war they were replaced by concentrated orange juice which was generally liked.

Coca Cola arrived with the Americans in Britain. Bottling plants were set up to provide the drink, sold cheaply to American forces, as a generous gesture by the Coca Cola Company.[5] It colonised the United Kingdom and remains to this day.

TOBACCO

Cigarettes, and to a lesser extent cigars and pipes, occupied a different position in society sixty years ago. Smoking was accepted as one of the pleasures of life. Working men frequently smoked, women perhaps rather less so. The troops were supplied with cigarettes as a matter of course. Smoking helped to calm frazzled nerves and reduce appetite. In the middle classes, smoking was regarded as sophisticated by both men and women. Winston Churchill waved his iconic cigar at the cameras. It was not realised how lethal the habit could be, and even King George VI was one of its victims.

As with many luxuries, imports of tobacco were reduced, though some were supplied from America under the Lend Lease programme. Smokers could not get their regular brands, nor as many as they were accustomed to. As tobacco is addictive, lack of nicotine made people irritable and restless. Substitutes were tried: the helpful Vicomte de Mauduit suggested collecting and drying stinging nettles, fennel and coltsfoot heads. Rubbed with honey and soaked in rum, if available, they were sewn into a canvas bag and pressed in a vice for three days. After that they were dried off, and then sliced into thin shavings.[6]

It was probably more satisfactory and much cheaper than buying cigarettes to cultivate real tobacco for yourself. The seeds could be bought and planted indoors or in a frame or greenhouse in spring. Then, giving them plenty of room, water and liquid manure, they could grow outside from June. The leaves were picked in September, and dried slowly, like washing, pegged on a line in a shed. The central rib of the large leaf was cut away, and the rest bunched and hung up in the sun if possible. After another three months in a cool dark place they were ready for shredding into pipe or cigarette tobacco. To begin with you needed a licence – tobacco carried duty – but later you could grow it for your own use without a licence, provided you informed the local Excise Office that you were doing so.[7]

EATING OUT

It seemed unfair that if you had the money you could dine in luxury. A compromise was reached, by which allocation of meat, in particular to commercial catering establishments, was reduced. By June 1942 the bureaucrats had moved in, with restaurant dishes classified as 'main' or 'subsidiary'. A main dish had a good proportion of protein, a subsidiary one much less. You were allowed one of each, though you could settle for a subsidiary dish in place of the main one, so that you had two subsidiaries. Three courses only were allowed, at a maximum cost of 5/- per meal.[8] In this way the very rich could not take unfair advantage, or so it was hoped. However, there was nothing to stop anyone eating a series of meals at 5/- a time in different places, if money was no obstacle. You could also stay at a hotel or boarding house for a while, though you had to surrender your ordinary ration book if you were there for more than five days.

From the restaurant's point of view there was a way of getting round the 5/-maximum. High cloakroom fees, or high prices for wine, were charged in exclusive restaurants. Entertainment and dancing cost an additional 2/6. These places also made a case for house charges to the authorities. They had high overheads, and claimed to be a necessary part of life even in wartime, when overseas diplomats, military top-brass and politicians expected a good standard of hospitality. Accordingly they were allowed house charges from 1/- to 6/- on a sliding scale to help them keep their status.[9]

However, the food served was often recognisably a wartime compromise. In 1944 Simpson's in the Strand was offering Creamed Spam Casserole, for instance, hardly *haute cuisine* with its potatoes, tomatoes – and Spam. Even the diners in the House of Lords restaurant had to make do with creamed (tinned) salmon and a risotto of rice and mixed vegetables.[10]

In spite of the danger of being caught in an air raid, dinner dances or dinner and cabaret were popular with the richer layers of society and off-duty servicemen. In 1940 people went out to dine at the Dorchester Hotel, but instead of going home afterwards they settled down in the lobby with rugs[11] and probably pillows too.

In London during the Blitz some people who took a chance to have a good time did not live to remember it. The Regent Palace Hotel took two hits, The Savoy, three. The Ritz itself was bombed, but most notorious of all was the carnage at the Café de Paris, when thirty people were killed in March 1941. Looters moved in more quickly than rescuers, and there were horror stories of corpses and the dying having the rings snatched off their fingers.[12]

PARTIES IN GENERAL

Naturally there were still birthdays to be celebrated, servicemen came home on leave, or young people went off to join up and needed a send-off to wish them luck. There were many weddings, as the pressure was on to make sure of a little happiness before an uncertain future. Births, christenings, anniversaries … and perhaps one should include the meals after funerals too.

In the summer of 1940 it was still possible to provide an almost normal menu for a gathering. *Woman* magazine of 1 June 1940 suggests a buffet meal for Party War Fare. Included were toast

Mrs Buggins' Brownie Party Cake. It is a plain fruit loaf, mixed with cold tea, festive enough for a celebration.

Jellies were prized for children's parties. Coffee frequently had a proportion of chicory added to it.

spread with home-made shrimp paste, Scotch eggs (eggs were not yet controlled), canned salmon set in aspic-type jelly (canned fish was not yet on points), liver rolls – a liver forcemeat rolled up in bacon (bacon was on the ration, liver was not, though it might be difficult to get). Chocolate Delight was dessert, made with plain chocolate not yet rationed, tinned condensed milk not yet on points, decorated with whipped cream and pistachio nuts (maybe from your store cupboard). Neapolitan sandwiches and Harlequins were savoury offerings.

Later on, no one household could provide all the food for children's parties, but co-operation was a great thing. One mother would promise some cupcakes, for instance, another would make the jelly, a third would bring along some neatly cut cucumber sandwiches, with plenty of salt and pepper to disguise the margarine. If the children themselves helped, as for instance in cutting out biscuit dough, so much the more exciting. Cakes were not rationed, so you could go along to a baker, such as Bexon's, for whatever they could offer. Mostly I remember rather plain and stodgy cakes, though in Cornwall there were always saffron buns, bright yellow and with a token amount of mixed peel included. (In order to make sure that bakers were doing their essential work of supplying bread, there was a mandatory simplification of cakes.)

A party was still possible even if a mother could not even provide a whole cake. The Buggins family, created by Mabel Constanduros, took up the idea in a *Kitchen Front* broadcast on 7 April 1942.[13] Grandma Buggins, a feisty eighty-year-old, her daughter Mrs Buggins and granddaughter Emma are in conversation. Emma has asked if she could invite some of her Brownie friends to tea. Mrs Buggins at first refuses, as she hasn't enough rations to make a cake. She can't buy any because money is short too. Then inspiration strikes:

Mrs. B:	… I tell you what we might do. 'Ow many Brownies do you want to arst?
Emma:	Well, there's Vi'let … and Heffie … and Shirley, … and Greta, and Marlene. Those are all the ones I like.
Mrs. B:	Well, we'll call it a Brownies Cake party, and all your Brownies can bring somethink towards it, and you shall make it. 'Ow'd that be?

Emma:	Oo, lovely, Mum. What do they 'ave to bring?
Mrs. B:	Well, there's 'alf a pound of National Wheatmeal flour, to start with.
Emma:	I better put it down. 'Alf a pound of flour. I'll arst Heffie for that. 'Er Mum always 'as 'eaps of flour, because she's Scotch, and makes 'er own bread.
Mrs. B:	3oz. of margarine and lard.
Emma:	3oz. … marge and lard … Vi'let can bring that, because 'er Mum lives out of tins and never does no cookin' so she can spare it.
Mrs. B:	'Alf a pound of dried fruit …
Emma:	'Alf a pound … Shirley's Mum's got some raisins. That's easy.
Mrs. B:	Three ounces of sugar. Can anyone spare that, d'you think?
Emma:	Three ounces! Greta and Marlene'll 'ave to manage that between them or I won't 'ave them to the party.
Mrs. B:	Well, that's ½lb. of flour 3oz. margarine and lard ½lb. of dried fruit. 3oz. of sugar I think I can manage all the rest myself. We shall want:- 1 teaspoon of cinnamon 1 teaspoon of baking powder 1 tablespoon of jam, or marmalade, or syrup or treacle A pinch of salt One cup of milk or cold tea.
G'ma:	I never 'eard of cold tea in a cake before.
Mrs. B:	It does very well if you 'aven't got the milk. Now, 'ere's 'ow you 'ave to make it Emma …

She goes on to say that first the fat is rubbed into the flour. Then the baking powder, jam or an alternative, the cinnamon, sugar, fruit and salt are added. It is mixed with the milk or tea, put in a greased tin and baked for one and a half hours at regulo 4 (gas) or 350°F.

It makes a good, plain cake, festive enough for a little girl's party, and simple enough for the child to make herself. Mrs Buggins was bringing up her daughter very well in spite of wartime conditions.

CHRISTMAS

The same kind of co-operation took place in schools. Muriel Gibson, who was a young teacher in Hartlepool at the end of the war, wanted to bake a cake for the children at Christmas. There were forty-eight pupils in her class at that time – or ninety-six if another teacher was absent. She sent a request home with each child to bring back anything the mother could spare. She had enough for her own mother to bake the cake, and still remembers what a big day it was when it was cut.

Earlier, hints from the Ministry about children's party food were given in one of their advertisements in December 1941: 'Let's talk about Xmas Food'.[14] As it said, there could only be 'simple treats, served gaily.' There were squares of parkin covered with a little melted chocolate, figures of animals or people like gingerbread men, cut from pastry or biscuit dough, and a chocolate icing made of cocoa, sugar and milk for the Christmas cake. For decoration you could dip holly into a strong solution of Epsom salts, which dried to a frosty sparkle. Instead of a bowl of fruit you could have a bowl of salad. 'Vegetables have such jolly colours – the cheerful glow of carrot, the rich crimson of beetroot, the emerald of parsley'. An open sandwich of raw vegetables with a sardine and a little cheese completed the party feast.

Clearly the home economists were doing their best to put on a brave show. I think that the children probably appreciated it. They too knew that there was a war on, and besides, at that time children were generally very much less sophisticated than they are today. There was certainly a great effort by mothers to make Christmas special. Parties complete with home-made cakes and biscuits, jellies and sandwiches were thought to be an essential part of childhood. At the end of the war there was a little extra confectionery at Christmas time for children, which also helped to make it festive.

Nevertheless substitutes often had to be used. For instance there were no ground almonds, so soya flour made a fairly creditable imitation almond paste for the Christmas cake. Some recipes for

Christmas cakes and puddings suggested dates or prunes in place of the usual currants, raisins or sultanas, and grated carrot helped to make the pudding sweet. Icing sugar was almost impossible to find, but you could make a frosting out of boiled sugar and egg white (if you had the egg).

In my childhood the neighbourhood party was one of the highlights of the year. It took place on Christmas Eve, in a community hall.[15] There were games to start with, such as pass the parcel, musical chairs, musical bumps and blind man's buff. Then came the tea, and afterwards an impressively costumed and cotton-wool-bearded Santa Claus called up each child to receive a present. As the sack emptied, the last ones became ever more anxious in case they were going to be left out, but none ever were.

I can also remember the home-made paper chains and party hats we constructed with great pride from left-over wallpaper and similar scraps. If we had decorated the house, perhaps a frugal Christmas lunch didn't matter too much.

Once the Americans landed, children's parties entered a different dimension.

OUR AMERICAN FRIENDS

Under the Lend Lease agreement, starting in 1941, Britain imported many American foods and other essential war materials. When America entered the war in her own right, Americans themselves arrived in this country in large and increasing numbers, preparing for the invasion of Europe. Camps for soldiers and airmen dotted the countryside, especially in East Anglia where there were many air bases. Towns and cities, particularly London, were full of off-duty men having a good time.

The WVS had set up 200 British Welcome Clubs for the servicemen. The American Red Cross set up some more. Meeting British families was encouraged. However, even though there were few language problems between the servicemen and their hosts, Britain was undoubtedly a foreign country. The Americans, though mostly welcome, had different habits and food preferences. Many were very young men who had not been abroad before. The same of course applied to the Canadian, New Zealand and other allied soldiers.

British families made an effort to make these visiting servicemen feel at home. Even Mrs Buggins invited a couple of Canadian soldiers to spend an evening with her and Grandma.[16] I do wonder if they visited her more than once though. They were to be offered 'scrap samwidges', filled with some chopped cooked vegetables including mashed potato, possibly a minced rasher and a few leftover bits from the Sunday joint. These 'samwidges' were then baked. The afters were bread and jam fritters – that is jam sandwiches dipped in a batter made from dried milk and dried egg powder, and then fried. As this was on 30 December 1941, perhaps there was enough New Year goodwill to make the evening a success.

Coffee could be a problem, as there was no strong tradition of good coffee in England at that time. Maybe the guest, having sampled the local variant, made a present of an American blend from the camp stores if he came again. Salads were comparatively easy, and there was a book tactfully written by Ambrose Heath, published in 1943, *Simple American Dishes in English Measures*.[17] They were still economy recipes of course. Baked Bean Soup and many other baked bean dishes, Potato Chowder, Fish Cakes Creole Fashion (using damp custard powder in place of egg to coat them with crumbs), and of course Apple Pie were all within the range of the British hostess.

Although the American authorities welcomed this hospitality, there was also caution, as they were aware of possible friction. They issued a booklet of *Instructions for American Servicemen in Britain 1942*.[18] One of the suggestions was that the G.I. should eat sparingly if he was invited to a meal. He might be consuming a family's entire weekly ration! Another was to avoid waste. After Lord Woolton's campaign to save even the outermost cabbage leaf, the contents of dustbins at American bases, or even the leftovers on plates, could give great offence. Waste represented lives lost at sea.

There did not seem to be any criticism of generosity though. The Americans were well supplied with their own rations (except possibly not enough liquor), and they were lavish with their gifts, which included cigarettes, bars of soap and the coveted nylon stockings which appealed enormously to girls at the glamorous age. Children learnt to ask for chewing gum, which was handed over with good humour, along with chocolate. Grace Bumphrey lived as a child in South Norfolk. 'The Americans were generous,' she said. 'They had plenty of sweets for the children. They came to the school to entertain us sometimes.'

Parties for children were high points, and they also held dances for local people. My sister was at a secretarial training college, which had been evacuated to the Cotswolds, in 1943. The Americans nearby sent transport to collect the girls, and deliver them safely back home. There were always very good refreshments as well as a party feeling in spite of careful chaperoning on the College side.

Quite a lot of American food seems to have found its way from the bases and camps into the local economy. Sometimes when the Americans moved on, they left supplies behind, as they did at Rosneath Castle in Scotland, which was handed over to the Royal Navy.[19] Civilians were employed at the various bases, and surplus stores were sometimes distributed, whether entirely legally or not it would be difficult to say now.

VICTORY STREET PARTIES

The official Victory in Europe Day – VE Day, was 8 May 1945. The war in the Far East did not finish until 15 August, VJ Day, after atomic bombs were dropped on Hiroshima and Nagasaki. Rejoicing was very properly muted. But VE Day was celebrated in various ways throughout the country, and people's memories of it vary accordingly. In towns there were parties held in the streets, especially for children. It was as if survivors wanted to mark the occasion in young minds as the time of the rebirth of hope. There were parties for adults too. A publication by the Age Exchange Theatre Trust gives many first-hand accounts and recollections of the celebrations. Here is one, for example:

> I remember the parties we had up Blackheath – Bonfires, baking potatoes in the old bonfire, everybody all dressed up in red, white and blue. It was fantastic. Dancing in the street. And somebody brought out a piano and was playing the old songs. We had long tables down the middle of the street and all the children sat outside. The food was whatever we could find, jellies, sandwiches, I don't know where

> we found the food from at the time, but we did. Everybody did. Everybody contributed a little bit towards the party.
> (Ladies Fellowship member, Christchurch, Greenwich.)[20]

Another writer, Tony Fawcett, remembers several different parties. She lived in Woolwich, where there was a bonfire at a junction of three streets.

> That was the start of the celebrations. Each street in the area started with a tea party for the children. Trestle tables covered with sheets, with long benches each side, were placed in the centre of the road, the traffic being diverted. Goodies that must have been hoarded for months appeared – sandwiches of all sorts, cakes, jellies, blancmanges – it could not have been from the black market, surely? Anyway, the children had a fantastic party in the afternoon. In the evening, it was the turn for us older people – I was well over fifteen at the time …
>
> Happily for us youthful types, the parties did not all occur on the same day. All we had to do was to look to see which street was having a stage erected, then we knew when and where the next one was to be. 'Hokey-cokey', 'Knees up Mother Brown', 'There'll always be an England', they all remind me of those far off days when I knew we wouldn't have to dive into the shelter again.[21]

One of my acquaintances was also involved in a street party. Her mother sent her to a neighbour with a jam jar of sugar for a cake to be made for the afternoon. She was a young child at the time, and tripped and fell. The precious sugar was spilt, the jar smashed. She realised what a dreadful thing she had done, so she went home, collected another jam jar and a dustpan and brush, swept up all the sugar she could find and delivered it to the right address. 'I nearly became a mass-murderer', she said. 'If the neighbour hadn't spotted the little bits of glass in the sugar …'

10

Austerity and Recovery

The war was over, but shortages and rationing were not. If anyone had expected a quick return to pre-war attitudes and plenty they were to be disillusioned. On 14 August a new Minister of Food, Sir Ben Smith, held a press conference. He told the nation that there was no hope that rationing could be improved quickly, though tomatoes, oranges and shell eggs might become more plentiful, and there was to be a new fish distribution scheme. Denmark was exporting bacon and eggs again, but not necessarily to Britain. Burmese rice would go first to Eastern people.

He warned that meat supplies would still be a problem. Corned beef would not be replaced by fresh meat, nor would there be any extra tinned meat. Bacon, oils and fats rations would not be increased. Sugar would need further restrictions, though he would not let it fall below half a pound a week. Fewer dried eggs would be compensated for by more shell eggs. The cheese ration was unlikely to be increased. He acknowledged that, 'This was not a cheerful picture, but it was right that the country should know the worst.' There was a tiny lick of good news however: ice cream prices would be controlled, and would not rise more than 50 per cent above their pre-war levels.[1] (The manufacture of ice cream had been banned in 1943 to save transport.)[2] The usual draconian penalties of withdrawal of ingredients would apply to profiteers.

It was not only the continuation of food rationing that seemed shabby. Everything was. The lights were on again, true, but travel was still difficult, so you couldn't go very far to enjoy them. Vast areas of cities were waste acres of rubble. Clothing, fuel and furniture were rationed, and the housing situation was desperate. The population of Britain was tired. How much this was a psychological reaction to years of strain and deferred hope, how much to years of adequate but boring food, is difficult to estimate. The potato factor might have had something to do with it.

Clothes were a particular problem for women. Rationing had started in 1941 and did not end until early 1949. Garments had been patched and darned, re-knitted and re-knitted again. Make-do-and-mend campaigns had called out ingenuity on the same scale as that needed to cope with food rationing. For example, a pre-war dress might have been converted to a skirt and bolero jacket, then into a little girl's skirt, then into a patchwork cushion cover. At this point it might go into the rag box for cleaning windows. The Utility clothing scheme had produced well-designed clothes, but using the minimum cloth. Skirts were knee-length without pleats, pockets scanty. The shortage of fabrics had affected not only fashions, but also household linens of all kinds. Bits of bathtowel were resurrected as teatowels, sheets turned sides-to-middle and back again. Essential blackout curtains were cut down for smaller windows.

Returning servicemen and prisoners of war brought problems with them, naturally. Many women had been used to independence. They had earned their own money, made their own decisions. Demobbed husbands often wanted restoration of pre-war home comforts and marital power. Prisoners of war had sometimes been severely undernourished, and needed not only reassurance but suitable good food. Women went back, often willingly, to domesticity, but sometimes the strain on marriages, which might have been rushed into, resulted in a divorce boom. Housewives were still, really, in the front line, but now official recognition became more muted. They were the most disadvantaged group too as far as food was concerned. If they were no longer working they were no longer eligible to eat in canteens, and restaurant meals were often too expensive. They had to make do on basic rations. With hungry menfolk and children at home they might not even get their fair share of these.[3]

There was no longer a naval blockade, so in theory the remaining merchant shipping could resume imports as they had before the war. But the countries of continental Europe on both sides of the conflict were shattered. Their infrastructure, agriculture and economies were ruined. They were desperate for such food as the world could direct there. There had been real starvation in the Netherlands, Germany and Russia for example.

As far as Britain was concerned, the bank looked as empty as grocers' shelves at the height of the war. There was little chance of buying much on world markets. In 1945 a new Labour government had swept away the Coalition under Winston Churchill. Social grievances of pre-war days could now get a reappraisal. Returning soldiers expected better conditions and better housing. But the war had to be paid for, and Britain had no reserves left. Lend Lease arrangements ended abruptly. The Americans had helped Britain to win the war in a military sense, but the new Labour government had come as a surprise to them. It seemed suspect and too much like Communism.

J.M. Keynes, perhaps the greatest economist of the time, took the case for financial help to America. He was a radical thinker, who had warned that the treatment of Germany after the First World War would lead to bitter feeling and further war. He was right, of course. But in 1945 he felt that America had a moral duty to help Britain, who had stood alone at the beginning of the conflict. However, President F.D. Roosevelt, our ally, had died just before the surrender of Germany, and America did not see it this way. Many thousands of their servicemen had perished. Their food had helped to save us from starvation. Surely that was enough, without free handouts to a socialist experiment?[4]

In the end there was a large loan of $4.34 bn, from America and Canada, but no grant. The interest was low at only 2 per cent, but some of the conditions led to financial difficulties, especially over the conversion of sterling to dollars. Again Britain was nearly bankrupt. It was only on 29 December 2006 that the final instalment was paid off. It should have been done in 2000, but there were six years when we had to defer payment.[5] On the other hand, just in time, the Marshall Plan of 1948 benefited Britain as well as the rest of Western Europe. It was designed to prevent the spread of Communism, and helped to reconstruct economies that had been ruined by the fighting.

Without the loan there could have been no Welfare State or moves towards social justice such as full employment, but all the same the country had to economise severely in the immediate post-war period. Austerity was part of socialist ideology in its commitment to fair shares and reconstruction of a better Britain. Yet without the obvious need to sacrifice a great deal for the sake of victory, it became increasingly unpopular. To tighten your belt for your country's very survival was one thing, to take it in another notch for a much more abstract dollar crisis was quite another. The supply and variety of foods fluctuated, with some things actually becoming scarcer than they had been in wartime. Restrictions were lifted slowly. Of course we were thankful when something reappeared on the grocer's shelf. (Number 35 of 57 varieties perhaps, or the return of our favourite biscuits.) But there was never a euphoric sense of sudden plenty.

Disillusion with the Labour government followed austerity, and it was then the turn of the Conservatives to come back to power in October 1951. The strategy of this government was to allow market forces more room to bargain, and food restrictions continued to ease, but rationing did not end completely until the summer of 1954, with meat and bacon coupon-free. It had been a long fourteen years.

Kitchen planning started to improve however. Even before the end of war the women's magazines were looking to the future, with, for example, *Good Housekeeping* running an article in 1943 about post-war design.[6] A more streamlined place was envisaged, with a double sink set into the continuous working surface, an electric cooker and plenty of wall-cupboards. After the war many more people acquired refrigerators. Gas and electric cookers were recognisably of modern design, no longer standing on four feet, but going down to the floor. You could get a simmerstat for an electric cooker and steel cabinets for storage. Formica made its appearance as an easily cleaned surface. I can also remember an effective pressure-cooker that was useful for bedsitter meals.

1945–1947

The years 1946 and 1947 were especially lean, as both bread and potatoes were rationed or controlled, but at least the drive to improve the health of children continued.

In July 1946 the Welfare (Foods) Scheme was renamed the Welfare Foods Service. Milk was reduced to 1½*d* a pint instead of 2*d* for children, compared with a standard 5*d* per pint. Cod liver oil and Vitamin A and D tablets were free instead of 10*d* per bottle or packet, and National Dried Milk for babies sold at 10½*d* instead of 1/2*d*. The government might have hoped that cod liver oil would go down better if it were free, but even this was not enough to make it popular. Orange juice was still usually 5*d* a bottle. For very needy

Coffee became more popular after the war.

families milk and orange juice might be free too. In 1949 Vitamin A and D tablets were free to every mother for thirty weeks after the birth. The government was really trying to make a difference!

From 1942 to August 1946 all schoolchildren could have 1/3 pint milk on school days at a halfpenny per bottle. From that time onwards it was free, until 1968 for older children, and 1971 for those in primary schools.

Non-residential nurseries were also eligible for Welfare foods in addition to the children's usual home ration. In August 1947 disabled children not attending school were entitled to a pint of milk a day at 1½*d* a pint.

Milk from tuberculin-tested herds was available and from 1947 customers could register with different milkmen to get it. Proprietary infant milk formula was restricted to children under two years from October 1947 to April 1950, or to children under one from April 1948 to October 1949. This was to prevent its being bought up for general use. It could be obtained as an alternative to the government issue, but was not provided at the cheap rate. (If you wanted something more upmarket you had to pay for it.)

Household milk – that is dried skimmed milk – was shifted onto the points' scheme in the summer of 1946, and became uncontrolled in the spring of 1947. It had been a valuable standby when liquid milk was short.

Dried eggs were on points, but mothers and children under five had one packet free of points every eight weeks, equivalent to a dozen shell eggs.

Meat

Men were generally dissatisfied with the amount of meat available, but that was tough! The ordinary ration was at its lowest from 1947 to 1949, being only 1/- worth per adult head, and this sometimes included a proportion of corned beef. However, an extra shilling's worth was allowed to coalminers at the end of 1946.[7] As meat prices had increased it was not as generous as it seemed. The rest of us could try the whalemeat then on sale. Whales are mammals, and the flesh looks somewhat like beef. It was an acquired taste though, which many people did not acquire, asserting that it tasted fishy. Concern about the ethics of whaling came much later.

Bread

All during the war there had been no limit to the amount of bread you could buy, though it had to be the National Loaf from March 1942. But there was a world shortage of cereals during 1946, so bread was rationed from July. It was not de-rationed until July 1948. The coupons were named bread units, and were cut out by the shopkeeper. You could buy the bread anywhere and did not have to register.

Unlike ordinary rationing, entitlement varied. A child under four got five units a week, and from four to eleven years, and ordinary adults, nine. Adolescents were recognised as hungry and needing more, so they got thirteen units. Expectant mothers and female manual workers had eleven units, and a male manual worker fifteen, though workers who had the extra cheese ration had an additional six units a week. (There had to be some sandwich round the cheese.) Nine units translated into a couple of large loaves each weighing 1lb 12oz and 7oz of rolls. Flour was included in the bread ration, so for the first time you had to go easy on home baking as well. Flour confectionery was also included.

For those people who did not eat a lot of bread, it was not a bad time, as the units could be exchanged for points, at first one for one, then reduced to two bread units for one point. This must have been too popular, putting strain on the points system, so later you could exchange points for bread units, one for one, but not the other way round.

As far as points themselves were concerned, the allowance had risen to twenty-four per person per month in the spring of 1944, but fell back to twenty in 1945, rising again to twenty-four in March 1946. In July there was a further increase, to thirty-two points.

Potatoes

The winter of 1946–47 had been exceptionally severe – the sea froze in places, and in Cornwall I can remember snow, usually unknown there at that time. The potato crop failed in 1947, so potatoes were controlled during the autumn and winter, until the spring of 1948. Northern Ireland escaped, however. Ordinary adults could buy up to 3lb a week, or half that for children under five years. Expectant mothers could get 4½lb, but weekly seamen seemed to be a special case, and could get 7lb. Potato Pete made a discreet exit.

Instant mashed potato was one of the modest heralds, instead, of the convenience foods to come once the famine was over.

Bananas

These began to be imported again. You did not have to register, but sales were restricted to expectant mothers, children under eighteen, and later to old people too. You could only buy half a pound for the first three days, but if there were any left you could get more, if you were the right age. I remember going to get mine with excitement, as they were an epicurean delicacy for children. 'How did you have yours?' 'Banana custard.' 'Banana flan.' 'I ate mine whole …' Perhaps if they had not been scarce they would not have seemed so special. The distinction between gourmet and common foods depends a lot on how rare and expensive they are.

Soap

Not having enough soap remained an irritation. The ration was reduced in June 1946 until 1949,[8] when it was restored to the previous level, though it was available for industrial wash-places in 1948. (Soap rationing ended in 1950.)

Soap was also rationed. Laundry starch was hard to get, but 'dip' was a post-war alternative.

Alcohol

Drinks were definitely coming back. A compilation of recipes from *Vogue* magazine, 1945–47,[9] carried advertisements for a Cotswold Vintage Cider and Perry Wine (made from pears), Cognac, Sherry, Brandy, Jamaica Rum, Hennesy Brandy, Booth's and Gordon's Gin, Real Orange Juice (bottled) and Angostura Aromatic Bitters. The latter was not only for pink gin, the pre-war cocktail, but could be used to flavour prunes, as a nightcap with hot milk, and as an addition to soups, gravies, dressings, even sweet dishes such as ice cream and grapefruit. (If your grapefruit needed jazzing up, that must have been available too.) Empire wines are advertised, and supplies were growing, so that you could once again choose wine to complement your meal. There are some good recipes for drinks in the book text as well.

1948–1949

At last milk was supplied in unrestricted quantities in the spring to domestic consumers and establishments. (Completely unrestricted in 1950.)

All remaining preserves were de-rationed in December 1948. They had been emerging slowly for some time. As bread had also been de-rationed in July of this year, the bread-and-jam meal was now available in plenty. (Jam today *and* jam tomorrow!)

Snoek came in at only two points a tin in May 1948, and made a quick getaway at the start of 1950. It was caught in Australian waters, but never caught on here. It is like a predatory fish, barracuda or barracouta, which was also marketed in January 1949, at two points a time, but only lasted on points until September.

Most cereals and cereal products came off points during 1948. Sago and tapioca were now freely available to make milk puddings, for instance. I can remember my school dinners in this year, when even the staff referred to tapioca as 'paperhangers' paste'. This was a pity, because if made carefully it is not at all bad – or not all bad. Only the lumps. It was greatly improved with the newly de-rationed jam.

Home-produced canned fruit no longer required points to buy them, perhaps because no foreign currency was involved.

Even *paté de foie* could be spread around – well, perhaps.

Dried eggs on points were suspended from January 1949 for ordinary customers, and from February 1950 for priority ones. The dried eggs had dried up! But fresh eggs were often not very fresh either, and there still weren't all that many. The Ministry's recipes for baking without eggs were needed more than ever.

Imported quick frozen pre-cooked meat meals appeared on the list of point-bearing foods until February 1950, when they came off. Frozen foods were to become part of the convenience foods revolution as households began to acquire freezers as well as refrigerators. (It was not until 1993 though that most people had a freezer at home.)[10]

Many imported cheeses were free of points too. A cheese board could now appear on the table, and 'cheese' was no longer a synonym for 'cheddar'. The main cheese ration remained, however.

Pulses such as dried peas, beans, lentils and split peas had always had low points values, because they were a valuable source of protein, and satisfying as well. They came off points altogether in April 1949.

Also in April 1949 sweets were de-rationed, but demand was too great and they reverted to 16oz per month in August.

1950–1954

Points rationing was finally abolished on 19 May 1950. This was real progress, though goods had gradually been trickling back, with corresponding lifting of points.

From now on you could buy biscuits of all kinds, including chocolate ones, canned fish such as pilchards and sardines, canned fruit, canned meat, poultry and rabbit, meat loaf and meat roll, just for money. Canned milk was available, and many people used evaporated milk, that is unsweetened condensed milk, in place of cream. Baked beans, the students' standby, which had taken up eight points in 1947, were now there to fall off the toast in abundance.

Dried fruit had been restricted since 1942, but now you could make your Christmas cake and pudding, your Simnel cake, birthday or wedding cake to pre-war recipes if you wished. Shredded and flaked suet, syrup and treacle were available too, which meant that steamed puddings continued to haunt the waistlines of a post-war generation.

The 5/- limit for food charges on restaurant meals was abolished.

In 1951 the successful Festival of Britain was held, which was to commemorate and emulate the Great Exhibition of 1851. It was rather like the Millenium, complete with a Dome (of Discovery), and a cigar-shaped 'skylon' held up by thin cables. (Just like Britain, without visible means of support, went the saying.) The Festival brought welcome tourists back to London. Rationing had no major changes in this year, but in 1952 tea was de-rationed.

The year 1953 saw the year of the coronation of Queen Elizabeth II. It was, many believed, the start of a new era of hope and renewal. Certainly February 1953 was a red-letter month – no, a golden month – for the children of Britain. Sweets came off the ration for the second time, and, provided pocket money was sufficiently generous, there was no longer an agonising choice to be made between, say, a bar of chocolate or a bag of humbugs. Scarcity had made confectionery seem very special and desirable. Sweets had sometimes been used as currency in the playground. Now you could have it all … It was a pity about tooth decay, but the NHS had dentists available at that time.

In fact 1953 was a good year. In March eggs were no longer controlled, and were comparatively easy to find. In April the dairy industry was able to sell cream once more, and in September sugar was de-rationed.

It was in May 1954, with the spring flush of milk on farms, when the fat famine ended. Cheese, butter, margarine and cooking fat were de-rationed. Baking could be resumed at pre-war levels, and there was an explosion of fancy cakes. Finally on 5 July you could actually go to a butcher and order what you wanted. You no longer had to make do with the more peculiar parts of the anatomy of food animals. Beef cattle produced steak, not merely oxtail, you could get a whole leg of lamb and pig meat implied more than sausages or bacon.

CONSEQUENCES OF RATIONING

Rationing during the war was perceived as successful and fair by most people. There had been a national team effort to prevent hunger. The planners had done their job, the merchant seamen had done theirs at great personal cost and the machinery of control and distribution had worked pretty well. Information for housewives was, as Mrs Buggins remarked, in even greater supply than food itself. No doubt many women were encouraged to cook better, and to take pride in putting the best meals possible in front of their families. The health of children had been safeguarded, and nutrition for poorer people was better during the war than it had been beforehand. Poverty on the pre-war scale and food deprivation were no longer acceptable politically. The Welfare State had emerged.

But wartime food seemed monotonous to many and insufficient for some. The emphasis on bread and potatoes was wearisome. Standards had been raised for the poor, but reduced for the affluent. White bread was welcomed back. Protein foods in particular were longed for, and when the opportunity arose there was a return to richer cookery. Eggs had been especially missed, as they are integral to so many dishes both sweet and savoury. There was a desire for cream, for fruit and novel ingredients. Foreign food too was welcomed. There had been a cautious attempt to introduce a few dishes from abroad on the *Kitchen Front* broadcasts, with housewives from France, China, Sweden, Canada and so on giving simple versions of national dishes. The presence of allied forces from Europe and the Commonwealth, and from America, had suggested to ordinary people that different flavours and dishes could be exciting.

The demand for new foods coincided with the rise of supermarkets. Only ten self-service stores were known in Britain in 1947.[11] Through the 1950s and 1960s they proliferated. Shopping was easier and quicker, if more expensive. Holidays abroad and immigrant workers at home both influenced the goods on offer. For instance red and green peppers, yoghurt and sweet potatoes were all newcomers post-war.

Frozen foods expanded enormously in scope and appeal, and so did ready meals, as women took up employment again outside the home. The TV dinner made its appearance. Television itself presented food programmes, with Marguerite Patten and Philip Harben as pioneers in the medium.

A FEW COOKERY BOOKS

Cookery books published during the war were inevitably devoted to making the most of rationed foods, and those off-rationed things that you might be lucky enough to find – like offal, sausages and fish.

In the immediate post-war period the books still showed the influence of food rationing and shortages of course, though Josephine Terry's *Cook-Happy*, 1945[12] gave suggestions for better times, enhancing the austerity recipes with extra sugar, cream, using fresh eggs instead of dried, butter in place of margarine and even luxuries like tinned truffles.

In the *Vogue* book mentioned above (1947), many of the names of the dishes are in French, but most ingredients are still on the economy side. There is a *Potage Monte Carlo*, for instance, made with fresh or household milk, dried egg, seasoning and curry powder, all made into a savoury custard and poured over fried croûtons.

The need for improvisation had led to meals being assembled with whatever happened to be in the larder or, by now, in the refrigerator. The main meal of many courses had gone for good in most homes. Vegetables could become a course in their own right. Our old friend the potato was hanging on in curious disguises, including a chocolate potato cake without eggs. Salads and home-grown fruit were still much praised, including an unusual tomato jam. (My mother had a recipe for this as well.)

Nell Heaton and André Simon were well-known cookery writers before the war – André Simon was a wine expert. Their book *A Calendar of Food and Wine* was published in 1949.[13] There is one recipe for eggless cake in which saccharin may be substituted for sugar, but apart from that the eggs, butter, cream, beef, lamb and cheese ooze out of the delicious pages.

Perhaps a real turning point came in 1950, when Elizabeth David published her first work, *A Book of Mediterranean Food*. It described the dishes of the seaboard countries where she had lived and collected recipes at first hand. The basic ingredients of olive oil, wine, garlic, onions, tomatoes, herbs and spices were combined with fish, meat, eggs and vegetables in ways that were new. This was exotic and exciting cookery. In 1950 some of her ingredients were still difficult to get, but by the time the second edition was published in 1955 they were all available somewhere in Britain. Elizabeth David became a household name with her subsequent books which included *French Country Cooking* and *Italian Food*. Good food was not overly elaborate any more, but based on fresh ingredients that brought the sun into the kitchen. Britain was ready for a world cuisine.

CONCLUSION

'Food is a Munition of War' declared the posters, but this is not strictly true. What is true is that deprivation of food is a weapon of mass destruction – starving your enemy is just as effective as blowing him up. Food is life. Britain had entered the war in many ways unprepared, but when committed made heroic efforts to feed herself and make the most of what she had.

Has this any relevance for today? I think it has. Everyone now knows about global warming, a change in the world's circumstances now established beyond a doubt. Hoping for the best, as Britain did in the 1930s, is likely to lead to an even more threatening outcome. It would do no harm to see what we could do by applying *some* of the methods of co-operation and control that we used in the Second World War. It is hopeful that a number of things are being done already.

Salvage drives, for instance, are now called recycling. We do not need as much packaging as we use and waste. It would be silly to go back to wrapping the fish (from depleted stocks) in old newspaper, but equally it does not need to be in a plastic tray, which is then wrapped in clingfilm and taken away from the supermarket in a plastic carrier bag. There is a campaign at present to re-use the plastic, but we might start a fashion for strong, light string bags again.

Aluminium saucepans are no longer needed for Spitfires, but the cans and foil we use are being recycled, and so are paper, cardboard, glass and clothing.

Fuel needs saving now more than ever, both to conserve world stocks and reduce greenhouse gases. In our own kitchens we could follow the old advice on making best use of the cooker, and plan meals carefully. How about a modern hay box?

Where food itself is concerned, the principles behind rationing and food distribution were 'green'. Imports were reduced as much as possible, and waste regarded as criminal. This compares with the 33 per cent of bought food we now throw away.[14] Local produce was distributed locally if possible. People grew far more of their own food than we do today. We wouldn't want to dig up the remaining school playing fields, but we could do more to import less. As a small example it might be possible to put strawberry plants among the roses, enjoy the fruit in its proper season and avoid flying it in all the year round from warmer countries.

We could take more notice of the rules of nutrition. As in 1939, many children are poorly nourished. They are not half-starved any more, but they are not particularly well fed either. The recent campaign by Jamie Oliver suggests that school meals could benefit by a consideration of past practice.

Wartime advice was not always good. For instance the margarine provided was high in saturates, which we would avoid today. But we eat too much sugar and maybe not enough wholemeal bread. Potatoes are fine in moderation. No, I don't want to have them at every meal. But we might remember how many acres of land are needed to produce meat, in contrast to the amount of wheat or oatmeal that the same acreage will supply.

I have tried in this book to give a taste of what it felt like to live under food shortages and rationing at a critical time in our history. With hindsight we know we came through it with some dignity, a lot of ingenuity, and a respect for the rights of our neighbours. Now, looking at the future, we do not know what will happen. We will have to write the next chapter for ourselves.

11

Representative Recipes

The best wartime recipes were obviously not gourmet fare, but looked back to an economical tradition.

Here are a few that may still be useful today, while being faithful to the past. There is no point though in replicating the extremes of austerity, nor to repeat basic dishes which are well known. Authentic wartime dishes included plain stews, baked fish and fish pies, meat and fruit pies, pasties, fruit crumbles, scones, plain vegetable soups, milk puddings, steamed sponge and suet puddings, lots of cornflour-based custard, yeast buns, plain cakes and biscuits etc.

The ingredients have changed somewhat. Margarine is better and healthier than it was. Many people now prefer semi-skimmed liquid milk, but as with eggs, there is no need for dried. Flour can be wholemeal or plain white with a proportion of wholemeal to imitate the wartime kind, if you are going for a 1940s' experience. There was more salt and sugar than we might think necessary. But of course, war or not, the cook always makes the decision about what will taste good.

BEETROOT SOUP

Serves at least 4

Adapted from wartime leaflet on uses of soya flour. Soya was versatile, being used to thicken and enrich soups, stews, cakes, pastry, and vegetarian dishes.

8oz (250g) raw beetroot, peeled weight, grated
1 cooking apple, peeled and grated

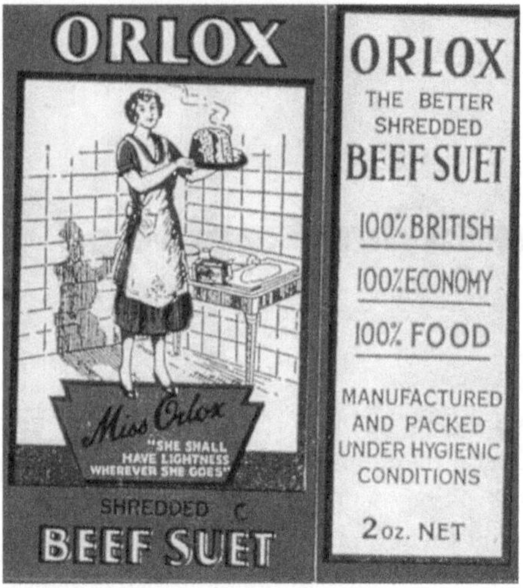

Packaging was kept to a minimum, and housewives were urged to put cardboard and paper out for salvage. Suet puddings had been a standby before the war and continued to be liked, though some of the other uses of suet don't look very appealing today.

1 pint (550ml) vegetable stock or water
Seasoning
1 teaspoon sugar
1 teaspoon vinegar
1oz (30g) soya flour
Sour milk, soured cream or yoghurt to finish

Simmer the beetroot, apple, seasoning to taste, sugar and vinegar together in ¾ of the liquid for thirty minutes. Tip the lid or the pan will boil over. Mix the soya with the rest of the liquid and stir into the soup when the beetroot and apple are cooked. Simmer for another ten minutes, stirring occasionally.

To serve, put into bowls and add a swirl of yoghurt etc. The wartime recipe used sour milk. This soup is a distant relation of the classic Russian bortsch.

SARDINE ROLLS

Makes about 4 rolls
Source: *Kitchen Front*: a recipe sent in by Miss Parke.[1] Adapted.

Beetroot soup, with added sour milk or (nowadays) yoghurt.

1 small can sardines in oil
4 tablespoons flour to each tablespoon of oil in the can
A little salt and 3 teaspoons water to 4 tablespoons flour.

Open the sardines, drain off the oil and measure it. Combine it with flour and salt in the proportion given, mix with the water to make pastry. Roll out to an oblong, and divide into as many pieces as there are sardines. Wrap each fish in pastry like a sausage roll, seal the join with a little water, slash the top once or twice with a sharp knife and bake in a hot oven, reg. 6 or 400°F for fifteen to twenty minutes. Eat hot or cold. Good with salad.

FISHCAKES

Serves 4

A general recipe to make almost any fish go further. Leftover baked or freshly cooked fish may be used, including salted haddock or cod, or drained canned fish such as pilchards or pink salmon.

8–10oz (250g or more) cooked fish, flaked
1oz (30g) fresh breadcrumbs
2–3oz (60–90g) well-mashed cooked potato
1 teaspoon chopped parsley, or other herbs to taste
Seasoning and a large pinch of ground nutmeg
1 egg, beaten
Milk or water if necessary
Egg and crumbs to coat, optional
Fat to fry, optional

Combine the ingredients, using a little extra milk or water if needed to make the mixture easy to shape. Form into eight equal flat cakes. If you like, these may then be dipped in more beaten egg and coated in crumbs, or the fishcakes may be left plain (as in wartime).

They may be shallow fried in a little fat, or baked in a fairly hot oven, reg. 6 or 400°F for about twenty minutes.

SPAM FRITTERS

Serves 4

For the batter:
4oz (100g) plain flour
1 dessertspoon wholemeal flour
1 egg
¼ pint (125ml) milk
Seasoning
8 thin slices of Spam dusted with plain flour
Fat or oil for frying

Sift flour into a bowl with a little salt and pepper, stir in the wholemeal and make a well in the middle. Drop in the egg and a little milk, and stir and gradually draw the flour into the liquid, adding more to make a smooth thick batter as you go. Beat well.

Heat a little fat in a large frying pan. Dip floured slices of Spam into the batter and drop into the pan. Turn when cooked on the first side and continue to cook until golden brown. Serve at once.

MOCK DUCK

Serves 4–6
Source: *Kitchen Front* : 'Your idea' – a listener's recipe.[2] Adapted.

1 fairly large onion or 2 leeks
1 rounded teaspoon dried sage or to taste
1 lb (450 g) sausage meat
1 lb 4 oz (550 g) peeled weight potatoes
Seasoning for potatoes
Gravy made with potato and onion water, and gravy powder.

Boil onions or leeks, previously chopped, in a little water. Strain and keep the water. Mix the onions with the sage. Boil and mash the potatoes, reserving liquid. Put layers of sage and onion, sausage meat, and potatoes into an ovenproof dish. Season the potatoes as you go and finish with potatoes.

Make some gravy with commercial gravy powder (such as Bisto), using the saved potato and onion waters.

Press down, make large holes with a skewer through the layers, pour over some of the gravy and bake in a fairly hot oven for an hour, reg. 5 or 375°F. The gravy will make it look similar to the roast skin of a duck (with a bit of imagination). Serve with more gravy.

It must be well baked to make sure the sausage meat is cooked through.

CORNED BEEF HASH

Serves 4
This is more of an idea than a recipe. The principle is to make the most of corned beef by mixing it with cooked potato and frying the result until at least some of the potato is appetisingly browned. Flavouring such as onions and herbs may be added to taste. Some people mixed the brown bits of potato into the rest as it cooked, others preferred to leave a thick brown crust undisturbed until serving. Quantities varied too. You just used whatever corned beef you could spare.

1 medium/large onion, diced
1oz (30g) fat
1¼lb (550g) cooked potato, diced. Or boil diced potatoes from raw
1 can corned beef (340g), diced
2 tablespoons water or milk
A pinch or two of dried thyme or other herbs to taste, optional
Seasoning – not much salt as the corned beef probably has enough

Fry the onion gently in the fat, using a large pan, until golden brown. Lightly mix in the diced potato and corned beef, together with the liquid, herbs and seasoning. Leave on low heat to brown on the bottom. Stir lightly from time to time if you like. Serve hot with a green vegetable. It may be rather dry for your taste, so you could serve with a brown or tomato sauce.

CORNED BEEF AND ONION SAUCE

Serves 4

No formal recipe is needed for this. Just make an onion sauce with plenty of sliced onions, say two or three, sautéed in 2oz (60g) of margarine, plus 2oz (60g) of flour and a pint of milk (550ml) with plenty of pepper and a little salt. When the sauce is thick stir in a can of corned beef cut into chunks, heat through and serve in a border of mashed potato. Garnish with watercress or parsley.

CORNED BEEF ON TOAST

Serves 4

Source: MoF early *Food Facts* advertisement found between pages of an old cookery book. Adapted.

1oz (30g) cooking fat
2 level teaspoons curry powder
¼ level teaspoon paprika pepper
Pinch of cayenne pepper
A little made mustard

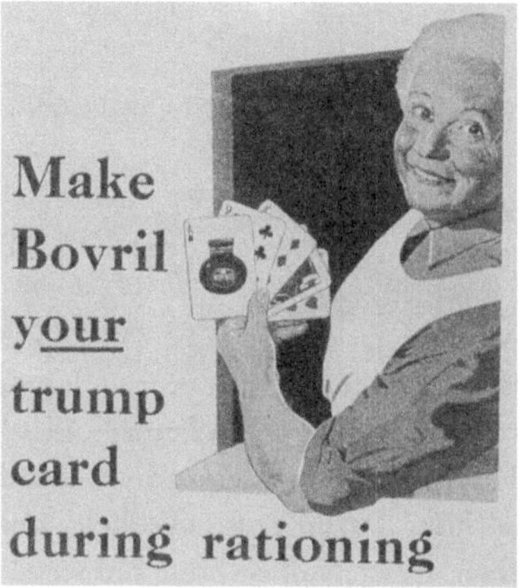
Make
Bovril
your
trump
card
during rationing

'Make Bovril your trump card'. Monotony was one of the problems of wartime cookery. Anything such as Bovril, Marmite, herbs, spices and bottled sauces helped to make boring foods more appetising.

Pinch of pepper
2 level tablespoons flour
6 tablespoons water
6oz (175g) corned beef, broken up with a fork

4 rounds of toast, spread with butter or margarine, to serve

Melt the fat, mix in all the seasonings and flour. Cook, stirring, for two minutes. Add water slowly, stirring, then simmer for two or three minutes until thick. Stir in the corned beef and heat through. Serve hot on toast.

RAGOUT OF BEEF

Serves 4–5
Source: *Kitchen Front* broadcast, given by 'A French Housewife'.[3] She said it was 'really only a stew, with a few extra touches.'

2oz (60g) margarine or cooking fat
1½lb (700g) any cheap cut of beef
2 onions or leeks 'if you can get them'
1 level tablespoon flour

About 1 pint (550ml) vegetable stock or water
Salt, pepper
A bunch of sweet herbs, tied together: thyme, bay leaf, parsley and fennel 'If you've got it'
1lb (450g) carrots, sliced across
1½lb (700g) potatoes, peeled or scrubbed

Melt the fat in a large pan, cut up the meat and onions and brown them. Add flour. Stir, cover with liquid. Add seasoning and a bunch of herbs which we in France call a 'bouquet Garni'. Cook on low heat for three-quarters of an hour. Add carrots, cook for another half an hour. Put in potatoes whole unless very big. Cook for another three-quarters of an hour and serve.

This is a good idea to save washing up. The meal is cooked in one big pan (or casserole) and needs only perhaps a salad on the side or a large amount of chopped parsley to garnish.

CHEESE AND SEMOLINA RISSOLES

Serves 4
Source: MoF leaflet No.29 *Meals without Meat* April 1946.[4] Adapted.

2oz (60g) semolina
½ pint (300 ml) water
3oz (90g) grated cheese
1 teaspoon salt
Pinch powdered mace
A few grains of cayenne pepper
Batter for coating made with 4 level tablespoons flour and 4 tablespoons water
Dried breadcrumbs (½ teaspoon of dried herbs is a good addition)

Mix the semolina to a paste with a little of the water. Boil the rest and pour onto the paste, stirring. Return to pan and cook for five minutes, stirring frequently. Add the cheese and seasonings, mix well and turn onto a plate to cool.

When cold divide the mixture into four large or eight small

portions and shape into rissoles (cork shapes), or leave in triangles. Coat with the batter, roll in breadcrumbs and bake on a well-greased baking sheet for twenty minutes in a hot oven.

This is economical with fat, as the rissoles are baked rather than deep-fried.

CHEESE PUDDING

Serves 4

Source: MoF War Cookery Leaflet No.11 (*Dried Eggs*).

Though this recipe was intended for dried eggs, it is still quick to make and thrifty. It is almost like a cheese soufflé.

½ pint (300ml) milk
1 teacupful of breadcrumbs about 1oz (30g)
2–3oz (60–90g) grated Cheddar or other hard cheese
Salt and pepper,
¼ level teaspoon made mustard
2 eggs, beaten

Boil the milk, stir in the crumbs, remove from heat and add cheese, salt, pepper and mustard, and beaten eggs. Pour into a greased pie dish and bake in a moderate oven, reg. 4 or 350°F for thirty to forty minutes, or until set and risen. Serve at once, with a green salad perhaps.

POTATO FLODDIES

To make 8

This is adapted from an early *Food Facts*, probably No.24 of Jan 1941.[5]

6oz (175g) grated raw potato.
Approx. 2oz (60g) plain flour to bind
Seasoning, including cayenne for savoury version
Herbs to taste for savoury version
Fat to fry (this would have been dripping in wartime)

Mix flour with the freshly grated potato, seasoning and herbs if used to make a soft mixture that can be spooned into a frying pan with a little preheated fat in it. Press out with the spoon to make thin cakes like drop scones.

Fry gently until golden brown on both sides, turning from time to time. They can be served with jam, but are very good in the savoury version. Any herbs and seasonings can be added to taste.

'WARTIME CHAMP'

Serves at least 4
Source: *Food Facts* No.28.[6]
A good filler that gets the potatoes and veg. done in a single pan. Said to be an old Irish dish.

> Scrub and slice 1lb potatoes and 1lb carrots [500g each]. Put in a saucepan with a teacupful of hot salted water and add a small cabbage finely shredded. Cover with the lid, cook steadily, giving an occasional shake, until tender (about 15 minutes) … add a small teacupful of hot milk and mash well with … pepper and salt if necessary. Serve at once with a pat of margarine to each helping.

WOOLTON PIE

One 8-inch pie, serves four
Another generic name for a vegetable pie to fill a hungry gap. It was said to have been invented by a chef at the Savoy Hotel, but seasonal variants were inevitable.

1lb (500g) approx. mixed vegetables cut into bite-sized pieces – e.g. a selection such as carrots, turnips, swedes, cauliflower, broccoli, leeks (but save potatoes for the topping)
½ pint (300ml) brown or cheese sauce
Topping (1) Potato Pastry 4oz (125g) wholemeal flour
2oz (60g) margarine or cooking fat

Potato Floddies. These could be either savoury or sweet.

1 level teaspoon baking powder
Pinch salt
2oz (60g) cooked potatoes, sieved
Water to mix

Or *Topping (2)* Mashed potato
A little grated cheese or margarine

Wash and cut the vegetables into bite-sized pieces. Cook briefly in salted water. Put in a greased pie dish.

Prepare a savoury sauce or gravy. Cheese sauce is good, but a brown sauce, home-made or otherwise will do. Pour over the vegetables and mix in.

Make pastry like ordinary shortcrust, but adding the potatoes to the rubbed-in mixture before binding with water.

Cover the pie with rolled-out pastry, flake the edge with a knife and make scallops. Slash the pie in several places to allow steam to escape. Glaze with a little milk. Bake in hot oven, reg. 6 or 400°F for about twenty-five to thirty minutes, until brown.

Or cover the pie with well-seasoned mashed potato, smooth and make a pattern with a knife, sprinkle with a little cheese or dot with margarine. Brown under the grill or in oven.

STEAMED JAM PUDDING

Serves 6

This pudding comes from a MoF Leaflet, *Puddings without eggs.*[7]

Muriel Gibson mentioned steamed puddings like these served up for dinner when she was at a teacher training college during 1941–43. There were six to a table, who shared a huge pudding between them. 'It might be ginger, currant or chocolate, with custard or sauce.'

The pudding is a useful economy recipe, quick to prepare, and can be varied in several different ways as well as by using different jams. Cook it in a saucepan with water coming halfway up the sides of the basin, or in the top of a steamer. (Don't let the water boil dry.)

8oz (250g) self-raising flour or 8oz plain flour and 4 level teaspoons baking powder
Pinch of salt
2oz (60g) margarine or cooking fat
2oz (60g) sugar
Just over ¼ pint (150ml) milk or milk and water
3 tablespoons jam

Mix the flour, baking powder if used, and salt together. Rub in the margarine or cooking fat and add the sugar. Mix with the milk or milk and water. Grease a basin, 1½ or 2 pint size (1 litre capacity), and put the jam at the bottom. Add the mixture, cover and steam for 1½ hours. In the war this would have been served with custard or a flavoured cornflour sauce.

Variations

1. Marmalade. Use marmalade instead of jam.
2. Chocolate. Omit jam. Increase sugar to 2½–3 oz (80g). Add 3–4 tablespoons cocoa with the sugar. Add a little vanilla essence with the liquid.
3. Mixed Fruit. Omit the jam. Add 1 level teaspoon mixed spice and 3oz (90g) dried fruit with the sugar.

Woolton Pie. This version is made from vegetables with a wholemeal and potato pastry on top.

4. Ginger. Omit the jam. Add 3 level teaspoons ground ginger with the flour etc., and 1 tablespoon syrup with the liquid.

BAKED FRUIT PIE

Serves 4

An adaptation of a standard fruit pie, using bread, rather like a fruit charlotte.[8]

Vary the amount of sugar used according to the fruit. If it is already sweetened you may not need any more.

2lb (900g) fruit, bottled or fresh
Sugar to taste
1 pint (full ½ litre measure) of bread cubes, cut neatly from left over pieces
3 tablespoons milk
2 tablespoons sugar

If fresh fruit is used, stew it and sweeten to taste. Put the fruit and juice in a pie dish. Cover with the cubes of bread. Pour the milk over the bread and sprinkle on the sugar. Bake in a hot oven for twenty to thirty minutes.

It is particularly good with soaked and cooked dried apricots.

SPECIAL PLUM PUDDING

Serves 4

Source: The same *Puddings without eggs* leaflet as above. Adapted slightly.

This is a creditable stand-in for a Christmas pudding. Like many wartime MoF recipes you might reduce the sugar, as it contains dried fruit as well as naturally sweet carrots.

8oz (250g) grated raw potato
6oz (200g) grated raw carrot
4oz (125g) plain flour
1 teaspoon salt
2–4 oz (60–120g) sugar
1 teaspoon bicarbonate of soda
1 teaspoon ground nutmeg
1 teaspoon ground cinnamon
10–12oz (300–350 g) mixed dried fruit
3oz (90g) melted dripping or margarine

Prepare and grate the vegetables. Mix all the dry ingredients together, add the fruit and vegetables and, lastly, the melted dripping. Put into a greased basin, 2 pint (1 litre) size and cover with greased paper or a lid. Steam for three to four hours.

Note. This pudding keeps only for two to three days. 'It makes a delicious rich tasting pudding with no trace of carrot or potato flavour.'

BLACKBERRY OR ELDERBERRY ROLY POLY

Source: MoF *Hedgerow Harvest* Leaflet.[9] Adapted.

Another traditional type of recipe.

For the pastry: ¾oz (20g) margarine or cooking fat
6oz (180g) self-raising flour, or 6oz plain and 3 level teaspoons baking powder
Milk to mix – about 6 tablespoons
8oz (250g) prepared blackberries or elderberries
3 level tablespoons sugar
½ teaspoons cinnamon
2 tablespoons syrup
1oz (30g) margarine
¼ pint (150ml) water
½ teaspoon lemon essence, or better, a little grated lemon zest

Rub margarine into flour. Mix to soft dough with milk. Roll out to oblong. Mix fruit, sugar and cinnamon and spread over pastry. Damp edges, roll up and seal the edges. Put in a pie dish. Warm syrup, margarine, water and lemon slightly. Pour over roll. Bake in hot oven about thirty minutes.

BOILED CAKE

This was a wartime family recipe. It must date from an eggless period, but you wouldn't guess that just by tasting it, as it is moist and rich. Quick to prepare too.

¼ pint water (150ml)
4oz (125g) raisins or sultanas
4oz (125g) sugar, demerara if possible
4oz (125g) margarine
8oz (250g) plain flour
1 level teaspoon mixed spice
¼ level teaspoon ground cloves
1 level teaspoon bicarbonate of soda
½ level teaspoon baking powder
Pinch of salt
Granulated sugar to sprinkle on top

Grease a shallow 9-inch diameter cake tin and line the bottom with greased greaseproof paper (or baking parchment today).

Put the water, fruit, sugar and margarine into a saucepan and bring to the boil. Stir and simmer for three to four minutes. This makes the dried fruit more succulent. Allow to cool a little.

Sift together the flour, salt, spices and raising agents (yes, two kinds) into a bowl. Make a hollow in the centre, pour in the water/fruit etc., hot but not boiling. Stir quickly together to blend. Turn into prepared tin, smooth top and dredge with a little sugar.

Bake in a moderate oven, reg. 5, 375°F or 190°C for about thirty minutes until firm to the touch.

HONEY BISCUITS

Makes about 24 small biscuits

Source: MoF Cookery Leaflet 21 *Making the Most of Sugar.*[10] Adapted.

2½oz (75g) margarine
2 level tablespoons sugar
2 level tablespoons honey
6oz (175g) plain flour
Scant level teaspoon cinnamon or other spice, optional
Pinch of salt

Cream the margarine and sugar together and beat in the honey. Work in the flour, cinnamon and salt, as if making shortbread. Roll out to -inch thickness on floured surface. Cut into rounds with a 2-inch cutter, put on a greased baking sheet and bake in a moderately hot oven, reg. 4 or 350°F for ten minutes.

These biscuits are rather hard at first, but they keep well and soften over time.

ORANGE RIND MARMALADE, OR APPLE AND ORANGE JAM

Makes 2 pots

Source: *Good Eating, A Second Book of War-Time Recipes.*[11] Adapted.

Seville oranges were even more difficult to obtain than ordinary ones, which had to be used to the last pip.

Peel only from 2 large oranges, raw weight 8oz (200g) each approx.
2 pints (1,100ml) water
1lb (450g) cooking apples
½ pint (300ml) extra water
1½lb (700g) granulated sugar

Wash and score the skins of the oranges so that the peel can be removed neatly in four quarters from each fruit. Eat the flesh of the oranges on another occasion.

Using a sharp knife, cut the peel into fine shreds. Put these into a large saucepan or preserving pan with the 2 pints water and leave to soak for at least five hours.

Meanwhile wash the apples but don't peel or core them. Put them into a pan with the ½ pint of water and simmer gently until they are very soft. Rub through a strainer or sieve to make a pureé. Discard whatever will not go through the sieve.

Add the apple to the soaked peel together with the sugar. Bring to the boil, stirring, and cook briskly for about half an hour, stirring often to prevent sticking. If you have a sugar-boiling thermometer cook to the 'jam' stage, or 220°F. If not, test for setting either by putting a little onto a cold plate or by taking some of the liquid on a wooden spoon. Twirl this round until you have only a few drops left, then watch as they fall off the side of the spoon. When the drops seem reluctant to fall the jam is ready.

Pour into clean warm jars, cover and leave to cool before wiping the jars and labelling them.

Yield is about 2½lb or just over 1kg. It is a pleasant breakfast jam, very economical to make. It is improved by adding a finely sliced lemon to the orange peel.

TOMATO JAM

Yield: approx. 3lb jam
This was one of the ways my mother used to use tomatoes when they

were plentiful, but the wartime snag was that lemons were essential. As tomatoes do not contain any pectin to speak of, the jam does not set, but makes a runny conserve useful to serve with plain baked cottage pudding, milk puddings, or on unbuttered scones which will allow it to soak in.

2lb (1 kilo) tomatoes
2lb (1 kilo) granulated sugar
2 level teaspoons grated lemon zest
Juice of 2 large lemons

Put the tomatoes into a large bowl and pour over boiling water. Leave for a short time until the skins can be removed easily. Cut the tomatoes in quarters and take out the hard centre core.

Put them into a bowl with the sugar and lemon zest. Leave for twelve hours, covered, to allow the juice to run.

Boil with the lemon juice in a preserving pan or large saucepan for at least thirty minutes, or until the syrup has reduced somewhat. Pour into clean warm jars and cover.

Appendix

Friends and Memories

Many people have talked to me about their experiences during the war. Some of them were children at the time, but maybe their memories are all the more vivid for that reason. Their remarks mostly confirm my printed sources and I have reported them in the relevant places. I have had to make a selection from all they told me, or this book would have overflowed its covers, but I thank them all for fascinating hours in their company, and for permission to use their stories.

David Bexon was born in Nottinghamshire, at Awsworth, where his father ran a bakery business. His autobiographical account about baking and selling bread forms a substantial part of Chapter 5. In adult life David became a language teacher, specialising in French and Spanish. He is a strong supporter of Dunstable U3A and a keen member of several book and poetry groups. He has had a number of poems published in magazines and anthologies. He is married, with one daughter, five step-daughters and numerous grandchildren.

Grace and Peter Bumphrey lived in Norfolk as children. Peter came from a farming family and loved horses, helping out in school holidays. One of his jobs was muck carting, another helping to thresh corn in the fields, for which he was paid *6d* an hour. At the end of the war he had enough to buy a watch for £9. Sometimes he was allowed to help drive the milk cart drawn by a pony – 'the fastest milk cart in the west'. He remembers many helpers on the farms: Land Army girls, Italian prisoners-of-war and Germans too towards the end. British troops also helped while waiting for D-Day. After his National Service post-war, he worked in local government on electoral registration, and then became an inspector in the insurance world.

Grace was in the school playground one day when it was machine-gunned from the air. 'There was a big pile-up of children by the door all trying to get in.' There were no school meals, as the school had only two rooms and no kitchen, but home was only 50yds away. Shopping was done in the village or at Aylsham 5 miles distant. A shop there made weekly deliveries of orders made the previous week. Grace worked as a legal secretary before marrying Peter.

Muriel Gibson was sixteen at the beginning of the war. She was evacuated informally from Hartlepool to Corbridge, near Hexham, on the road to Edinburgh, to live with her aunt. When her father died her mother moved there too. She liked voluntary work in a YMCA canteen for soldiers en route to Carlisle. One day though some dishcloth bleach somehow got into the tea, which led to complaints!

She spent two years at a Teacher Training College, sometimes playing in the netball team against WRAF girls from a nearby camp. She remembered a restaurant in Newcastle: Bainbridge's café, where she particularly enjoyed fishcakes and chips. These could also be eaten in Carrick's cafés. British Restaurants in London were rather like Lyons tea shops. She took up a career in teaching before her marriage, and remembers that though most children were all right a few looked under-nourished. Free dentistry was needed when the NHS was set up, as many children had decayed teeth.

Mrs Betty Neil was nineteen when the war broke out. Her husband, whom she married in 1943, was in the Navy, serving two-and-a-half years in Egypt. Then he was posted to Rosyth naval base, while Betty worked in a paper mill in Edinburgh. She remembers the difficulties experienced when her son was born, queuing for dried milk for instance, and gave him rose-hip syrup and cod liver oil because she wanted to do her best for him. She had a daughter too.

Food was difficult at times. 'We put oatmeal in meat to make it go further.' When the family moved house they took most of their possessions in a deep pram. Their identity cards were covered with new addresses. After the war she was a full-time housewife, living in Durham.

Mary Rowe came from Solihull, near Birmingham, but was evacuated to the country at first to relations with a small farm. She enjoyed helping to make butter there. Then she went to a convent school near Bridgenorth. She remembers buying her sweet ration 'in a little dark sweetshop which was run by two elderly ladies', and recalls the bottled plums her mother used to make. She went to college in 1950 and started to go out to restaurants, including Lyons tea houses. She became a teacher and then a secretary, and now has a great interest in Classical Greek and in baroque music.

Cliff and Dot Townsend both came from Cheltenham. They were thirteen and seventeen at the start of the war. Cliff's first job was in the laboratory at a local gasworks, but at seventeen he was sent to work in a tin mine at Camborne (described on page 106). He had an interest in botany even as a boy, collecting cigarette cards of plants. Once the war ended he became a Chartered Gas Engineer, then switched careers to go to Kew Gardens, where he became a Principal Scientific Officer, working on the classification of plants.

Dot had two brothers, one in the army and one in the air force. She herself was a civil servant in a reserved occupation concerned with P.O. telephones. She remembered fire-watching duty in Cheltenham, mostly at the gas works, one night a week for a four-hour stretch. She did a lot of knitting, using unravelled wool from old garments, steamed to get the kinks out. The families of both Dot and Cliff kept hens in their gardens and grew vegetables both there and in allotments. Tea was still on the ration on their honeymoon in 1950, but they thought rationing had been a success. 'We were never really hungry.'

Notes

A NOTE ABOUT WEIGHTS AND MONEY

1 Ministry of Information, *Home Front Handbook* (London, 1945), p. 69.

CHAPTER 1: FAIRER SHARES

1 Ina Zweiniger-Bargielowska, *Austerity in Britain: Rationing, Controls and Consumption 1939–1955*. Oxford: O.U.P., 2000, pp.12–13.
2 Ian Beckett, *Home Front 1914–1918: How Britain Survived the Great War*. London: The National Archives, 2006, p.120.
3 May Byron, *May Byron's Ration's Book*. London: Hodder & Stoughton, no date but time of First World War, pp.2–3.
4 *ibid.*, p. 2. Many of her recipes could be used also in the Second World War.
5 John Burnett, *Plenty and Want: A social history of diet in England from 1815 to the present day*. Harmondsworth: Penguin Books, 1968, p.302.
6 *ibid.*, p.306.
7 V.H. Mottram and E.C. Mottram, *Sound Catering for Hard Times*. London: Nisbet and Co., 1932, pp.9–10.
8 *ibid.*, pp.28–29.
9 Tom Earley, *All These Trees*. Llandysul: Gomer Press, 1992, p.66.
10 Mottram, *Sound Catering for Hard Times*, p.11.
11 Mrs Mabel Wijey, *Warne's Everyday Cookery: Economical, Practical and Up-to-Date Recipes*. London: Frederick Warne, 1937.
12 *ibid.*, pp.350, 352, 354.
13 *ibid.*, p.121.
14 Zweiniger-Bargielowska, *Austerity in Britain*, pp.14–16.
15 *Civilian Supplies in Wartime Britain* by Monica Felton. IWM: K13149. Held at the Department of Printed Books, the Imperial War Museum.
16 *ibid.*, p.9.
17 Cited in Angus Calder, *The People's War: Britain 1939–45*. London: Jonathan Cape, 1969, p.232.
18 Burnett, *Plenty and Want*, p.323.
19 Much factual information in this section comes from The National Archives, ref. MAF 102/14.

20 Zweiniger-Bargielowska, *Austerity in Britain*, p.17.
21 The National Archives, MAF 102/14, Ministry of Food, *Our Food Today* No.1, 1946, p.7.
22 *ibid.*, pp.17–19.
23 *ibid.*, p.17.
24 Cited in Calder, *The People's War*, p.381.
25 Nat. Archives, MAF 102/14, *Our Food Today* No.1, 1950, p.2.
26 Zweiniger-Bargielowska, *Austerity in Britain*, pp.21–22.
27 BBC Written Archive Centre Microfilm T664.
28 Nat. Archives, MAF 102/14, *Our Food Today* No.1, 1950, p.19.
29 *ibid.*, p.31.
30 Nat. Archives, MAF 102/14, *Our Food Today* No.1, 1946, p.9.
31 A.J.P. Taylor, *English History 1914–1945*. Oxford: O.U.P. 1979, p.466.
32 Burnett, *Plenty and Want*, p.332.
33 Mottram, *Sound Catering for Hard Times*, pp.133–4.
34 *Woman* magazine, 21 Sept 1940.
35 Felton, *Civilian Supplies in Wartime Britain*, p.27.
36 Burnett, *Plenty and Want*, p. 329.

CHAPTER 2: FOOD VALUES AND VALUABLE FOODS

1 J.C. Drummond and Anne Wilbraham, *The Englishman's Food: A History of Five Centuries of English Diet*. London: Jonathan Cape, 1939. The work was revised and an additional chapter added by Dorothy Hollingsworth, with a final edition in 1991.
2 *ibid.*, p.448.
3 *ibid.*, from the Introduction by Tom Jaine.
4 *ibid.*, p.449.
5 Most information in this section is taken from the Food Standards Agency, *Manual of Nutrition*, 10th Edition. London: The Stationery Office, 1995.
6 The eight essential amino acids are: isoleucine, leucine, lysine, methionine, phenylalanine, threonine, tryptophan, valine. The one needed by infants is histidine. *Ibid.*, p.19.
7 The rest of the amino acids are: alanine, arginine, aspartic acid, asparagine, cysteine, glutamic acid, glutamine, glycine, proline, serine and tyrosine. *Ibid.*, p.19.
8 *ibid.*, pp. 40–47.
9 *Recommended Intakes of Nutrients for the United Kingdom*. London: H.M.S.O. 1969.
10 *Manual of Nutrition*, estimations from Composition of food tables, pp.132, 136.
11 Derek J. Oddy, *From Plain Fare to Fusion Food: British Diet from the 1890s to the 1990s*. Woodbridge: The Boydell Press, 2003, p.137.
12 Ronald Sheppard and Edward Newton, *The Story of Bread*. London: Routledge & K. Paul, 1957, pp.124–126.
13 Oral communication. Peter Bumphrey. See Appendix.
14 Andrew Whitley, 'The shocking truth about bread.' Article from *The Independent Extra*, 24 August 2006.
15 H.E. Jacob, *Six Thousand Years of Bread: Its Holy and Unholy History*. New York: Doubleday, Doran and Company Inc., 1944, p.380.
16 *Manual of Nutrition*, 10th ed., p.136.
17 Cited in introduction, p.3, of *The Englishman's Food*, 2nd ed.

18 Nat. Archives, MAF 102/15.
19 Article in *The Independent* newspaper, 'What are the properties of trans-fats, and should they be banned?' 1 November 2006.
20 Drummond & Wilbraham, *The Englishman's Food*, 2nd ed., p.451.
21 Oral communication. Muriel Gibson. See Appendix.
22 Nat. Archives, MAF 102/14, *Our Foods Today*, 1950, p.29.
23 R.J. Hammond, *Food, Vol.II, Studies in Administration and Control*. London: H.M.S.O. & Longmans, Green 1956, pp.770–776.
24 Cited in John Burnett, *Liquid Pleasures: A Social History of Drinks in Modern Britain*. London: Routledge, 1999, pp.65–66.
25 Burnett, *Liquid Pleasures*, pp. 44–46.
26 Zweiniger-Bargielowska, *Austerity in Britain*, p.137.
27 Nat. Archives, MAF 102/4, *Kitchen Front* broadcast, 5 January 1942.
28 Nat. Archives, MAF 102/15, *Keeping in Touch*, various dates during 1945.
29 *ibid.*

CHAPTER 3: THE HOUSEWIFE, HER KITCHEN AND WHAT SHE WAS TOLD

1 Bette Anderson, *We Just Got On With It: British Women in World War II*. Chippenham: Picton Publishing, 1994, p.10, and Zweiniger-Bargielowska, *Austerity in Britain*, p.103.
2 *The Times*, 10 July 1940, p.4.
3 Nat. Archives, MAF 102/15 *One-Pot Meals*, MoF Leaflet 35, 27 Sept. 1946.
4 For example, Imperial War Museum, MoF Leaflets Q (41) 15, Leaflet 9 and *Let's talk about Food and fuel-saving cookery*, Nov. 1941. Also Elizabeth Craig, *Cooking in War-Time*. Glasgow: The Literary Press Ltd., pp.6–10.
5 Imperial War Museum, Ministry of Food *Food Facts* Vol. II.
6 Gill Corbishley, *Ration Book Recipes, Some Food Facts 1939–54*. London: English Heritage, 1990, p.26.
7 Imp. War Mus., MoF *Food Facts* Vol.I.
8 Imp. War Mus., MoF Leaflets Q(41)15. War Cookery Leaflet 1.
9 Nat. Archives, MAF 102/15, *Meals without Meat* MoF No.29 April 1946.
10 Nat. Archives, MAF 102/15, Leaflet 1, 1946.
11 Nat. Archives, MAF 102/3, *Kitchen Front*, Ambrose Heath, 5 April 1941.
12 Nat. Archives, MAF 102/4, *Kitchen Front*, Mabel Constanduros 7 April 1942.
13 Nat. Archives, MAF 102/7, *Kitchen Front*, Mabel Constanduros 22 June 1945.
14 Nat. Archives, MAF 102/2, *Kitchen Front*, Elsie & Doris Waters, 26 December 1940.
15 Nat. Archives, MAF 102/3, *Kitchen Front*, March 1941.
16 Nat. Archives, MAF 102/15, MoF War Cookery Leaflet 19, no date.
17 Byron, *Rations Book*, p.8.
18 Nat. Archives, MAF 102/15, MoF Leaflet 36, Sept. 1945.
19 Nat. Archives, MAF 102/15, MoF War cookery leaflet 25, no date.
20 Ambrose Heath, *The Queen Cookery Book*. London: Weidenfeld & Nicolson, 1950, p.10.
21 Craig, *Cooking in War-time*, pp.119–120.
22 John Lewis, *A Doctor's Occupation*. London: New English Library, 1983.
23 *ibid.*, p.130.

CHAPTER 4: DIG FOR VICTORY AND VEGETABLES

1 Ministry of Information, *Home Front Handbook*. London: Imperial War Museum reprint of 1945 edition, p.7.
2 Gill Corbishley, *Ration Book Cookery: Recipes & History*. London: English Heritage, 1985, p.8.
3 Ministry of Information, *Land at War*. London: The Stationery Office, 2001. Facsimile of 1945 ed.
4 Much of the information in this section comes from *Land at War*.
5 *ibid.*, p.8.
6 Juliet Gardiner, *Wartime Britain 1939–45*. London: Headline Book Publishing 2004, p.162.
7 Calculated from Gardiner, *Wartime Britain 1939–45*, p.161.
8 *Land at War*, p. 67.
9 Raynes Minns, *Bombers and Mash: The Domestic Front 1939–45*. London: Virago Press, 1999, p.76.
10 Gardiner, *Wartime Britain 1939–45*, p.162.
11 Jennifer Davies, *The Wartime Kitchen and Garden*. London: BBC Books, 1993, p.14.
12 Calder, *The People's War*, pp.424–5.
13 *ibid.*, p. 422.
14 *Land at War*, p.95
15 Much of the information in this section comes from Nicola Tyrer, *They Fought in the Fields: The Women's Land Army*. Stroud: Tempus Publishing, 2007.
16 By Shewell Cooper, a horticultural journalist.
17 Joan Snelling, *A Land Girl's War*. Ipswich: Old Pond Publishing, 2004, p.16.
18 *ibid.*, p.18.
19 Calder, *The People's War*, p. 419.
20 For example, *What Did You Do in the War, Mum?* London: Age Exchange Theatre Trust, 3rd ed. 2000, p.3, Mrs Crane had inedible food, and pp.6–7, Dorothy had trouble with the cowman.
21 *Land at War*, p.94.
22 *The Times*, 22 April 1943. 'Labour for the Harvest', p.2.
23 Ministry of Agriculture, Dig for Victory poster/advertisement. In Davies, *The Wartime Kitchen & Garden*, p.78.
24 Imperial War Museum. EPH.C. AGRIC.
25 Davies, *The Wartime Kitchen and Garden*, p.41.
26 Imp. War Mus., EPH.C.AGRIC. *Dig for Victory* Leaflet No.1.
27 *ibid.*, *Dig for Victory* Leaflet No.7.
28 *ibid.*, *Dig for Victory* Leaflet No.12. Seed Potatoes.
29 *ibid.*, *Dig for Victory* Leaflet No.24.
30 *ibid.*, *Dig for Victory* Leaflet No.10.
31 Davies, *The Wartime Kitchen and Garden*, p.129.
32 Tyrer, *They Fought in the Fields*, p.228–229.
33 Davies, *The Wartime Kitchen and Garden*, p.126.
34 Oral communication. Cliff and Dot Townsend. See Appendix.
35 Oral communication. Mary Rowe. See Appendix.

CHAPTER 5: COUNTRY LIFE

1 Nat. Archives, MAF 102/14, *Our Food Today 3 The Agricultural Worker* 1945.
2 *ibid., Our Food Today*, 1950 ed.
3 R.J. Hammond*: Food, Vol. I, The Growth of Policy*. London: HMSO & Longmans, Green 1951. p.394.
4 Oral communication. Cliff Townsend. See Appendix.
5 Nat. Archives, MAF 102/14, *Our Food Today*, 1950 ed. pp.7–8.
6 *ibid., Our Food Today 3.*
7 *ibid.*, p.3.
8 *ibid.*, Appendix D.
9 *ibid.*, p.3.
10 Much of the information in this section comes from Helen Carey, *Bows of Burning Gold*. Skipton: Alfresco Books, 2005.
11 Marguerite Patten, *We'll Eat Again*, London: Hamlyn, 1985, p.8.
12 Imp. War Mus., EPH.C.FOOD.
13 Written communication. David Bexon. See Appendix.
14 National Archives, MAF 102/14 *Our Food Today No.3*, p.4, and Davies, *The Wartime Kitchen and Garden*, pp.177–181.
15 Nat. Archives, MAF 102/14, *Our Food Today No.3*, p.5.
16 Davies, *The Wartime Kitchen and Garden*, p.173.

CHAPTER 6: THE WILD HARVEST AND PRESERVING

1 E.R.Chamberlin, *Life in Wartime Britain*. London: B.T. Batsford, 1972, p.80.
2 Imp. War Mus., MoF *Food Facts & Let's Talk About Food* Vol.1.
3 Oral communication. Peter Bumphrey. See Appendix.
4 Nat. Archives, MAF 102/15, *Hedgerow Harvest*, July 1946.
5 Vicomte de Mauduit, *They Can't Ration These*. London: Michael Joseph, 1940.
6 Dorothy Hartley, *Food in England*. London: Macdonald, 1954.
7 Richard Mabey, *Food for Free*. London: Collins, 1973.
8 Jan Orchard, *The Hedgerow Harvest: Traditional Recipes from Nature's Storehouse.* Marlborough: The Crowood Press, 1988, p.16.
9 Mauduit, *They Can't Ration These*, pp.39–42. Lewis Carroll knew about it too. 'There's nothing like eating hay when you're faint,' remarked the White King to Alice in *Through the Looking Glass.*
10 Hartley, *Food in England*, p.574.
11 Imp. War Mus., MoF Leaflets Q(41)15.
12 Oral communication. Peter Bumphrey. See Appendix.
13 Mabey, *Food for Free*, p.13–14.
14 C. Anne Wilson, *Food & Drink in Britain from the Stone Age to recent times.* London: Cookery Book Club, 1973, pp.169–170.
15 Min. of Agriculture & Fisheries, Leaflet No.14, no date.
16 Min. of Agriculture & Fisheries, Bulletin 21. First published in 1929 followed by many editions and reprints.

CHAPTER 7: TOWNS

1 Nat. Archives, MAF 102/14, *Our Food Today* 3, 1945, p.6.
2 Imp. War Mus. EPH.C.FOOD. Prices from *Shaw's Monthly Food List,* January 1944.
3 Chamberlin, *Life in Wartime Britain*, p.105.
4 Oral communication. Mrs Betty Neil. See Appendix.
5 Cited in John Burnett, *England Eats Out: A Social History of Eating Out in England from 1830 to the Present*. Harlow: Pearson Longman, 2004, pp.245–246.
6 Nat. Archives, MAF 102/14, *Our Food Today 2, The Industrial Worker*, 1945, p.1.
7 *ibid.*, p.2.
8 Nat. Archives, MAF 102/15, *Meals without Meat*, 1946.
9 Imp. War Mus., 31(41)/5.421 *Canteen Catering.*
10 Most information from Hammond, *Food, Vol.II*, pp. 421–3.
11 Imp. War Mus., *Food Facts* Vol.II.
12 Donald Thomas, *An Underworld at War: Spivs, Deserters, Racketeers & Civilians in the Second World War*. London: John Murray, 2003, p.69.
13 Gardiner, *Wartime Britain*, p.371.
14 Thomas, *An Underworld at War*, p.70.
15 Gardiner, *Wartime Britain*, p.379.
16 Nat. Archives, MAF 152/34 *Emergency Feeding in Air Raid Conditions 1940–45*, p.13.
17 *The Times*, 15 November 1940, p.2.
18 John Gregg, *The Shelter of the Tubes: Tube sheltering in wartime London*. London: Capital Transport, 2001, p.47.
19 Nat. Archives, MAF 152/34, *Emergency Feeding in Air Raid Conditions 1940–45*, p.8.
20 *ibid.*, p.15.
21 Hammond, *Food Vol. II*, pp. 364–366 & Nat. Archives MAF 152/34.
22 The main source of information in this section is Katharine Bentley Beauman, *Green Sleeves: The Story of the WVS/WRVS*. London: Seeley Service, 1977.

CHAPTER 8: THE BLACK MARKET AND GREY AREAS

1 Oral communications given by various people among the list in the Appendix.
2 Zweiniger-Bargielowska, *Austerity in Britain*, p.158.
3 *ibid.*, p.152.
4 Ministry of Information, *Home Front Handbook*, p.69.
5 Thomas, *An Underworld at War*, pp.160–161.
6 *ibid.*, p.136.
7 *ibid.*, pp.138–139.
8 *ibid.*, p.143.
9 *ibid.*, p.148.
10 Oral communication. Cliff Townsend. See Appendix.
11 Hammond, *Food, Vol.I*, pp.158–160.
12 Chamberlin, *Life in Wartime Britain*, p. 59.
13 Imp. War Mus., *Food Facts* Vol. II.
14 BBC Written Archives Centre Microfilm T207. Charles Hill, 21 March 1941.
15 *ibid.*

16 *ibid.*
17 *The Times*, Friday 19 February 1943, p.2.
18 Oddy, *From Plain Fare to Fusion Food*, p.212.
19 Mabey, *Food for Free*, p.184.
20 Imp. War Mus., *Food Facts* Vol. II.
21 Article in *Metro* newspaper, 11 October 2006
22 Chamberlin, *Life in Wartime Britain*, p.75.
23 Imp. War Mus., EPH.C.FOOD.

CHAPTER 9: LET'S HAVE A PARTY

1 Chamberlin, *Life in Wartime Britain*, p.102.
2 Davies, *The Wartime Kitchen and Garden*, p.177.
3 Cited in Burnett, *Liquid Pleasures*, pp.136–137.
4 *ibid.*, p.175.
5 *ibid.*, p.106.
6 Mauduit, *They Can't Ration These*, p.126.
7 Davies, *The Wartime Kitchen and Garden*, pp.102–105.
8 Cited in Burnett, *England Eats Out*, p 235.
9 *ibid.*, p.234.
10 *ibid.*, p.239.
11 *ibid.*, p.232.
12 Calder, *The People's War*, p.176.
13 Nat. Archives, MAF 102/4.
14 Imp. War Mus., *Food Facts* Vol.I.
15 The local community is described in the Introduction.
16 Nat. Archives, MAF 102/3.
17 Ambrose Heath, *Simple American Dishes in English Measures*. London: Faber and Faber, 1943.
18 Republished by The Bodleian Library, University of Oxford, 2004.
19 Davies, *The Wartime Kitchen and Garden*, p.212.
20 *'When the Lights Go On Again' Memories of V.E. Day and After*. London: Age Exchange Theatre Trust, 2000, pp.6–7.
21 *ibid.*, pp.11–12

CHAPTER 10: AUSTERITY AND RECOVERY

1 *The Times*, 15 August 1945, p.2.
2 Hammond, *Food, Vol. I*, p.344.
3 Zweiniger-Bargielowska, *Austerity in Britain*, p.261.
4 BBC TV programme, *Mortgaged to the USA*, 6 January 2007.
5 *The Independent*, 29 December 2006, p.46.
6 Brian Braithwaite and others, compilers, *The Home Front: The Best of Good Housekeeping 1939–1945*. London: Ebury Press, 1987. p.103.
7 Nat. Archives, *Our Foods Today*, 1950, p.3 and Appendix.
8 Nat. Archives, *Our Foods Today*, 1950, p.12 and Appendix.
9 Doris Lytton Toye, *Contemporary Cookery: Vogue Receipts* 1945–1947. London: Conde-Nast Publications, 1947.
10 Oddy, *From Plain Fare to Fusion Food*, p.186.

11 T.K. Derry & T.L. Jarman, *Modern Britain: Life and Work through Two Centuries of Change*. London: John Murray, 1979, p.286.
12 Josephine Terry, *Cook-Happy*. London: Faber and Faber, 1945.
13 Nell Heaton and André Simon, compilers, *A Calendar of Food and Wine*. London: Faber and Faber, 1949.
14 'Waste not, want not.' *The Independent*, 17 March 2007.

CHAPTER 11: REPRESENTATIVE RECIPES

1 Nat. Archives, MAF 102/4, *Kitchen Front* 1942.
2 *ibid.*
3 Nat. Archives, MAF 102/3, *Kitchen Front* 1941.
4 Nat. Archives, MAF 102/15.
5 Imp. War Mus. *Food Facts* Vol.1.
6 *ibid.*
7 Nat. Archives, MAF 102/15, MoF Leaflet No. 32, *Puddings without eggs*, reprinted 1947.
8 *ibid.*
9 Nat. Archives, MAF 102/15.
10 *ibid.*
11 *The Daily Telegraph Home Cook. A Second Book of War-Time Recipes*. London: Macmillan 2006 (reprint of wartime cookbook), p.115.

Bibliography and Further Reading

Anderson, Bette, *We Just Got On With It: British Women in World War II.* Chippenham: Picton Publishing, 1994.

BBC Written Archives Centre, Microfilm T207. Dr Hill ('A Doctor'). Microfilm T664. Lord Woolton.

Beauman, Katharine Bentley, *Green Sleeves: The Story of WVS/WRVS.* London: Seeley Service, 1977.

Beckett, Ian F.W., *Home Front 1914–1918: How Britain Survived the Great War.* London: The National Archives, 2006.

Braithwaite, Brian & others, *The Home Front: The Best of Good Housekeeping 1939–1945.* London: Ebury Press, 1987.

Brown, Mike and Harris, Carol, *The Wartime House: Home Life in Wartime Britain 1939–1945.* Stroud: Sutton Publishing, 2001.

Burnett, John, *England Eats Out: A Social History of Eating Out in England from 1830 to the Present.* Harlow: Pearson Longman, 2004.

Burnett, John, *Liquid Pleasures: A Social History of Drinks in Modern Britain.* London: Routledge, 1999.

Burnett, John, *Plenty and Want: A Social History of Diet in England from 1815 to the Present Day.* Harmondsworth: Penguin Books, 1968.

Burrows, Ian, *Food from the Wild.* London: New Holland Publishers (UK), 2005.

Byron, May, *May Byron's Rations Book.* London: Hodder & Stoughton, no date (First World War).

Calder, Angus, *The People's War: Britain 1939–45.* Cape, 1969.

Cantwell, John D., *The Second World War: A Guide to Documents in the Public Record Office.* London: H.M.S.O., 1993.

Carey, Helen, *Bows of Burning Gold.* Skipton: Alfresco Books, 2005.

Chamberlin, E.R., *Life in Wartime Britain.* London: B.T. Batsford, 1972.

Corbishley, Gill, *Ration Book Cookery: Recipes & History.* London: English Heritage, no date.

Corbishley, Gill, *Ration Book Recipes, Some Food Facts 1939–54.* London: English Heritage, 1990.

Craig, Elizabeth, *Collins Family Cookery.* London: Collins, 1957.

Craig, Elizabeth, *Cooking in War-Time.* Glasgow: The Literary Press Ltd, no date.

Craig, Elizabeth, *Cooking with Elizabeth Craig.* London: Collins, 1932.

Daily Telegraph, Home Cook, *Good Eating: A Second Book of War Time Recipes.* London: Macmillan, 2006 (reprint).

David, Elizabeth, *A Book of Mediterranean Food.* Harmondsworth: Penguin Books, 1955.

Davies, Jennifer, *The Wartime Kitchen and Garden.* London: BBC Books, 1993.

Derry, T.K. and Jarman, T.L., *Modern Britain: Life and Work through Two Centuries of Change.* London: John Murray, 1979.

Drummond, J.C., and Wilbraham, Anne, *The Englishman's Food: A History of Five Centuries of English Diet.* London: Jonathan Cape, 1939. Revised by Dorothy Hollingsworth. London: Pimlico, 1991.

Earley, Tom, *All These Trees.* Llandysul: Gomer Press, 1992.

Felton, Monica, *Civilian Supplies in Wartime Britain.* London: Imperial War Museum, 2003 reprint.

Food Facts for the Kitchen Front: A Book of Wartime Recipes and Hints. (Foreword by Lord Woolton.) London: Collins, no date.

Food Standards Agency Manual of Nutrition, 10th ed. London: The Stationery Office, 1995.

Gardiner, Juliet, *The 1940s House.* London: Channel 4 Books, 2000.

Gardiner, Juliet, *Wartime Britain 1939–45.* London: Headline Book Publishing, 2004.

Gregg, John, *The Shelter of the Tubes: Tube sheltering in wartime London.* London: Capital Transport, 2001.

Hammond, R.J., *Food. Volume I The Growth of Policy.* London: H.M.S.O. and Longmans, Green & Co., 1951 (History of the Second World War.)

Hammond, R.J., *Food. Volume II Studies in Administration and Control.* London: H.M.S.O. and Longmans, Green & Co., 1956 (History of the Second World War).

Hammond, R.J., Food. *Volume III Studies in Administration and Control.* London: H.M.S.O. and Longmans, Green & Co., 1963 (History of the Second World War).

Hartley, Dorothy, *Food in England.* London: Macdonald, 1954.

Department of Health and Social Security, *Recommended Intakes of Nutrients for the United Kingdom.* London: H.M.S.O. 1969.

Heath, Ambrose, *The Kitchen Front: 122 recommended recipes selected from broadcasts by Mabel Constanduros, Freddie Grisewood, etc.* London: Nicholson & Watson, 1941.

Heath, Ambrose, *More Kitchen Front Recipes* … London: A. & C. Black, 1941.

Heath, Ambrose, *Kitchen Front Recipes & Hints* … London: A. & C. Black, 1941.

Heath, Ambrose, *New Dishes for Old: Food Values & Substitute Recipes.* London: A. & C. Black, 1942.

Heath, Ambrose, *The Queen Cookery Book.* London: Weidenfeld & Nicolson, 1960.

Heath, Ambrose, *Simple American Dishes in English Measures.* London: Faber and Faber, 1943.

Heath, Ambrose, *There's Time for a Meal.* London: Robert Hale, 1941.

Heaton, Nell and Simon, André, *A Calendar of Food and Wine.* London: Faber and Faber, 1949.

Hylton, Stuart, *Their Darkest Hour: The Hidden History of the Home Front 1939–1945.* Stroud: Sutton Publishing, 2003.

Jacob, H.E., *Six Thousand Years of Bread: Its Holy and Unholy History.* New York: Doubleday, Doran and Co. Inc., 1944.

Imperial War Museum, Ministry of Food Leaflets Q(41)15.

Imperial War Museum, *Canteen Catering* 31(41)/5.421.

Imperial War Museum, *Food Facts*, vol. I & vol. II.

Imperial War Museum, EPH.C. Agric. Leaflets.

Imperial War Museum, EPH.C.FOOD.

Lewis, John, *A Doctor's Occupation: The dramatic true story of life in Nazi-occupied Jersey*. London: New English Library, 1983.

Longmate, Norman, *How We Lived Then: A history of everyday life during the Second World War*. Hutchinson, 1977 (Arrow Books).

Mabey, Richard, *Food for Free*. London: Readers Union/Collins, 1973.

Mauduit, Vicomte de, *They Can't Ration These*. London: Michael Joseph, 1940, and London: Persephone Books, 2004. (www.persephonebooks.co.uk)

Marwick, Arthur, *The Home Front: The British and the Second World War*, Thames & Hudson, 1976.

Ministry of Information, *Home Front Handbook*. London: Imperial War Museum, 2005, reprint of 1945 ed.

Ministry of Information, *Land at War: The official story of British farming 1939–1944*. London: The Stationery Office, 2001. Facsimile of 1945 ed.

Ministry of Information, *What Britain Has Done 1939–1945*. London: Imperial War Museum 2005, reprint of 1945 ed.

Minns, Raynes, *Bombers and Mash: The Domestic Front 1939–45*. London: Virago Press, 1999.

Mottram, V.H. & E.C., *Sound Catering for Hard Times*. London: Nisbet and Co., 1932.

National Archives, MAF 102/2, 1940 *Kitchen front* broadcasts

National Archives, MAF, 102/3, 1941 *Kitchen front* broadcasts

National Archives, MAF 102/4, 1942 *Kitchen front* broadcasts

National Archives, MAF 102/7, 1945 *Kitchen front* broadcasts

National Archives, MAF 102/14, 1943–50 Min. of Food leaflets on food etc.

National Archives, MAF 102/15, 1943–52 Min. of Food leaflets on food etc.

National Archives, MAF 152/54, *Emergency Feeding in Air Raid Conditions*

Northwood, Owen T., *Call Back Yesterday: People of Lincolnshire remember the war*. Lincoln: Lincolnshire Books, 1995.

Oddy, Derek J., *From Plain Fare to Fusion Food: British Diet from the 1890s to the 1990s*. Woodbridge: The Boydell Press, 2003.

Orchard, Jan, *The Hedgerow Harvest: Traditional Recipes from Nature's Storehouse*. Marlborough: The Crowood Press, 1988.

Patten, Marguerite, *We'll Eat Again: A collection of recipes from the war years*. London: Hamlyn, 1990.

Patten, Marguerite, *The Victory Cookbook*. London: Hamlyn, 1995.

Patten, Marguerite, *Post-War Kitchen: Nostalgic Food and Facts from 1945–1954*. London: Hamlyn, 1998.

The Real Good Life. London: Cassell Illustrated and The Soil Association, 2005

Schweitzer, Pam & others, eds. *What Did You Do in the War, Mum? Women Recall their Wartime Work*. London: Age Exchange Theatre Trust, 2000.

Schweitzer, Pam & others, eds. *When the Lights Go On Again: Memories of V.E. Day and After*. London: Age Exchange Theatre Trust, 2000.

Sheppard, Ronald & Newton, Edward, *The Story of Bread*. London: Routledge & K. Paul, 1957.

Snelling, Joan, *A Land Girl's War*. Ipswich: Old Pond Publishing, 2004.

Taylor, A.J.P., *English History 1914–1945*. Oxford: O.U.P., 1979.

Terry, Josephine, *Cook Happy*. London: Faber and Faber 1945.

Thomas, Donald, *An Underworld at War: Spivs, Deserters, Racketeers & Civilians in the Second World War*. London: John Murray, 2003.

Tyrer, Nicola, *They Fought in the Fields: The Women's Land Army*. Stroud: Tempus Publishing, 2007.

Toye, Doris, *Lytton Contemporary Cookery: Vogue Receipts 1945–1947*. London: Conde-Nast Publications, 1947.

U.S. War Dept., *Instructions for American Servicemen in Britain*. Washington, D.C., 1942. Republished by The Bodleian Library, Oxford, 2004.

Waller, Jane and Vaughan-Rees, Michael, *Women in Wartime: The Role of Women's Magazines 1939–1945*. London: Macdonald Optima, 1987.

Waller, Maureen, *London 1945: Life in the Debris of War*. London: John Murray, 2004.

Wilson, C. Anne, *Food & Drink in Britain from the Stone Age to recent times*. London: Cookery Book Club, 1973.

Wijey, Mabel, ed., *Warne's Everyday Cookery: Economical, Practical and Up-to-Date Recipes*. London: Frederick Warne, 1937.

Zweiniger-Bargielowska, Ina, *Austerity in Britain: Rationing, Controls and Consumption 1939–1955*. Oxford: O.U.P., 2000.

Index

agricultural workers 23, 85-88, 91–97
alcohol, alcoholic drinks 41, 81, 175–177, 196
allotments and town gardens 97–103
aluminium 62, 202
American foods 29, 185, 187
American Red Cross 159, 185

backyard farming 119–124
bacon 17, 23, 27, 122, 189, 192
bakers 109, 114–119
bananas 27, 195
BBC broadcasts 29, 60
  Kitchen Front 56, 71–75, 170, 182, 199
beer 175–176, 177
bees, beekeeping 122–124
Bexon, David 114, 221
Bexon's Bakery 109, 114–119
Biscuits 18, 29, –30, 53, 67, 117, 198
black market 160–163
blackout 49, 87, 172
bombing, air raids, Blitz 26,104, 138, 148–157, 167–168, 172, 175 ,180
bovine tuberculosis 54, 169–170
bread, *see also* National Loaf 17, 19, 24, 33, 34, 45–46, 47, 62, 114–119, 154, 194, 202
  brown 17, 45–46
  white 17, 19, 45–46, 47, 199
bread and potatoes 23, 34, 38, 97, 108, 192, 199
breakfast 20, 109
British Restaurants 23, 52, 73, 109, 138, 141–142, 143
Buggins Family 72–73, 181–182, 186, party cake, 181–183
Bumphrey, Grace and Peter 47, 93, 121, 128, 131, 187, 221
buying permits, retailers 28
Byron, May 14, 7

Cable & Wireless Ltd 10, 61
cakes and puddings 47, 48, 53, 64, 75, 77, 116, 124, 146, 182–185
calcium 42
calories 16, 17, 43, 44–45, 48, 75, 176
Camden tablets 74, 136
canned goods 24, 28, 29, 38, 52, 174, 197–198
carbohydrates 33, 37, 38, 40–41, 53, 108
catering establishments 105, 109, 142, 179–180
cereals 29, 47, 86, 197
cheap foods 17, 18
cheese 17, 23, 24, 38, 51, 86, 105, 189, 197, 199
children 23, 24, 26–27, 36, 54–55, 95, 96, 111, 112, 125, 148 , 159, 169, 184, 187–188, 192, 202
Christmas 31, 39, 117, 184–185
Churchill, Winston 36, 178, 191
cigarettes, tobacco 163, 164, 178–179, 186
clothes rationing 190
cod liver oil 44, 52, 56, 192
coffee 54, 181, 186, 193
Colorado beetles 102
compost, manure 100
Constanduros, Mabel 182
consumers *see also* shopping 14
control systems 21–22, 32
cookery books
  post-war 129, 200–201

pre-war 16, 17, 19
wartime 63, 68, 78–79
cookery methods 48, 62–66, 74
corned beef 52, 189
cost of food:
in 1932 17, 33
in wartime 32, 113, 140
country foods 125–133
country wines 177
country workers 105–108
County Herb Committees 125, 132, 170
Craig, Elizabeth 76, 78–79

David, Elizabeth 201
de Mauduit, Vicomte 128–130, 131, 179
Denman, Lady 91, 92, 94, 111
Depression, The 15, 54, 85, 93, 111, 125, 158
Dig for Victory campaign 34, 43, 97–99
digestion 38–39 *see also* nutrition
digging 99
dinner 20, 109, 179
disease 152, 168–170, 171, 172
distribution schemes for milk, eggs 24, 33
dried fruit 17, 24, 29, 198
Drummond, Sir Jack 36, 48, 144
dysentery 169, 171

Earley, Tom 18
economy recipes 16
eggs:
dried 24, 51, 67, 189, 194, 197
fresh 18, 19, 24, 51, 86, 106, 131, 189, 197–199
emergency feeding 151–157
evacuees 58, 112, 129, 138, 159, 175,
expensive meals 20

Farm Survey 1940 88–89
farming:
agriculture 85–97,
living conditions 93
fat:
butter 18, 19, 23, 24, 39, 49, 50, 75–76, 199
cooking fat 23, 24, 49, 50, 199
dripping 50, 51, 76
in diet 19, 37, 38, 41, 44, 108
margarine 17, 23, 24, 38, 43, 49, 50, 199
suet 17, 51, 204
fats rations 23, 24, 49, 76, 189, 199
first-aid food 154–156
First World War 13, 14, 32, 33, 38, 57, 86, 91, 123, 168, 191
fish 18, 19, 34, 38–39, 40, 52, 104, 132, 189
flies 67, 170, 171
food:
foreign 199–200, 201
hazards 168–170
hoarding 75
imports 13, 18, 21, 22, 38, 85, 105, 190, 202
in and after air raids 148–157, 167–178
nutrients 38–45
poisoning 66
post-war 189–199
storage, 66–67, 99, 167
Food Facts 30, 67, 69, 126, 127, 148, 161, 174
Food Offices 25–26, 27, 28, 68, 163, 164
foods, essential basic 45
fruit 18, 19, 39, 70, 86, 97, 125–127, 199
preservation 53, 84, 112, 134–137 *see also* preserving
fuel 21, 61, 63, 124, 163, 202
fungi, mushrooms 125, 127–128, 170

game 19, 34, 104, 131
gas masks 26, 149, 150
Gibson, Muriel 52, 148, 184, 214, 221
Grisewood, Freddie 71, 74

ham 23, 122
hay as food 129–130
hay box 65–66, 202
Heath, Ambrose 71–72, 75, 78, 186
herbs 101–102, 130, 132–133, 134
Hill, Charles (The Radio Doctor) 71, 168–169, 170
Hitler 175
hoarding, shop crawling 162, 173, 174
housewives 57–77, 190, 199
ice cream 133, 189
identity cards 11, 26

industrial canteens 142–147
inflation 9, 17, 32
insecticides, fungicides 102–103
jam, preserves, syrup, honey 23–24, 29, 53, 76–77, 112–114, 122–124, 135, 197

Jersey, Channel Islands 80–84

Keynes, J.M. 191
kitchens and kitchen equipment 60–68, 192
Knox, Ronald 103

Labour Government 1945 142, 191, 192
land use 89–91
legal offences 28, 161–163, 165, 166, 174, 186, 202
Lend Lease 22, 28, 51, 89, 133, 178, 185, 191
leptospirosis 172
Lewis, John 81
Lloyd George, David 128
lunch, luncheon, midday meal 20, 105, 109, 144–147

Mallet, Cecile 82
meat 17, 18, 19, 22, 23, 24, 27, 39, 51–52, 81, 86 , 144, 146, 165, 192, 194, 199, 202
medicinal herbs 132–133
milk 18, 19, 23, 38, 39, 51, 54–55, 76, 105, 109, 111 , 144, 145, 169–70, 192–194, 196
minerals 16, 19, 38, 41–42, 47
Ministry of Agriculture 97, 101, 125
Ministry of Food,
  after 1939, 21, 23, 26, 30, 36, 60, 71, 79, 101, 105, 112 , 129, 154, 169
  Food Facts & leaflets 30, 62, 67, 69–71, 126–127, 128, 144, 148, 161, 174, 180
  in First World War 13, 19
mobile canteens 155–157
Mottram, V.H. 16

National Flour, National Loaf 38, 46–47, 53, 72, 74, 145, 194
National Fruit Preservation Scheme 112
National Registration 26

Neil, Betty 141, 149, 222
night blindness 49
nutrition 36–56, 68–71, 74, 202

offal, sausages 34, 35, 52
orange juice 43, 55, 192

packaging 67
parties 180–185, 187–188
Patten, Marguerite 79–80, 200
personal points 24, 30
pests and diseases, garden 102
pets 166–167
Pie Centres 108–109, 110
pigs and pig clubs 86, 120, 121–122, 169
points rationing 24, 28, 29, 30, 52, 138, 174, 193–195, 198
poisoning 170
Porthcurno, Cornwall 10, 61, 95
Potatoes 17, 48, 76, 82–83, 86, 89–91, 97, 101, 103, 145, 146, 170, 195, 200, 202
poultry 19, 34, 86, 120
poverty 15, 17–20, 112, 199
pregnant women 23, 24, 26, 36, 42, 44, 54–57
preserving: bottling, canning etc. 101, 133–137
price controls and subsidies 32
prisoners of war 95
protein:
  animal 16, 19, 34, 37, 38, 39–40, 51, 52, 199
  vegetable 39, 70
pulses 24, 29, 38, 197

Queen Elizabeth (Queen Mother) 94, 156
Queen Elizabeth II 26
Queen Mary 26
Queen's Messenger Convoys 74, 156–157
queues 22, 138

rabbits 34, 120–121, 131, 140
railway buffets 141
ration books 14, 24, 26–27, 163
rationing:
  amounts of foods 23, 25, 73, 110
  consequences of 199–200

end of 24, 192, 195–199
organisation 22–32
post-war 189–199
preliminary planning 21
registration with shop 27, 28, 164
start of 23
First World War, amounts of foods 13, 33
rats 171–172
Recipes:
Apple Marmalade 219
Baked Fruit Pie 215–216
Beetroot Soup 203–204
Blackberry Leaf Tea 130–131
Boiled Cake 217–218
Buggins Party Cake 181–183
Cheese Pudding 211
Cheese Rissoles 210–211
Corned Beef & Onion Sauce 208
Corned Beef Hash 207
Corned Beef on Toast 208–209
Fishcakes 205–206
Fruit Roly-Poly 217
Honey Biscuits 218
Mock Duck 207
Potato Floddies 211–212
Ragout of Beef 209–210
Sardine Rolls 204–205
Spam Fritters 206
Special Plum Pudding 216
Steamed Jam Pudding 214–215
Tomato Jam 220
Wartime Champ 212
Woolton Pie 212–213
refrigerators 61, 66, 134, 139, 171, 192
restaurants 179–180, 198
retailers 14, 28, 30, 163–165
roofs and window boxes 101
rose-hip syrup 126, 133, 135, 136
Rowe, Mary 103, 149, 222

saccharin 77
salvage, recycling 159, 167, 201–202
school meals 147–148, 202
seaweed 132
shampoo, toothpaste, shaving soap 31
shelters, air-raid 139, 148–154
shops, shopping 67, 68, 105, 114, 138–141, 163, 200
Snelling, Joan 93
snoek 197
soap rationing 27, 31–32, 84, 195–196
soft drinks 178
South Crofty Tin Mine 106
soya beans, flour 39, 70, 77, 184
Spam 10, 29, 52, 67
Stella, Lady Reading 158
submarines, U-boats 13, 22
subsidies 14, 32
farming 86, 89
substitutes 75–77
sugar 17, 23, 27, 29, 38, 53, 76, 77, 83, 86, 109 , 189, 198
supermarkets 200
sweets and chocolate 24, 30, 186–187, 197–198

tea 23, 27, 28, 53–54, 109, 130, 198
tea (meal) 109
television 200
Thatcher, Margaret 55
Townsend, Cliff and Dot 103, 106, 166, 222
trichiniasis 169
typhoid 168–169, 171

Underground shelters 139, 151–154
unrationed foods 33, 35

vegetables 18, 19, 34, 38, 43, 48–49, 70–71, 85–86, 97–99, 129, 145, 170, 200
cooking 64, 70, 71, 74
vegetarians 27, 39, 50, 74
Victory parties, street parties 187–188
Vitamins 16, 23, 37, 38, 42–43, 50 *see also* fats, fruit, meat, milk, vegetables
volunteers for agriculture 95–97

wages 9, 92, 163
War Agricultural Committees 87, 90
waste 162, 166–167, 186, 202
Waters, Elsie and Doris (Gert and Daisy) 73
weights and measures:
household 63
Imperial and metric 8, 63
Welfare Foods 54–56, 192–193
Welfare State 191, 199
whalemeat 194

wild foods 125–132, 138
wines and spirits 176–177
women, emancipation, Women's Lib. 57–58, 111, 190
women's employment 57–58
women's health 59, 190
Women's Institutes 72, 91, 109, 110–112, 133, 157
Women's Land Army 57, 87, 91–94, 111
women's magazines 31, 33, 58, 136, 180, 189, 192
Women's Voluntary Service (WVS) 21, 62, 155, 156, 157–159, 185
Woolton, Lord, Minister of Food 28, 29, 36, 38, 69, 141, 147, 153, 161, 162, 170
workers
  country 105–108
  heavy industry 143–144